Praise for *Circling Home*

"Terry Repak's honest book captures not only the ...... and landscapes and wildlife they encountered at every turn, but the moments of stark loneliness and confusion. She quickly learned to make friends and seek out local women and expats who became mentors and confidantes. This is how she found "home" wherever she landed. The difference a friend can make stands out as this book's most valuable bit of wisdom."

—**Melissa Fay Greene,** *New York Times* **best-selling author of** *Praying for Sheetrock* **and** *The Temple Bombing*

"Whether she's recounting a trek up Mount Kilimanjaro with women friends or describing what it's like to raise children during stints in Africa and Europe with her husband, Terry's memoir is a graceful and inspiring book about the rewards and challenges of an adventurous, fulfilling life as a global citizen."

—**Misha Berson, former Arts Reporter for the** *Seattle Times* **and author of** *Something's Coming, Something Good: West Side Story and the American Imagination*

"Terry Repak draws on her sharp eye as a journalist and her heart in connecting with others wherever her husband's career took their family in the early days of AIDS work. She shows us how home is a place we must access within ourselves while raising children over-seas, taking care of ageing parents, and building community again and again. The take-away from this absorbing memoir is one worth pondering: 'After years of living overseas, I concluded that connecting with people instead of focusing on differences was the most fulfilling way of being in the world.'"

—**Jennifer Haupt, best-selling author of** *Alone Together* **and** *In the Shadow of 10,000 Hills,* **and recipient of the Washington State Book Award for General Nonfiction**

"If you have ever been overseas—especially to Africa—or are planning to go, you must read Circling Home. The book is written with such honesty and vivid details of both people and places that readers are guaranteed to find many inspiring gems. It's the author's ability to be open and honest about relationships with friends and family that struck me as unusually perceptive and enlightening. I found myself nodding and smiling—and occasionally crying—from the first page to the last. A great read."

—**Pamela White, former US Ambassador to Haiti and The Gambia, and former USAID Mission Director in Tanzania and Liberia**

"Anyone contemplating living abroad for either her own or a spouse's career will find Terry Repak's memoir about her family's long stints in two African nations and in Europe invaluable. While offering lots of practical advice, Terry shines in contemplating both the difficulties and the lasting enrichment she, her husband and children experienced."

—**Liza Nelson, author of *Playing Boticelli***

Circling Home

What I Learned
by Living Elsewhere

Terry A. Repak

SHE WRITES PRESS

Published 2023
Printed in the United States of America
Print ISBN: 978-1-64742-545-6
E-ISBN: 978-1-64742-546-3
Library of Congress Control Number: 2023906755

For information, address:
She Writes Press
1569 Solano Ave #546
Berkeley, CA 94707

Interior Design by Kiran Spees

She Writes Press is a division of SparkPoint Studio, LLC.

Names and identifying characteristics have been changed to protect the privacy of certain individuals.

Credit: Wendell Berry, "The Peace of Wild Things" from New Collected Poems. Copyright © 2012 by Wendell Berry. Reprinted with the permission

For A & H, my heartstrings

Life can only be understood backwards, but it must be lived forwards.

Soren Kierkegaard

I wish someone had told me when I was young that it was not happiness I could count on, but change.

Terry Tempest Williams

Chapter 1

Departures

My move to a West African country whose name I could hardly pronounce followed a series of jarring events, although it was nothing like being a Polish refugee at the end of World War II as my mother-in-law had been. Anna fled war-ravaged Europe to follow her fiancé to the Belgian Congo where he went to work as a public health veterinarian. They stayed in central Africa for thirteen years and had three sons there, but they were forced to leave when Congo erupted in civil war in 1960. My husband, Stefan, was six years old and recalls cowering in a church with dozens of other children and their parents as fighting raged outside. Fleeing another war-torn country, his parents emigrated to the US after his father accepted a job at the University of Pennsylvania.[1]

Stefan dreamed of returning to Africa to work one day, and he arranged several rotations in southern African countries while he was in medical school. I knew it when I met him—that he hoped to work overseas—although it sounded like speculation at the time. Mutual friends had invited us to dinner when we were about to turn thirty. It wasn't my first "blind date," yet it was the first time that a man's open curiosity ignited mine. A year after that dinner, we moved in together and I started working on a PhD.

I had my own ambition about living abroad after studying in London for graduate school. Yet I hadn't envisioned moving to West

1

Africa with two young children; especially since becoming a mother had been an excruciating process for me, involving several miscarriages and rounds of tests and treatments before I delivered a healthy baby. Two years later, after more tests and treatments, I got pregnant a second time; but it turned out to be a molar pregnancy—a false pregnancy that could become cancerous—and I was devastated by the news. We decided to forego more tests and treatments and try to adopt a baby instead. It took a year to complete a home study, and then we had to wait for a birth mother to choose us or for a child to be identified.

We were living in Santa Fe in the early 1990s while Stefan was working at New Mexico's Health Department as an epidemiologist in training. With the Pecos Wilderness to the east and the Jemez Mountains in the west, it was a stunning refuge from the distresses of trying to have another child. Those landscapes provided the best balm for our sore hearts as did the presence of our precocious son. In our second year there, I finished my PhD and secured a contract from a university publisher to turn my thesis into a book. But my professional aims were on the backburner due to my focus on having a second child.

While we were waiting for news of a baby, Stefan was offered a position at an AIDS Project in Cote d'Ivoire (aka Ivory Coast), and he accepted it with my blessing. The idea of moving to West Africa when we were trying to adopt a baby was a stretch for me; and I had reservations about taking young children to a country where AIDS and malaria were the leading causes of death. But his contract with the Centers for Disease Control (CDC) would be for two years, and I thought I could make the best of things for that amount of time.

Meanwhile, Stefan's mother let her contacts in Poland know that we were looking to adopt. One of her friends—an ob-gyn—informed her that his colleague had an eight-month-old granddaughter in an orphanage in Lodz, and he offered to facilitate the adoption. We flew to Poland after packing up our house in Santa Fe and preparing for the move to Ivory Coast.

To adopt a child in Poland in the 1990s, you had to have family ties in the country and be willing to spend a few months there to complete the process. Stefan had close relatives in Poznan, and he spoke fluent Polish. I had a family link too since one of my grandparents had emigrated from Poland in the early 1900s.

We were elated to be with our baby girl as soon as we arrived in Poland, although it wasn't easy to manage two small children in the cramped apartment of friends; especially when it rained every day, and we couldn't take the kids out to play. It took three months to complete the required paperwork, and I had to learn enough Polish to answer questions in court and promise to uphold Polish traditions in our home. We also had to submit documents to the American Embassy that would allow our daughter entry to the US. Through the kindness of friends and relatives, we finally had two children instead of one; something that had been important to me as one of seven myself.

Upon our return, we stayed with my parents in Maryland for a month while preparing for our big move overseas. They helped us immensely with childcare when we had to do errands and go for medical checkups. But things got complicated when one of my brothers decided to hole up in a basement bedroom and kick his crack habit cold turkey. Mike's life had spiraled out of control as had his marriage, and he'd recently lost his house and custody of his son on account of his habit. With nowhere to go, he took refuge in our childhood home.

My parents were understandably upset by his situation. I worried about Mike too since we'd always been close, and I adored his six-year-old son. Mike had often confided in me about problems with his marriage and job. Now, he rarely left his bedroom and slept all the time. Between his long bouts of sleep, my parents and I tried to help him strategize about how to put his life back together. After weighing his options, Mike decided to accept our brother's invitation to join his family in Texas and get away from the temptations that dogged him.

In November 1993, a few days after Mike left for Dallas, Stefan and I flew to Ivory Coast with Aaron and Elena, ages four and one. As we sat in the airplane, I thought of Stefan's mother who was in her early twenties when she boarded a plane for the first time in 1948, eager to embrace a new life in Africa. By contrast, I'd just turned forty and was physically and emotionally drained from the jarring events that year. I didn't feel the least bit brave, nor was I looking forward to the sea changes that lay ahead of us.

If only Anna had kept a journal of her early days in Congo, I might have gleaned insights into her adjustment process as well as guidance in smoothing the way for my children. If only the older, wiser me could have told the frightened new mother that after a bumpy first year in Ivory Coast, I'd fall in love with the place and hate to leave. At the time, I never expected to remain overseas for fifteen years and have to redefine "home" again and again, nor did I have a clue that foreign settings and people would enrich our lives and transform the way we viewed ourselves and the world.

Chapter 2
Adjusting to Life in the Tropics

The heat was thick as agave as we emerged from the cocoon of an Air France jet and stepped onto the tarmac in Abidjan. It coated my skin and didn't lift when we entered an un-airconditioned terminal along with masses of other travelers. We'd arrived in a tropical country at the hottest time of year, at the end of the *petite saison de pluie* or small rainy season.

The humidity amplified the din of foreign tongues as we merged with hundreds of others into two customs lines. With Aaron clinging to my sweaty hand and Stefan steering Elena's stroller, we entered a stream of fellow passengers being funneled through a narrow hallway. Stefan's fluent French got us through immigration as uniformed men asked brusque questions that I couldn't comprehend in my sleepless state after two long flights.

In the terminal, I gazed wide-eyed as men in pajama-like outfits and women in colorful robes piled boxes on their heads and babbled in languages I didn't recognize, waiting like us for luggage that never seemed to come. All the while our tired kids clung to me as the saturating heat glued the clothes to our bodies.

Out of the blue, Stefan's new boss appeared with balloons for the children and flowers for me. A few years younger than Stefan and roughly the same height, Alan had a robust build, a trim beard, and a hearty voice and laugh. The CDC driver, who also acted as an expeditor, steered us through customs and out of the terminal past a crowd of men milling around the entrance asking in French if they could help us with suitcases or taxis.

The strangeness of the night intensified as Alan and his aide piloted us through teeming city streets. My mind was addled by exhaustion and the effort it was taking to process the seismic shift in our environs. In the dark night, car horns bleated and traffic converged on all sides onto a boulevard with no clearly delineated lines. After inching across a congested bridge and along a palm-lined lagoon, we eventually pulled into a leafy neighborhood and stopped in front of a single-story house with a flat roof. A uniformed man opened the metal gates to admit us to the driveway and a yard surrounded by cinderblock walls topped with barbed wire.

"Is he our guard?" Aaron asked sleepily as he stared at the smiling man.

"I guess so," I replied, as surprised as he was. Stefan had mentioned that our house would be guarded round the clock, seven days a week, although I hadn't registered the fact until a tall man with a cudgel in his belt greeted us in French.

The rest of the night was a blur as we unpacked the few suitcases we could take on the plane and put the children to bed before falling into it ourselves.

I opened my eyes on the new day the way Dorothy did when she woke up in Oz. My senses went into overdrive as unfamiliar sights, sounds, and smells inundated them, all of it magnified by the clammy humidity. Intrigued by glimpses of palm trees and bougainvillea ringing the front porch, I unlocked the security grates and pushed open sliding-glass doors to hear the bird chatter outside. Miniature parrots wolf-whistled at each other from the tops of mango and avocado trees while weaver birds and doves cooed in the branches. It was a feast for the ears and eyes while my nose filled with an orangey fragrance.

I liked the house immediately. Two sets of sliding glass doors flooded the living/dining areas with light and opened onto a wide porch that wrapped around the front and side of the house. High ceilings and stone floors made the rooms seem spacious and airy, though my eyes were invariably drawn to the flowering trees and shrubs outside.

While taking in the surroundings, I heard a knock at the kitchen door and hurried to open it. An African American woman in a business suit introduced herself as our community sponsor, assigned by the US Embassy to help us settle in. Maggie said she was a diplomat in the political section at the Embassy, and her quiet authority and warmth were reassuring.

"Thanks for stocking our refrigerator," I said, remembering that Alan had told us our sponsor was responsible for the casserole and breakfast fixings in the fridge.

"It won't last you long," Maggie said with a dismissive wave. "I could take you to the market later if you like, and you can pick up more groceries."

"Thanks," I bobbed my head. "But this morning we have to go to the Embassy to get IDs and have a briefing with the Regional Security Officer."

"I know the drill," she nodded. "We could go to the market this afternoon or tomorrow."

After I thanked her, Maggie stepped aside and introduced a petite woman in African dress who smiled demurely. "This is Gladys. She's a housekeeper and nanny I thought you might need. My cook recommended her. She's worked for expats before."

"Hi, Gladys," I said, a little confused. I hadn't thought about hiring someone to clean my house or watch my children, and the introduction put me on the spot.

"Hi, madame," she said in perfect English, extending her hand for me to shake. She held her left hand under her right as a sign of deference and shook mine limply.

"I don't think we need a housekeeper full-time," I said hesitantly.

"You could hire her part-time and let her split her week with another family," Maggie suggested. "Most expats have housekeepers and cooks. Our kitchens don't have dishwashers, and she can help you with shopping and cleaning produce, which is a chore. You have to be careful about cleaning fruit and veggies because of parasites that westerners aren't used to."

"Oh, okay." I smiled at Gladys, who moved around me and stepped inside without asking. She immediately started washing the dishes to demonstrate how helpful she might be.

"You have thirty days to decide whether to sign a contract with her or not," Maggie said quietly. "I left my number on the buffet if you need anything. See you this afternoon."

"Thanks, Maggie," I called after her as a CDC car pulled into the driveway.

I left Gladys to putter around the house and went with Stefan and the children to the Embassy for a mandatory security briefing and IDs. The Regional Security Officer warned us that car jackings were common in Abidjan as were home burglaries and muggings in local markets. He also advised us to stay away from crowds since political tensions were high in Ivory Coast and riots could break out any time. He emphasized the need to be vigilant since the State Department categorized Abidjan as a "critical security risk." In my jet-lagged state, the RSO's briefing fanned the flames of my overactive imagination, and I left the Embassy scared.

The CDC driver dropped me and the children at home and took Stefan to his office downtown. While the kids were exploring the yard, I tried to converse with our day guard, Adama. All Americans attached to the US Embassy were required to have a full-time guard even though Stefan was a medical epidemiologist working for the CDC and not the State Department.

Adama's French was hard for me to understand. A tall, thin man with crooked teeth and a deeply lined face, he looked much older than his forty-six years. I could tell he liked children by the way he grinned and spoke to them. With a lot of gesturing and nodding, I learned that he was Muslim and had six children with a wife in his home country of Burkina and a baby with his second wife in Abidjan. He'd been working at our house for a decade and spoke several languages including French, but not much English. I had studied French in high school and took a refresher course in college, yet I struggled to understand his accent. It was clear that I needed to find an intensive French class ASAP.

Exhausted by that point, I went into the house and told Gladys she could leave while the children and I napped. She insisted that she needed to clean the terrace because it was dusty.

"Gladys," I asked timidly, "would you mind speaking French when you're here so the kids and I can practice?"

Her face lit up in a wide grin. "Of course. I come from Togo and French is my language."

"Bon." I nodded. "A plus tard." ["See you later."]

"A bientôt," she responded warmly.

That afternoon, Maggie took me to an outdoor market where the venders—all women—wore colorful headwraps and boubous/robes. They spoke in rapid French with such forceful presence that I was shy about opening my mouth and responding in French. Listening to Maggie discuss prices with them, I couldn't imagine being comfortable and fluent enough to dicker with these venders.

At the crowded market, people bumped against each other as they moved from one stall to the next. Competing scents wafted my way—of sweet perfumes mixed with sweat and over-ripe fruit, and of spices like cloves and cinnamon. Mangos and papayas had a blush to them that I hadn't seen in grocery stores. In the afternoon heat and sensory overload, I suddenly grew light-headed and had to ask Maggie to take me home.

Over the next few days, I had to take it easy while adjusting to the heat and humidity—and to a stomach bug that I'd picked up. There were more orientations and appointments at the Embassy, and I wanted to tour preschools for the children. Yet most days all I could do was play with the kids until lunch. After the midday meal, Elena and I took naps while Aaron had quiet time.

On one of our Embassy jaunts, I met a lively older woman who inquired about my background and told me about a French class at the university. She was clearly a connector and said she would introduce me to other women I should meet. When I mentioned that the RSO's warnings had alarmed me, she shook her head. "I like to think that people are basically good and they're not out to hurt me. I've lived in Africa for ten years, and I haven't been disappointed." Her optimism boosted my confidence, and I resolved to venture out more on my own.

After a week I mustered the courage to drive our secondhand car to a grocery store alone. I managed to find my way to the store through congested city streets, maneuvering around *daladalas* (local taxis) that darted in and out of traffic whenever people flagged them down. I figured out where to park, how to pay the deposit for a shopping cart, and how to respond to the cashier in French and give her the proper currency. What threw me were the clogged streets and intersections on my return trip home.

Every time I stopped at a red light, panhandlers swarmed around my car. Most of them appeared to be polio survivors, and they hobbled over to tap on the windows and hold out their hands for spare change. When I shrugged my shoulders with palms up to show that I didn't have any coins, they moved on to solicit other drivers. One boy sprayed water on my windshield and rubbed it vigorously with a dirty cloth. As the light turned green, I didn't have time to lower my window and explain that I had no change. But when I gave him the palms-up sign, he gestured angrily and kept his hand outstretched as if I owed him something.

The encounter shamed and embarrassed me. As I drove on, I saw policemen flagging drivers to the side of the road and my heart started pounding. The RSO at the Embassy had warned us that local police often stopped cars, ostensibly to check on documents, although they also asked for money. The RSO had advised us to say that it was against US Embassy policy to give them money, but I didn't think I could make myself understood in French. So I averted my eyes and drove past them without stopping.

Eventually I made it home and collapsed in a chair, drained by the heat and my cloying fear. It was discouraging that a simple trip to the grocery store could be so unnerving.

That night I had a troubling dream about my brother Mike. As if he'd read my mind, he called the next morning and told me that he hadn't used crack in a month. Yet he said he wasn't ready to plunge back into the working world and spent most of his time sleeping and watching TV. He was also seeing a counselor twice a week and was involved with a support group for addicts.

It depressed me to think how Mike's life was on hold and how much he must be missing his son. It weighed on me since my life was on hold too. Both Mike and I found ourselves in unfamiliar settings without any friends. At least I had a partner and children and knew what I needed to do in coming months. But what did he have to look forward to?

It was the first time I felt like a foreigner in every sense of the term: not connected or related, rootless, ungrounded, excluded; an alien, outsider, stranger. I was earmarked as a foreigner every time I left the house and opened my mouth. My skin color, clothes, accent, and body language gave away the fact that I was a newcomer who looked ill at ease, and foreigners were easy targets for carjackers and thieves. Far from being excited about my new environs, it was a burden to be a foreigner in those early weeks.

Such thoughts caused me to regret moving so far away from my family. Yet I had to make myself at home there for the children's sake as well as my own. "Home" had been in three different states in as many years, and it was up to me to redefine it.

It was clear that I needed to become proficient in French and get used to driving on my own. Above all else, I had to suppress my fears and trust that I'd know how to handle encounters with the police as well as with panhandlers and people on the streets. I couldn't rely on Stefan since he was working twelve-hour days to fill in for Alan, who'd left for the US as his wife was having a baby. Though daunted, I had no choice but to master these challenges on my own.

"Bonjour, madame," one of the Ivorian teachers intoned as she unlatched the gate of the preschool and welcomed me inside. It was a single-story house like ours with toys strewn around the yard and beneath the palm trees.

The teacher and I exchanged the usual greetings in French as I glanced around the yard for my children. I spotted Elena on the terrace with other toddlers who were watching a teacher feed the bunnies.

Stefan and I had visited several preschools before settling on a local one in our neighborhood. The Ivorian teachers had been warm and welcoming, and I could walk the children to and from school. Everyone spoke French, which meant that Aaron and Elena would quickly become familiar with the language. They'd also get to meet other kids in the neighborhood.

A week after they started attending preschool, Elena seemed to be adjusting smoothly and was elated to be with other children. Aaron, on the other hand, didn't like going to school three mornings a week. He was used to being home with me, and it frustrated him to not be able to express himself freely. He was reluctant to respond when people spoke to him in French, although he told me in confidence one day, "I'm keeping French a secret inside me until I can speak it better."

I called to Elena as I stepped onto the porch, but she only had eyes for the bunnies.

"Where is Aaron?" I asked a teacher in French.

"Inside, I think," he replied, pointing.

Entering the big main room, I didn't see Aaron among the groups of children playing with building blocks and doing puzzles. Then I spotted him lying on some cushions in a corner by himself and immediately went over to him. "Why aren't you playing with the other children, Aaron?" I asked, stroking his hair.

"I want to go home," he responded in a forlorn tone.

My heart ached for him, and I pulled him gently to me. "Isn't there anyone here you want to play with?"

"No," he moaned. "I just want to go home and play with Tony."

Tony was the guard who replaced Adama on his day off. Originally from Ghana, he spoke perfect English and was happy to chase the children around the yard and play with them. "Let's go home then," I said, helping him up. "You can play with Tony during quiet time."

It struck me anew how much Aaron was struggling to get used to a foreign language and country. He yearned to be "home" without having a clear idea of where it was or what it meant. Both children had been clinging to me more than usual in that first month, and they sometimes woke up with bad dreams or had trouble falling asleep. What made it hard for Aaron was the absence of grandparents, uncles, and aunts who knew and loved him. The fact that he'd landed in a French-speaking country made it even harder for him to adjust to his surroundings—unlike Elena, whose ear was already attuned to different languages and who didn't really know our relatives.

Aaron would gradually get used to communicating in French, and he'd enjoy preschool more after befriending an African American boy who lived in the neighborhood. But it was up to me to help them feel at home in that new place, and I'd have to manage it myself before I could assist them; like putting on my own oxygen mask before helping my kids put on theirs if we found ourselves on an airplane in trouble.

Right before Thanksgiving, I worked up the nerve to drive to the university and enroll in an intermediate French class that met three mornings a week. I'd been introduced to a woman from Ghana who was in the class, and she briefed me on what I'd missed in the first three weeks. Efua was a stout woman with kind eyes and a perpetual smile who dipped her head as she spoke in modest tones. She had two children a couple of years older than mine.

I invited Efua and her family to have dinner with us on Thanksgiving and bought canned pumpkin, cranberry sauce, and a frozen turkey at the Embassy commissary. The local flour was full of tiny bugs that I had to sift out before baking, and sweet potatoes from the market were the size of melons. We didn't have much kitchen equipment since our shipment had yet to arrive, and Maggie was kind enough to lend us baking dishes and utensils. I managed to bake pumpkin and apple pies and the usual Thanksgiving sides while Stefan roasted the turkey. He loved hosting dinners and was always willing to pitch in with cooking and cleaning.

Having guests to share the meal with us after cooking all day made it feel like a real Thanksgiving. We enjoyed getting to know Efua and her husband Atu, who was a diplomat at the World Bank. After five months in the country, Efua already knew scores of people at her children's school and in the diplomatic community. It made me a little envious and inspired me to try harder to make friends.

One week later, I accepted Efua's invitation to go to the big market in the center of Abidjan. It was a huge one that I'd been reluctant to tackle on my own, and I was excited to go with an aficionado. I watched in fascination as Efua bargained hard with venders as they brought out multiple trays of West African beads. But after an hour in the midday heat, I grew light-headed and had to ask Efua to take me home. I'd inadvertently picked up another stomach bug and had to spend the rest of the day in bed or in the bathroom.

It was a distressing turn of events since Stefan had to go to Morocco at the end of the week to attend his first AIDS-Africa Conference. I desperately wanted to go and take the kids instead of staying home. Fortunately, I was well enough after a few days to accompany him.

Marrakesh was an enchanting shopper's town with labyrinthine Berber markets fanning off of a central square. In a predominantly Muslim country with a low crime rate, the city pulsed with activity night and day as pedestrians shared the road with bikes, cars, and horse-drawn carts while crowds of people shopped or sat in sidewalk cafés.

I wasn't shy about speaking French with the market venders since they were friendly and bargained as if it were a game. As we ambled among the covered stalls, people stopped to talk to our towheaded kids and earned big smiles from them. The children seemed to enjoy the market as much as I did and were mesmerized by a snake charmer who played a flute to lure a cobra from its basket. The market felt so safe that I returned with the kids the following day while Stefan was at the conference.

One day he accompanied us on a short trip to the Atlas Mountains, and we were speechless along the way while gazing at mountains in the semi-arid desert that reminded us of New Mexico. We also saw similarities between the villages populated by Berber families selling handmade crafts and Native Americans who sold woven rugs and turquoise jewelry outside of Santa Fe. We bought a few decorative plates along the way and feasted our eyes on vistas that stretched for miles in all directions. I hadn't missed our home in New Mexico until I saw those mountains and arid landscapes in the desert light. It made me dread returning to tropical Abidjan, where we rarely had vistas and perspectives like those.

My spirits plummeted when I caught a cold toward the end of the trip. My immune system was clearly stressed, and I was sick of being sick. The cold kept me confined to an airless hotel room in Casablanca, where we'd stopped for a couple of days before returning to Ivory Coast. Casablanca wasn't as charming as it had appeared in the movie. More westernized than Marrakesh, it was a big city with white buildings and apartment blocks, and it felt less safe.

One afternoon I ventured outside the hotel for a walk with Stefan and the children. I was holding Aaron's hand and Stefan was pushing Elena's stroller when two men came up on either side of him and started jabbering at Stefan in French. He kept walking while trying to respond to them. When I saw one of the men reach for Stefan's wallet in his back pocket, I yanked on the guy's sleeve and started yelling in French, "*Au secours, Au secours!*" ["Help!"] The men ran away without getting the wallet, and Stefan and I stood there and stared at each other in shock. Then we started laughing, both of us amazed by my outburst in French. Aaron found it so funny that he kept chirping in his high voice, "Au secours! Au secours!"

Thwarting a petty crime turned out to be a serendipitous event. I'd had the wits to foil two pickpockets—while sick no less—and had saved us from having to deal with the police in a foreign country. The encounter showed me that I could muster courage when it was needed, and that I didn't have to be so afraid of burglars or pickpockets in crowded markets. I returned to Abidjan with newfound confidence, knowing that I could trust myself to act appropriately in sticky situations.

Back in Abidjan, Stefan was spending long hours at the office with Alan away, and I was sorely missing my friends and family that Christmas. Because the internet was in a nascent stage and unavailable in most homes, it was hard to stay in touch with friends and family. We didn't have cell phones and couldn't call the US from our landline; but people could call us, and my parents managed to reach us on Christmas Day. When my brother Nick called from Dallas, I teared up at the sound of his voice. I cried even more when he told me that Mike had slipped up and used crack a few times.

As the second of seven children, I was used to being with my siblings and felt needed by them; especially by Mike and by my youngest sister, Tink. She and I had bonded when our mother was sent to a TB sanatorium right after Tink was born. The baby spent her first year of life nestled on my nine-year-old hip when she wasn't staying with a family friend. When she was nine herself, she saw the movie *Peter Pan* and decided she wanted to be Tinker Bell. I started calling her Tink, and she liked it so much that she made it her legal name at age eighteen. Now she was divorced and living on her own in LA, and I worried about her as I did about Mike.

Worrying about my siblings had always been second nature to me. In some senses I'd reversed roles with my mother when she was in the sanatorium, and I had developed strong attachments to my brothers and sisters along with an acute awareness of their needs. Those bonds became a source of strength and made me feel like a linchpin in my family. Yet growing up in a crowded house hadn't been easy for an introvert like me. After an encounter with a dirty old man/groper that unnerved me during the pivotal time when I was nine and my mother was gone for a year, I grew up to be fearful and adventurous at the same time.

Now that we were living overseas—a goal that Stefan and I had shared—I was conflicted and found myself longing for home, not realizing that what I really yearned for was a sense of belonging.

After Christmas I got sick again and spent New Year's Eve alternating between vomiting and sitting on the toilet. I'd been in the same position for several nights running after drinking a fruit shake that had been prepared in our new blender. Stefan suspected that it might be an intolerance to papaya, which can cause allergic reactions in some people—including vomiting and diarrhea. We had a papaya tree in our yard, and I'd been eating the fruit twice daily. Between colds and stomach bugs, I had been sick for forty days out of sixty since we'd moved to Ivory Coast. Something had to change, so I gave up eating papaya.

On New Year's Day I felt well enough to go with Stefan and the children to a beach only an hour away. It was the season of Harmattan, when dry winds out of the Sahara caused the humidity to plummet. The winds sometimes carried sand that got in your eyes and covered every surface in the house. Yet Harmattan reminded me of New Mexico's weather, and I preferred it to the usual tropical heat.

We parked ourselves under a thatched cabana at a small hotel in Grand Bassam, the former colonial capital with dilapidated buildings and a few rustic hotels on the beach. Few people swam in the ocean because of the rough surf and dangerous riptides along that stretch of the Atlantic. Instead, we took the kids to a hotel pool that we liked because it drew more locals than expats.

Eating fresh fish and French fries at the beach, my spirits rose that day. The kids giggled nonstop as they wriggled through the pool to show us how they could "swim." I hoped that the day might herald a bright start to the new year.

But the healthy spell and high spirits didn't last. I got sick again a week later and broke down in tears after stomach and intestinal troubles kept me up at night. It depressed me that the adjustment wasn't getting easier with time. I couldn't help comparing myself to Efua—who'd traveled to Ghana for the holidays—and imagining her surrounded by friends and family. I'd never had trouble making friends before, and I knew that it was only a matter of time. Yet it was hard to be patient when I was ill and tired all the time.

When the children developed diarrhea too, we sent stool samples to the Embassy's health unit, and an astute lab tech identified the cause of our ailment. It was shigella, a highly contagious bacteria related to E. coli that can cause dysentery if left untreated. The Embassy doctor prescribed an antibiotic that knocked it out, and all of us felt better within days.

Stefan had noticed that at the preschool, children always washed their hands in a common bucket after playing outside. Suspecting that it was the source of the shigella, he suggested to the teachers that they change the hand-washing practice and not have everyone use the same bucket, and they immediately complied.

At the end of January, Stefan had President's Day off, and we drove to a distant beach near the Liberian border to spend a few days. With no electricity or running water, the local resort at Monogaga Bay had just opened, and we were the only family in a bungalow surrounded by empty ones. The kitchen staff went out of their way to cater to us at mealtimes, serving fresh fish twice daily along with avocados, mangos, pineapples, and bananas from the resort's trees.

December and January were the best months to visit Monogaga since it was cool enough to sleep without air conditioning and there were few mosquitos. In the half-moon bay, the lapis sea was calmer than most Atlantic beaches and the shore unblemished by garbage and algae. The ocean temp was in the low eighties and the water clear enough to see the sandy bottom. A bonus was the absence of jellyfish and other sea creatures that might inhibit swimming.

Utterly content after so many bouts of illness and a lonely Christmas, I wrote in my journal, "It doesn't get any better than this: waking up at dawn under a mosquito net in a bamboo hut with one child asleep in my arms and the other breathing softly beside us in her porta crib. Stefan's arms encircle me as I listen to the waves break onshore, pulsing as if the sea is breathing along with us. If only I could replay such moments of contentment when I need them."

That weekend it felt as if my shaky little skiff had finally found a berth after being adrift for months in choppy seas. Thanks to the blissful respite, the prospect of living in a foreign place didn't seem as daunting. In making peace with my surroundings, I could soldier on with whatever life held in store for us in Abidjan.

Chapter 3

Making Peace with a New Place

O n a sultry day in February, Efua and I were sitting next to each other in class when a dozen students marched past the building blowing loud whistles and shouting in French. A handful of men barged into our classroom, and one of them barked, "You must leave now. We are on strike, and you must support us."

Efua sprang to her feet and bolted for the door. I followed her out, though our teacher pleaded, "Stay in your seats, please, and continue working." As we hurried to our separate cars, I asked Efua, "Do you think we should've listened to the teacher and stayed?"

She shook her head decisively. "I know student strikes in Ghana, and they can turn violent at any moment. I won't stay around to see what happens."

It was a big disappointment to curtail the French class. I'd been relieved to put the holidays behind us and establish a routine with the children going to preschool three mornings a week while I studied French at the university.

When we returned to the university the following Monday, we were listening to the teacher explain the subjunctive case when our class was interrupted again. A group of students with loud whistles yelled as they marched past our building, and several men burst into our classroom. When one of them commanded us to leave, a British classmate started arguing with him. The exchange quickly turned into a shouting match. "You foreigners shouldn't be having your classes when we can't have ours!" he yelled.

Efua bolted from her seat again, and I tried to follow, but an administrator blocked our exit as he stood outside the door arguing with students. It looked like it might turn into a shoving brawl as Efua and I slipped past the staff member and strikers.

Efua hurried to her car and waved goodbye before driving off. But I was concerned about the British woman and her friend and decided to check on them. Making my way back to our building, I found them standing in the quad, talking to one of our teachers. The teacher was saying, "Ivorians are peaceful people, and you have no reason to be afraid. You should go back to class and ignore the strikers."

Suddenly we heard whistles and saw a much bigger crowd of students marching toward the quad. Worried that they'd be angry with us for sticking around, I hurried back to my car as a handful of students at the front of the crowd started throwing rocks at the admin building. My legs shook as I ran, afraid that they might aim their rocks at the foreign strikebreakers. As more students joined the protest, the road I usually took from the university was blocked, and I didn't know which way to turn. I followed the cars in front of me, hoping that eventually I'd find my way home.

The timing of the protests was unfortunate as I was just beginning to feel settled and ready to get out and meet people. Less afraid to drive on my own, I'd started taking the children to hotel pools and to the Abidjan Zoo on the days they didn't go to preschool. Our favorite outing was to a hotel that had a big outdoor pool where I could swim laps and keep an eye on the kids while they ate lunch under the palm trees. Once a week I took them to an English-speaking play group so they could be with kids who spoke their language.

The Saturday after I'd left the university in a hurry, Stefan and I went to the British HASH to meet other expats and explore new sections of the city. The HASH was a weekly gathering of runners and walkers who did a ten-kilometer course in different parts of the city. I was delighted to see Efua there, and the two of us talked the entire time as we walked. At the end of the course, I asked Efua, "Will I see you at class on Monday?"

She shook her head with a somber expression. "I'm not going back until the strikes are over. I just don't feel safe there."

"You don't think they'll end soon?" I asked, my spirits sinking.

She shook her head no. "Political tensions are too high in this country. Until Boigny is buried, rival political groups will keep fighting, and it won't be safe for foreigners." (Houphouet Boigny, who ruled Ivory Coast for thirty-three years after the country's independence in 1960, had passed away soon after we arrived in the country. His funeral was imminent.)

"You really think foreigners would be targets," I asked, "with so many French here?"

"You never know what Ivorians will do. It's the custom for leaders like Boigny to be buried with a hundred heads, and they say crime is up as a result."

My eyes widened as Efua continued. "Burying heads with him is done on the sly, but he was a prominent chief, and such traditions must be followed. I escort my children everywhere these days and keep a close eye on them."

"Would they want the heads of white children too?" I asked, a chill running through me.

"They don't discriminate that way," she said, grimacing.

Her news added a new element of anxiety to my overactive imagination and caused me to worry even more. The US Embassy had recently issued an alert that dependents of official Americans—which included us—would be evacuated if riots broke out around Boigny's funeral. Tensions in the Embassy community were high since there was little confidence in the Ivorian army (which was small) or the police (who were purportedly corrupt). The RSO held weekly radio checks that all official Americans were expected to answer so the Embassy could account for our wellbeing.

Stefan was better at ignoring rumors of political unrest and not letting them disrupt his movements. He had to drive through town to reach his office, and he found crowd scenes exciting rather than enervating. When he returned from work each day, he was exhausted yet elated from nonstop meetings with his Ivorian colleagues. In contrast, I was on edge whenever I had to drive in town and wondered if it was safe to go to the beach on Sundays as we usually did.

The last Sunday in February, we drove to Grand Bassam and spent the day playing with our children at the beach hotel we liked. On our way home, we were driving through Abidjan when a big soccer match had just ended. The stadium was perched above the highway between downtown and our neighborhood, and traffic came to a complete halt as disappointed fans poured onto the highway. We heard on the radio that the Ivorian team had lost to the Ghanaians as we watched angry fans blocking the street. Some of them pounded on stopped cars and peered into windows as they marched by. I wondered if they were looking for Ghanaians to fight or if they'd be mad at all foreigners. With our kids buckled into their car seats, I was terrified as angry men peered in our windows and pounded on the hood of the car. I tried not to let my fear show for the children's sake, yet my hands shook as I gripped the window crank to keep it closed.

Once the crowd passed and cars were able to move again, we made our way home, and I collapsed in the living room.

Fortunately, around that time I met several women who would alter my perspective on life in Ivory Coast a hundred and eighty degrees.

The first was Lorna, a pediatrician who'd been living in Abidjan happily for five years with her journalist husband. Though she wasn't affiliated with the US embassy, Lorna had a membership at the American Recreation Center, and she invited my kids to swim with her boys there. She was a poised African American with soulful eyes, and we immediately clicked. She was an avid reader and invited me to a monthly book group that met in another expat's house.

That expat was Carol Squire, who impressed me with her confidence and savvy. She was very much at home in Ivory Coast after living there for a decade, first as a Peace Corps volunteer and then as a business owner who was married to an Ivorian. At my first book group gathering in her home, Carol introduced me to a Mexican American woman who was also married to an Ivorian and taught physics at the university. Both women had children the ages of mine, and they invited me to visit them anytime. I left the book group meeting with a lighter heart, grateful that I was getting to know women with deeper ties to Ivory Coast. They were the kinds of friends I needed in order to feel at home in that country.

I stopped attending French class as the student strike carried on. The days my children went to preschool, I focused on rewriting my PhD thesis with the intention of delivering the manuscript to the university press when we returned to the US in the summer. I also intended to write articles for academic journals, an exercise that new PhDs had to do if they wished to pursue a career in academia; although I wasn't sure about my career path, especially if Stefan's work kept us overseas.

After majoring in journalism in college, I'd worked for famed investigative reporter Jack Anderson on his daily column, which was syndicated in a thousand newspapers around the US. But after a year, I found that I wasn't cut out to be a reporter in Washington, DC. Female role models and colleagues were few and far between,

and I simply wasn't tough enough, especially when older men in positions of power made comments about my looks or came on to me. (It
was forty years before the #MeToo movement would challenge such
behavior.) I left the reporting job to enroll in graduate school at the
London School of Economics and Political Science, hoping to bolster
my confidence with a master's degree.

After returning to the US with the degree, I worked as a TV
reporter for a while—again with Jack Anderson—but that compet-
itive fast-paced medium didn't suit a reflective person like me who
shunned the limelight. I applied for and won a scholarship at Emory
University to do my PhD, thinking that I might want to teach someday even though I was far more interested in writing than in teaching.
After two years of coursework and several more of research—during
which time Stefan and I started a family—I got the PhD. But I wasn't
allowed to work in Ivory Coast as a "trailing spouse," so I had a good
excuse to stay home and write.

Both Aaron and Elena developed fevers when Stefan was away in early
March and I was alone with the kids. By the third day, Elena's fever
inched up instead of abating, and I got scared. Unable to reach the
Embassy doctor on the phone, I called Stefan's boss, who lived near
us and was also a doctor. I broke down in tears on the phone while
describing Elena's symptoms, and Alan picked me up and drove us to
the embassy. The health unit doctor tried to give Elena medication
that would lower her temperature, but she couldn't keep it down. My
body shook as I held her, realizing how vulnerable my children were
in a country where hospitals weren't up to US standards. Elena clung
to me and wouldn't let the nurse or anyone else near her. I took the
children home after the doctor did a rapid test to be sure it wasn't
malaria. The test was negative, and we just had to wait for the fever to
go away.

All of us were taking a weekly prophylaxis to prevent malaria. The long-term effects of mefloquine weren't known, but after consulting malaria experts at CDC, Stefan considered it the safest option. Some people had a hard time tolerating it, yet Aaron and Elena had no trouble with the small weekly dose we gave them—in a spoonful of frosting to help the medicine go down.

I had no choice but to get over my fear of driving in the city since the Embassy was in the center of town and the kids often had to go to the health unit. When Elena developed terrible diarrhea in early March, we had her tested and found that she'd picked up shigella again. Another course of antibiotics quickly knocked it out.

Some weeks later, after walking the children to preschool, I was sitting at my desk working on my manuscript when the guard knocked at our door.

"Aaron is here, and he has someone with him," Adama announced in French.

Surprised that Aaron could get home from school on his own, I went outside and found the director of the preschool standing beside him. She had never been to our house and had to ask Aaron to show her where we lived.

With a concerned look on her face, the director pulled out a piece of paper and asked in halting English, "Excuse me, madame, can you tell me if Elena's teeth looked like this when you brought her to school this morning?" She proceeded to draw a smiling face with a jagged line where front teeth should be.

"I don't think they looked like that," I said with growing concern. "Where is she?"

"I left her at the school, playing happily."

Grabbing my purse and car keys, I drove the director and Aaron to the preschool. Elena was indeed playing happily and didn't pay any attention when she saw me. But when I cupped my hand under her chin and asked her to smile at me, I was shocked to see that both front teeth were broken and there was blood on her gums. "How did this happen?" I asked a teacher who stood nearby.

"Sorry, but we don't know," the director apologized. "She must have fallen, although she didn't cry. As soon as we noticed it, I asked Aaron to take me to you."

Frantically trying to figure out what to do, I drove the children home and called Stefan. He told me to wait while he phoned the Embassy to get a recommendation for a dentist. A few minutes later, he called back and told me to meet him at the office of a Belgian dentist nearby.

I managed to get both kids in the car and drive there with shaking hands. Elena was perfectly composed until she was seated in the examining chair and the dentist tried to look in her mouth. As soon as she began wailing and thrashing, the dentist asked me to sit in the examining chair and hold Elena against me face up, pinning her arms to her side. I hugged her tightly while Stefan held her mouth open wide.

The dentist couldn't give Elena anesthesia since it was impossible to insert a needle in the mouth of a thrashing child, but she promised us that it would be over quickly. Elena screamed as the dentist pulled off part of a jagged tooth and cauterized the nerve that dangled from it. Then she filed the other tooth to smooth it out. Hugging Elena's writhing form against me as the dentist worked in her mouth, it felt as if my body was buffering hers and absorbing her pain. I let out a whimper in tandem with her cries.

This, I realized, was the root of my fears: that something bad might happen to my children, and I wouldn't be able to stand it if they didn't survive this foreign adventure of Stefan's and mine. With an active imagination, I worried every time they spiked a fever—that it might be malaria or another tropical malady—or that we might be in an auto accident, and they couldn't get treatment in time. "What if the worst happened?" was always lurking in my mind.

For Elena, the incident had indeed been awful, but the procedure was over quickly, and no permanent damage had been done. They were her baby teeth after all, and Elena was easily mollified. As soon as we got home, she ran to the playroom to find her toys.

A surprise silver lining was that Elena and I seemed to bond in a profound way as I held her in the dentist's chair and tried to cushion her pain. She must have felt it too since she clung to me for days after the incident.

Four months after we landed in Abidjan, our household goods arrived (by sea), and we were finally able to put pictures on the walls and use our kitchen implements. The children rediscovered favorite books and toys, and Stefan and I were able to sleep in our own bed and return the old box spring set provided by the Embassy. Yet instead of being elated, I cringed at the prospect of Gladys and Steve watching us unpack fifty boxes of food and personal items.

Steve was the part-time cook we'd recently hired, a thin young man from Ghana who spoke English and French. I drove him home from work one day and was shocked to see the shantytown where he lived with his wife and three children. It was in a muddy field on the outskirts of our suburb, and most of the "houses" were shacks with tin sheets on top. Running between long rows of shacks were narrow dirt corridors, and I could only imagine how noisy and unsanitary it must be for the inhabitants, most of them from neighboring countries like Steve.

I'd also driven Gladys home one day when taxi and bus drivers went on strike. The rutted roads in her district were unpaved, and my car had bumped slowly over potholes to reach her block. She'd invited me in to see the room she rented, which was the size of a one-car

garage and was attached to other single-story dwellings. With cinderblock walls and a tin roof, the building was more substantial than
Steve's. Gladys had artfully decorated her room by arranging colorful
cloths on the walls and a frilly spread on the bed. She had a hot plate
for cooking, a dresser, and a table with four chairs. She even had a sink
and toilet inside.

As a housekeeper who worked for expats, Gladys earned more
than most migrant workers in Abidjan.[2] When I asked about her
family, she told me that her mother was raising her daughters in Togo
so she could work at a higher-paying job in Abidjan. The father of
her two daughters had gone to Germany two years before in search
of a higher-paying job, and he hadn't returned or sent any money
for child support. Yet Gladys's optimism was unflagging on account
of her faith. She'd walk around our house in bare feet and sing Jesus
songs while cleaning. An attractive woman at thirty, she had a round
face like Elena's and perfect skin the color of walnuts. She also had
shoulder-length black hair and perfect posture at five feet two.

Though she had only completed second grade, Gladys read the
bible and other religious books and was good at figuring sums in her
head. She also had a sharp eye and intellect when it came to dealing
with venders. If a stranger came to our door, she could size them up in
a heartbeat and tell me whether a request for funds was legitimate or
not. We got constant requests—from guards to garbage collectors—
for "loans" to pay for children's school fees or for relatives' funerals.
Working people like Gladys also fielded constant requests for money
from unemployed relatives, and most of them sent money to their
natal villages.

As I unpacked the many boxes of clothes, books, toys, and food
from our sea shipment, I couldn't help viewing the scene through
Gladys's and Steve's eyes. I imagined that to them, it looked like we'd
imported a Target or Walmart to satisfy the whims of four spoiled
Americans.

It was impossible for me to ignore the huge gap between people with resources and those who had very little—a divide that was based largely on skin color and where one happened to be born. The gap seemed more evident in Abidjan due to the large numbers of migrant workers and expats. Dubbed the "Paris of West Africa," the city's economy was booming in comparison to its neighbors, with record-high prices for Ivorian coffee and cocoa, the two main exports. It was also headquarters for the African Development Bank, which brought thousands of professionals to Abidjan from other African countries. With them came a demand for low-wage workers to fill service jobs.

The children's excitement upon seeing their old toys and books made it seem like Christmas to them. We gave some of the toys and clothes to Gladys and Steve for their children as well as to our guards, Adama and Ousmane. The guards asked if they could have the boxes we'd emptied to line the walls of their homes for insulation. They took empty plastic bottles to sell and writing paper that was blank on one side for their own use. With no formal recycling in Abidjan at the time, it was an informal system that seemed to work.

In late March, Stefan got the phone call from home that every expat dreads—that a family member was in critical condition and might not survive. He returned from work in the middle of a workday and told me with tears in his eyes that his brother had called from Colorado where he was skiing with their mother. Anna had suffered a cerebral hemorrhage and had to be driven by ambulance to Denver for emergency surgery. Five hours later, his brother called back to say that a surgeon had clamped an aneurism in her brain and drained most of the blood from her head. But there was a chance she'd have complications and might not recover all her faculties.

Stefan left that evening for Denver and had to take three flights to reach her bedside. Left alone for two weeks with the children, I appreciated Gladys's quiet competence more than ever. One day when Elena threw an epic tantrum, Gladys strapped the wailing child to her back with a long piece of fabric and took her for a walk. Elena promptly fell asleep on Gladys's back.

It was also helpful to have friends nearby. The afternoon of the tantrum, I drove the kids to Jeane's house so they could play with her children while she and I talked. Jeane, who was a "trailing spouse" and writer like me with two children the same ages as mine, also attended the monthly book group meetings. Whenever we got together, we'd talk about our families, her previous posts in Africa, the books we'd read and the ones we hoped to write. Her daughter quickly became Aaron's closest friend and classmate.

Jeane was an excellent baker who'd taught her cook how to make homemade bagels, which were better than any bagel I'd tasted in the US. Jeane sent us home with a bag of them that day, and I relished the gift like it was manna from heaven.

When Stefan returned to Abidjan, I was anxious to see his mother, and he encouraged me to go so she'd have company at the rehab center where she was staying. I made the long trip home in mid-May with Aaron and Elena. My parents met us at Dulles Airport, and it was a huge relief to be in my childhood home where dinner and comfy beds waited. To get nine hours of uninterrupted sleep after twenty-four hours in transit with two young children was a dream.

Waking up on a pristine spring morning, I was captivated by the bright green sheen of pollen coating every surface outside my window. I found Aaron and Elena in the living room, giggling as my father crawled on the floor after them while my mother talked to them in goofy tones as she made breakfast. With the kids playing happily, I slipped outside to take a walk in the crisp spring air, a rare treat after the stifling heat in Abidjan. That afternoon, when the kids went down for a nap, I snuck out again for a bike ride on the C&O Canal.

The next day I offered to go grocery shopping and was shocked by the huge variety of food choices at relatively low prices. I was already viewing my country through outsider's eyes. In Abidjan, wage workers—particularly immigrants from neighboring countries—didn't shop at grocery stores frequented by expats and Ivorian professionals, whereas in America people from all walks of life shopped at the same chain stores.

That first trip home made me realize how oppressive my surroundings in Abidjan felt at times. Living behind high walls with barbed wire and a guard outside—and with constant warnings from the embassy about crime—I was hyperalert whenever I ventured outside our gate or drove through the city, especially when my children were with me. At home in the Maryland suburbs, I could suspend such vigilance and roam around carefree.

Our neighborhood in Bethesda was a feast for my tired eyes. All senses were engaged in the crisp air as I drank in the sight of pink and white azaleas and green fuzz on budding trees, which seemed to pulsate with new life. The sunlight was stark and unfiltered with a sapphire sky clear of clouds and humidity. There were so many pleasures to process in the spring that I couldn't get enough of being outside.

The opposite sort of sensory shock awaited when we drove to Philadelphia to see Stefan's mother. My mother came along to watch the children while I visited Anna every day in the rehab place. Wheelchair bound and unable to feed herself, she was lucid enough to know me, yet she couldn't remember anything that had happened a day or a week before. She didn't even recall that Stefan had just been there to visit her. She wore no makeup, and a punky grey stubble had replaced her honey-colored hair since her head had to be shaved for multiple surgeries. Most telling of her altered state were her sagging shoulders and dribbled chin.

It was distressing to see her in that condition and to ponder what might lie ahead for her. She was braver than anyone I knew and had been an incredible role model of an independent woman who came of age during the Second World War. I was eternally grateful to her for having raised a sensitive son like Stefan and for coming to our aid during the adoption process. She had kept me company in Poland when Stefan had to work in Ivory Coast for a month, and she'd helped me haul luggage and groceries up several flights of stairs and cooked for us.

Now she lay in a hospital bed unable to form coherent sentences. While sitting at her bedside and watching her sleep, I was flooded with renewed admiration and love for her. It had never occurred to me that we might not have her around for years to come, and it was awful to ponder what life would be like without her. I begged God or the universe to let us have her for a few more years, not wanting to lose the mother I'd recently found.

Anna would have to remain in rehab for months learning how to walk and function on her own again. Although her short-term memory was impaired, her long-term memory was returning slowly. The aneurism and surgeries appeared to have aged her by a decade.

The ordeal seemed to age Stefan too. When he'd returned to Abidjan, he told me with wet eyes that he'd never imagined having to wipe drool from his mother's chin and clip her face hair. Seeing Anna transformed overnight, Stefan and I stared mortality in the flesh for the first time. Could this happen to my mother and father as well?

It rocked our world and made us realize how little time we had on this earth, and how someday we might be the cause of great sadness to our children too.

After a month in the US, I returned to Ivory Coast in an altered state with Aaron and Elena. My mind was once again in transit like my body, only this time I was excited about going to Abidjan rather than dreading it. I was glad to escape the noise of Rockville Pike, the drabness of Anna's rehab place, and the incessant driving one had to do in American suburbs. In Abidjan, we lived calmer lives closer to nature and alongside people who'd seemed so different from us at first. Now they were more like friends and an integral part of what was becoming "home."

When we pulled into the driveway, Adama and Ousmane greeted us with warm smiles and helped us with our luggage. I exchanged news with them about our families as the children ran inside to get straws. They'd noticed a heap of coconuts beside the driveway that Adama had culled from the trees, and they begged him to cut a few open for them. After they had their fill of coco water, they asked Ousmane and Adama to hoist them up on the metal gates so they could watch the street life outside—a pastime they'd enjoyed with both guards.

Gladys was washing dishes when I stepped into the kitchen and greeted her. She had tears in her eyes as she held my hand and told me how much she'd missed me and the children. I asked about her trip to Togo, and she told me about the month she'd spent with her kids. Then she opened the fridge to show me the wholewheat bread and fruit salad Steve had prepared for us. I scooped a big helping of pineapple and mango into a bowl while avoiding the papaya.

Wandering through the airy dining and living rooms, I was surprised to see that the porch running along the front and side of the house had been screened in—per Stefan's request to the Embassy. It seemed to add a whole new room to the house, and there was new porch furniture too. Now we'd be able to spend hours outdoors since mosquitos would no longer be a problem. I would relish the chance to sit outside in the mornings listening to the birds chatter, and to eat dinners there with the family in the evenings.

In the quiet dusk, our tropical garden seemed more exotic than ever. I watched as clouds gathered in the sky and looked forward to the impending downpour that would drum a raucous beat on our metal roof that night. The rain in that part of Africa was a phenomenon I'd never witnessed before. It plummeted straight down on our flat roof instead of blowing in at an angle, the clatter waking us as it rose to the pitch of a generator—which is what I thought it was the first time it poured.

Sitting on our porch eight months after we'd moved to Ivory Coast, it dawned on me that our time was limited and our sojourn there would be over all too soon. I vowed to take less for granted and stop pining for my life in the US.

Chapter 4
Migrations of Both Hearts and Minds

One reason I was glad to embrace my life in Abidjan was the prospect of deepening friendships with women like Lorna and Carol. But when I went to lunch with Lorna after my return, she broke the news that she and her husband would be leaving Abidjan at the end of the summer. My spirits did a nosedive, and I bemoaned the short time remaining to get to know her better. She was a wise, searching soul with whom I shared many interests, and she'd been an inspiration to me with her balanced perspective and aura of inner peace. It was the first time I faced the prospect of losing a friend who had walked into my life and enriched it.

Fortunately, Carol was entrenched in Ivory Coast as a key player in the effort to stop the spread of AIDS at the height of the epidemic in Africa. Her company's yellow condom-shaped kiosks distributed information about HIV along with prophylactics. The kiosks were highly visible and outlandish in central Abidjan and cities up-country. I looked forward to the monthly book group meeting at her house and found a sense of community among the dozen women who attended regularly. Carol would ask provocative questions to spark debate and then sit back and listen to people argue with a bemused grin on her face.

After one meeting, she invited me to stay for tea. Carol had dazzling blue eyes and a pageboy haircut, and she dressed in a flowing

Ivorian robe/boubou. I was eager to hear more about her early days in Ivory Coast, and she obliged me. A French major at university, she'd entered Peace Corps after graduation and was sent to Ivory Coast in the early 1980s. After a year in the country, she happened to be in Washington, DC on medical leave when she learned that Peace Corps was cancelling the program in Ivory Coast because of Reagan-era budget cuts. Her superiors told her she couldn't return to her post. But Carol was so keen on resuming her work that she bought her own plane ticket to Liberia and snuck back into Ivory Coast by bus. When she showed up at her job, the Peace Corps country director fired her.

Instead of returning to the US, Carol stayed and secured her own contract to teach English at a local school in Abidjan. One evening, while eating dinner with friends at a *maquis* (an outdoor bar and grill), she met an Ivorian who'd just returned from the US with a graduate degree in business. Mamadou and Carol started dating, and two years later, they married.

Her story intrigued me. She'd had the guts to remain in Ivory Coast on her own and to face racial biases in her WASP milieu in Chicago when she married an Ivorian and traded her home for a foreign one. In the ten years she'd been in Ivory Coast, she'd made big contributions to public health with her social marketing campaigns broadcasting the dangers of HIV/AIDS.

As attached as I was to my home and family, I couldn't imagine a permanent move to a country so different from my own. While I was struggling to find my place in Ivory Coast, Carol became my model of an expat who'd adapted to the culture. She scoffed at official Americans who worried about carjackings and crime and was fearless about driving through the poorest parts of town for her work. She'd managed to accomplish a lot professionally with two children at home. (I wasn't allowed to work outside the home since I was considered a "trailing spouse" by the US and Ivorian governments, a term that I found demeaning.)

Carol's house became a base and haven for me. It's where I con-nected with other women who would become close friends—like Chris, who was also married to an Ivorian. Chris was the astute lab tech at the Embassy health unit who'd diagnosed the shigella that plagued us soon after we arrived. Chris's family and mine were invited to Carol's house for Thanksgiving and Christmas that year.

Each day, when Stefan returned from work, the kids would run to him and ask, "Any boxes?" since all our mail was delivered to his office. Care packages and letters from home were precious to all of us, and Stefan's mother and mine sent packages stuffed with gifts and treats for the kids. My sister Tink—who was godmother to our children and like a kid herself—sent VHS tapes of holiday movies along with *Bill Nye the Science Guy* and other children's shows.

The weeks leading up to the holidays were busy with visitors coming and going in our home. Tink flew from LA to spend a week with us while Stefan was away on business, her suitcases loaded with Christmas gifts and movies for Aaron and Elena. A British woman who worked at Stefan's project also came to stay for a few days so as not to be alone on the holiday. We invited Efua's and Jeane's families to join us on Christmas Eve, when Stefan made his traditional Polish dinner. After cooking for fourteen people, we were exhausted by the time Christmas Day rolled around. Still, we rallied in time to attend Carol's party that night.

Besides Chris's family, Carol had invited other friends, including Mona and her family from Nigeria. Twenty-five guests milled around the living and dining rooms drinking hot apple cider and eating samosas before sitting down to dinner. Some of us balanced plates on our laps while others sat at the dining room and kitchen tables when local turkey and a variety of sides were served. Carol was unruffled at having to feed a large group with a dozen children underfoot. She made sure everyone had Secret Santa gifts to open after dinner and allowed the children to hand them out. Then we sang carols while she and Mona played the piano. Each adult took different parts in a full rendition of "The Twelve Days of Christmas" with the kids joining in. Stefan's refrain of "five golden rings" made them laugh each time he belted his lines off-key.

I was tired but grateful when we left Carol's that night after being welcomed by a group of new friends. It was a far happier holiday than our first lonely Christmas in Abidjan.

I found it ironic to be writing a book about Central American immigrants while we were living in West Africa. Before we moved, I had interviewed hundreds of Salvadorans and Guatemalans—most of them women—to find out why they left their countries, why they chose to migrate to Washington, DC, and how they had fared there. My research revealed that a surprising number of women led the migration to the nation's capital in the 1950s and '60s instead of men, partly because American families had recruited them to work.[3]

By the end of our first year in Abidjan, I'd finished the book based on my dissertation and gave it to the publisher on time. I had also written four articles based on my research, and all of them had been accepted by academic journals.

In casting around for a new writing project, I hit upon the idea of interviewing expats like Carol and Chris who were married to Ivorians and living in Abidjan. The project excited me since I was curious to know how these women had adjusted to Ivorian cultures. I'd made big sacrifices by moving to Ivory Coast for Stefan's work, yet these women made even bigger sacrifices and managed to do what I longed to do: integrate into a foreign culture and make themselves at home there. I was also hoping to write an article about Americans living in Ivory

Coast that might counterbalance the negative reporting about West Africa in the US press.

In 1994, an article had appeared in The Atlantic that made me question my fears all the more.[4] Robert Kaplan's "The Coming Anarchy" was an alarmist view of African countries that read like a modern version of *Heart of Darkness*—a white traveler's nightmare about children "who swarmed like ants" and "groups of young men with restless, scanning eyes . . . hordes of them." The article depicted West Africa as a monolithic entity beset by crime, poverty, disease, hunger, and intertribal warring. I knew that Ivory Coast wasn't the economic basket case he described, nor was it interchangeable with warring countries like Liberia and Sierra Leone. Kaplan's article typified the kind of reporting about Africa that Chimamanda Ngozi Adichie would later lambast in her TED talk, "The Danger of the Single Story." It was the story of Africa as a unidimensional place full of negative stereotypes.[5] Kaplan drew his doomsday scenario and predictions after spending a month riding around in bush taxis and interviewing people in six West African countries. I was drawing very different conclusions after living in Ivory Coast for a year and meeting expats who chose to live there instead of in the US.

In subsequent months, I managed to interview two dozen Americans—all but two of them women—who had married Ivorians and stayed in Abidjan.[6]

The day I sat with Sue in her living room, I had to concentrate hard to hear what she was saying. Her three-story house resembled a local YMCA with small children running in and out while older kids watched TV in an adjoining room and a handful of boys shot hoops outside. "How many children do you have?" I asked, unable to hide my surprise.

Sue wasn't much older than I, although her long black hair was streaked with gray and deep lines creased her cheeks when she smiled. "Seven." Sue grinned. "We adopted my husband's nephews after their father passed away, and I had five of my own." She added thoughtfully, "It was the biggest adjustment I had to make after I moved to Abidjan, the lack of privacy in my own home. You wouldn't survive here if you were a very private person."

"That would be me." I nodded sheepishly. I couldn't imagine living with the hubbub that Sue did. It was too reminiscent of my noisy childhood with seven children and two adults crammed into a small suburban rambler. Now, as an adult, I cherished time alone to think and write when my children were in preschool. Yet I also knew that adopting a child had enriched our lives immeasurably.

Sue told me she'd met her Ivorian husband at university in Syracuse and had agreed to return to Ivory Coast with him. Some of the early adjustments she had to make sounded familiar to me. She was the only white woman in the squalid neighborhood where they initially settled, and without a car or telephone, she found it difficult to do anything on her own. "We're talking about serious isolation, and I don't know how my husband survived me. It got easier once I got my independence back." She did so by learning French, buying a second-hand car, and going to work for a friend's computer company.

Sue said that another big adjustment was coming to terms with different views on infidelity and polygamy. "I didn't marry my husband for sexual exclusivity. Still, I'd be really ticked off if he told me he was having an affair." She paused before continuing. "I know I'd be hurt, but if I refused to let him live in his culture, I'd be invalidating his parents' relationship. My husband grew up in a polygamous family, and he said he's seen the bad side of polygamy and wasn't interested in it." She added as an afterthought, "But I would rather he took a second wife who has responsibilities in the family than have mistresses on the sly. A mistress is a parasite, but a wife contributes."

It surprised me that she was so open-minded about infidelity in a country where sexually transmitted diseases were rampant. Few of the other women I interviewed shared Sue's views. She told me she was a pragmatist who believed marriage was more of an economic arrangement between families than a romantic one. "Girls aren't always expected to remain celibate here, and they aren't ostracized if they have children outside of marriage. All these things—infidelity, illegitimate children, etc.—are a lot less dramatic here than in our puritanical world in the United States. People just accept life for what it is."

After my interview with Sue, I met an African American woman who was even more open-minded about polygamy. At thirty-eight, Sean was several years younger than I, with a sweet demeanor and soulful eyes. As we sat in her living room drinking tea one day, she told me how she'd come to Ivory Coast when she was thirteen. Her parents had grown up in the Deep South, and they'd joined the Peace Corps Family Recruitment Program in 1970 because they wanted to raise their children in an environment free from the kind of racism that killed Martin Luther King Jr.

Sean was living in an openly polygamous marriage with her Ivorian husband and seven children along with a co-wife with four of her own. Sean said that when her husband asked her to let him live in a polygamous relationship, "I thought it was either agree or go back to the US. I didn't want to raise children in the States on my own and didn't think I had a lot of options. I didn't even have the money to go back to the States. It was totally against my grain, but I thought I could do it for my kids' sake. Other people in Africa live with polygamy, so why couldn't I?"

Sean admitted that she and her co-wife were unhappy when they combined households, and she and her husband even discussed divorcing. Then, twelve years into her marriage, Sean became a born-again Christian and shared her faith with her husband and co-wife. All three adults joined a charismatic church that welcomed members who kept African customs like polygamy. "After we became committed Christians, there was total reconciliation, and God made it work." Sean said she tried to think of her co-wife as a sister. Still, she admitted she wouldn't want to see her daughters in polygamous relationships. "It's just a very difficult proposition."

It was a revelation to me—that sexual exclusivity and monogamy weren't part of the marriage contract in some ethnic groups, and that polygamy was still practiced in Ivory Coast even though it was officially banned in 1964. I knew that many churches had adapted to African customs, but the fact that an evangelical Christian church tolerated polygamy also surprised me[7]

A teacher friend who was married to an Ivorian helped me see these relationships in another light. "I've lived by myself and taken care of myself. But some of my African friends married not for love but because the man had enough money to take care of them. They just went into the relationship with different expectations." It was an apt reminder that women in every culture—including my own— might have mixed motives for marrying.

A few years after our interview, curiosity would compel me to ask a friend how Sean was doing, and I would learn that Sean moved to California with her children. I could only assume that it had been too much of a stretch to make her polygamous marriage work after all.

On World AIDS Day in December 1994, Carol shared her own marital troubles with me as we marched in a parade through downtown Abidjan to raise awareness about AIDS.

"Mamadou has been seeing other women, and sometimes he doesn't come home at night," she confided as we hoisted our banner amid throngs of others. "His brother called a family council and had

Mamadou sit down and discuss the situation with me. Mamadou apologized and promised to change his ways, and he assured me that he wanted to save our marriage. But I don't know if it can be saved."

Her revelation came at the end of an emotional day. I had just finished telling her the story of our guard, Adama, even though it was hard to talk about him without getting choked up. Adama had developed stomach problems the previous summer, and I'd driven him to a clinic where the doctor prescribed medications. When we'd returned to Abidjan after our summer vacation, it had shocked me to see how much weight Adama had lost. I'd driven him to another clinic where they gave him medicines to treat worms and bacterial infections, and he saw a traditional healer who gave him herbal remedies. Initially his health had improved, but after a month he'd taken a turn for the worse.

Stefan had driven him to a clinic for blood tests, and Adama came back with the dreaded result: he was HIV positive. Within weeks he was unable to work, and a replacement guard had shown up at our house. I'd asked Ousmane, our night guard, to help me find Adama's place, and we had visited him together. His dwelling was in a shantytown on the outskirts of Abidjan, a flimsy shack with a tin roof on top. I had cried when I'd seen Adama, alarmed by his transformation. He stared at me out of yellow eyes in a skull that looked as if transparent skin were stretched over it. Lying in a fetal position, he was unable to close his mouth due to fungal infections on his lips and gums. I held his boney hand as tears leaked from his eyes and mine.

Ousmane and I had returned to his place the following day with medicines to treat his fungal infection and stomach pain. I went to see him once a week, though it was excruciating to watch Adama decline over the next two months after he developed full-blown AIDS. When his wife could no longer care for him at home and he couldn't eat on his own, he was admitted to the university hospital in Abidjan.

Stefan and I visited him there, and we were appalled by the

conditions. His narrow bed was situated in a hallway among dozens of other AIDS patients while relatives slept on floor mats and brought food to them each day. Adama's mouth was blue from the medication for fungal infections, and he had nasty bed sores on his hips and groin. He told us that the pain in his throat and chest was so bad he couldn't eat or swallow.

The morning of the AIDS walk, Ousmane came to our house to tell me that Adama had passed away. I was shaken and bereft when I met Carol for the march that day. Adama was forty-three years old from a country where the life expectancy was forty-nine.[8]

It wasn't the first time that the ravages of the epidemic hit home to me. Two years prior, a close friend from college had revealed that he had AIDS, and he'd asked me to help him rewrite his memoir. We worked on it together during the last year of his life, and I'd attended his funeral right before we moved to Ivory Coast.

The next time I saw Carol, she told me more about her marriage and said that religion hadn't been a stumbling block between them even though she'd never converted to Islam. She fasted with Mamadou during Ramadan, and he celebrated Christmas with her. "There's a much milder form of Islam here than in Saudi Arabia or Pakistan, which is why religion isn't an issue. He isn't a devout Muslim, and he didn't insist that we raise our children in his faith."[9]

They did have major disagreements when it came to child-rearing, however. "In every other facet, we've basically lived an Ivorian life, and he didn't have to adapt to anything alien to his own experience," she said wryly. "I could accept that. But in raising children, we don't see eye to eye. I wanted to raise my kids as I'd been raised, reading to them at bedtime and talking about personal matters that concern them. Mamadou agrees in theory, but he finds it impossible to involve himself with the children. I didn't expect him to change diapers. That would have been too extreme for him. But I wanted to see him bonding with his children, and he can't relate to them as I'd like."

Carol valued the fact that "in Ivory Coast, children are taught to respect their elders and to cooperate and share their belongings rather than claim things as their own." She was also grateful that professional and working women didn't have to choose between home and career. Domestic help was affordable and easy to find as legions of people from neighboring countries sought domestic work in booming Abidjan. Their help allowed middle- and upper-class women to work all day and return home to clean houses and prepared meals, leaving them more time to spend with their children. Carol said that women could accomplish more in Ivory Coast than the US because they weren't expected to play supermom roles.[10]

My interviews with Americans married to Ivorians took a year to complete. Getting to know this select group of women gifted me with a handful of new friends, and I was deeply grateful that they shared their struggles with me. They'd offered invaluable insights into Ivorian culture and an entrée into broader circles than most diplomats and "trailing spouses" had. They helped me see that many of my fears about my children's health and our safety were overblown. (Most of the women had lived in Abidjan for years and felt safer there than in many US cities.)

Hearing about their issues helped me put my own in perspective and made me appreciate the way Stefan and I communicated, especially when it came to our children. With similar views on child-rearing, fidelity, and communication, we trusted and relied on each other in tough times.

Having adopted a child after giving birth to my first one, I knew that there were many ways to form a family. The interviews showed me that there were also many ways to manage family dynamics and deal with external pressures that might tear couples apart. Americans married to Ivorians had to negotiate how much meddling they could handle from relatives and how much they'd bend for the sake of their partners, as Carol, Sean, and Sue did. (The article I wrote was never published, unfortunately. It took weeks to get responses by mail when I queried magazines and newspapers, and I quickly got discouraged by a handful of rejection letters.)

Three months after Carol shared her marital troubles with me on World AIDS Day, she broke the news that she was preparing to leave the country. Her news depressed me since she'd become my closest friend during a difficult first year in Abidjan. It was her attitude and example that helped me find my place, and we'd shared everything from politics and books to our spiritual paths and what we hoped to do someday. But Carol said she needed to find a way out of the stalemate she was in since Mamadou hadn't changed and was still seeing other women.

Knowing she was a trailblazer who was used to problem-solving, I sympathized with her whole-heartedly. It was hard for her to feel stuck and not know how to work things out in her marriage. When the US-based Population Services International (PSI)—which was in partnership with her company—offered her a job in Pakistan, she was so eager to move that she left two months later with her daughters and few belongings. Soon after she left, Mamadou's mistress moved in with him.

I saw Carol later that summer in Washington, DC when she attended a conference and I was visiting my parents. Over lunch in a K Street café, she told me how thrilled she was with her new job and life in Pakistan. She relished the challenge of heading up PSI's office and the opportunity to immerse herself in different cultures on the Indian sub-continent.

Though I missed her terribly, her enthusiasm inspired me. When I returned to Abidjan after summer vacation, I took over hosting the monthly book group and joined the board of the Professional Women's Network (which Carol had co-founded) after attending their meetings for a year. I also formed a writing group with Jeane, Mona, Octavia, and another teacher-writer. Friendships with other embassy spouses, like Michele and Marybeth (my next-door neighbor) and Stefan's CDC colleagues, were also incredibly supportive.

These deepening ties were the main reason I said yes when Stefan asked me if I'd be willing to stay in Ivory Coast for two more years. His contract was up for renewal in the spring of our second year, and with his research projects ongoing, he wanted to see them through. The children and I had just settled in, and it had taken a year for me to make close friends and get involved in several communities. Both of us agreed that it would be a shame to leave so soon and not give it two more years.

I'd realized early on that friendships would be critical components of my emotional well-being while living overseas. Writing was an isolating endeavor that brought me little affirmation or monetary reward, whereas Stefan was a respected scientist at a big CDC project with a staff of over a hundred. He spent ten hours a day working with people while I juggled writing at home with children's needs. I'd come to rely on friends to help me through hard times and to stand in for our families when we celebrated holidays and birthdays.

Making ourselves at home in foreign countries would become synonymous with making friends and connecting to various communities. Small wonder that the hardest part about living overseas would be watching friends leave. It was sad for Aaron and Elena since some of their playmates left too. The only positive aspect about the annual turnover of expat families was that new people were always arriving, which presented opportunities to make new friends.

Chapter 5
Two Faces of Friendship

At the start of our second year, Elena remained at the neighborhood preschool, and we transferred Aaron to a French preschool for older children. He turned five that year and started attending school four half-days a week, as did Elena. Wednesday was our day to go to a pool or the zoo.

A month or so after Aaron's school started, a German couple showed up dragging their defiant daughter to his class. The girl spoke no French, and she looked as lost as Aaron had when we'd arrived in Abidjan.

Her father caught my eye when he stepped into the classroom in loose cotton trousers with a flashy indigo design. A shock of silver hair brushed his shoulders, though it was cropped short in a crew cut on top. His pike nose, narrow lips, and darting eyes under a jutting brow reminded me of a falcon's head.

His wife was a few steps behind him, leaning over her daughter and entreating her in German. It was easy to recognize wheedling in any language, and it clearly wasn't working. Ula wore Birkenstocks and a tank top over billowing pants cut from Ivorian fabric. She had short spikey hair with a maroon tint in it and dangling silver earrings.

In subsequent weeks, Ula and I struck up a casual friendship as we hung around the playground at pick-up time and our kids played on the swings or slide. She'd ask me where she could find a tailor or dentist and what to do on weekends—questions I had posed not long before. But after a year in the country, I knew the ropes.

Despite her punky look, there was an air of vulnerability about her that I recognized. In fact, the two of us looked alike with the same boney build, narrow faces, short brown hair, and hazel eyes, except that she seemed much more spontaneous and carefree. Ula told me that she and Detlef had been teaching in a small German city when he convinced her to take a sabbatical from her job so he could work in West Africa. Like Stefan, Detlef had roamed around Africa before she met him, and he'd hoped to return and work there someday. Like me, she'd agreed to put her life on hold and move for his job. But then a lot of expat wives were in the same bateau.

Within weeks, Ula's daughter became Aaron's closest friend at preschool. I invited her to his birthday party in December, and Ula and Detlef arrived at our house at the invitation time with their daughter and toddler son. Unlike most parents who dropped off their children for a couple of hours, they hung around and wanted to socialize.

Listening to Ula's fluted laugh ripple over the party noise, I could tell she was more comfortable with life in Abidjan. She spoke in belabored Queen's English, pronouncing words like "told" and "sold" as if they were two syllables instead of one, which I found charming.

Detlef and Ula started turning up at Embassy receptions that Stefan and I attended. Not being part of the diplomatic corps, I was always self-conscious at such gatherings and dreaded the question, "What kind of work do you do?" It was a relief to pair up with another stay-at-home mom and free spirit like Ula, her piccolo laugh ringing over the crowd as we sipped wine and conversed.

Just as I had done the previous year, Ula made a heroic effort to embrace her life in Ivory Coast. She enrolled in an African dance class, bought a tall drum, and started taking lessons that left thick calluses on her fingers and palms. She also took intensive French and was soon speaking it better than most expats, including me. Frequenting local markets to look for fabric and beads, she designed her own patterns for dresses and slacks, which tailors made for her.

I told Ula about the monthly book group meetings at Carol's house, and she started attending even though she was shy about speaking English. She also came to Professional Women's Network meetings where speakers gave presentations on local politics and culture, and she volunteered to teach a dance class at our children's school.

Ula never complained when Detlef had to travel for his job, though he often stayed away for days or weeks at a time. When I'd notice dark circles under her eyes and ask if she was sleeping okay, she'd shrug her shoulders and exhale with an audible sigh. Hearing reports from other expats about carjackings and burglaries, I could relate to her concern about crime since I didn't sleep well when Stefan traveled.

Security had been a big worry for me and was one reason I'd gravitated toward bolder women who didn't have my underlying anxieties. I wanted to be more like Carol and Chris, who frequented local markets and drove through the poorest parts of town without second thoughts. It occurred to me later that spending time with them was like trying to play tennis with better players so I could improve. Maybe it was the same with Ula—that she wanted to be around someone who was bolder and more confident—and in her eyes, I was that person.

Whenever I took my kids to Ula's for a playdate, she'd talk about how much she missed her sisters and friends back home, and how glad she was that she'd met someone like me with whom she could share everything. Although I liked spending time with her, I was less available since I worked at home and already had a network of friends.

After Carol's departure, I started spending more time with Mona, who missed her as much as I did. We walked together several evenings a week and shared a love of books and writing, music and theatre. I came to appreciate the richness of the cultures around us after attending arts events at the Alliance Francaise and dance and music performances with Mona.

She was a rare friend for me: a West African woman whose professional and family demands didn't prevent her from being active socially. Our friendship satisfied my desire to get to know women from African countries and not just hang out with expats like me. Beyond that, Mona was an insightful thinker whose opinions I respected. I was a little in awe of her when I'd see her at Carol's parties and at book group meetings, where she'd offer alternative perspectives that I found intriguing. An education specialist at the African Development Bank, she was an accomplished pianist and an opera singer who'd sung on the BBC.

Mona became my closest companion and confidante after Carol moved away. We talked about everything from our personal lives to life in general and what we believed in. Although she worked full-time at the African Development Bank, Mona made time whenever I needed to talk, sometimes taking long lunch hours during her workday.

We often discussed issues that troubled us, particularly regarding our children. I was concerned about Aaron's adjustment, for example, since he was an introverted child who liked to read but didn't like going to school. By contrast, Elena was an extrovert who loved being with children in the neighborhood and at school. She could be delightful and funny at times, yet she also threw legendary tantrums.

Mona was usually able to intuit my underlying concerns, and I valued her insights, yet she wasn't an easy friend for me. When she was in a good mood, she radiated warmth with unselfconscious brio. She was adept in any setting and could converse with anyone from government ministers to guards at friend's gates. Yet she could also be abrasive and scornful at times and had little patience for certain people. Both Ula and Mona attended the monthly book group as well as Professional Women's Network meetings, but Mona didn't give Ula the time of day at such gatherings.

We were from such radically different backgrounds that sometimes it was a stretch for us to understand each other. As a teenager, Mona had been forced to flee her Igbo homeland during the Biafran War, and she remained in Lagos until her family emigrated to the UK. I never saw the kinds of privation and cruelty that she must have witnessed as a youth in Nigeria, which probably molded her into the fearless, accomplished woman she became. She was a single mother who had to work full-time to provide for herself and her children, whereas I was a stay-at-home mom and part-time writer. Mona longed to write too, and she jumped at my suggestion that we form a writing group, although she rarely found time to write after her long workdays. These differences between us made me uncomfortable at times—that in accompanying Stefan overseas, I didn't have to work outside the home and could stay home and write.

At the end of our second year, Aaron was old enough to attend kindergarten at the International School of Abidjan (ICSA). He was much happier after switching schools since everyone spoke English and his closest friend—Jeane's daughter—landed in his class.

Apart from a couple of family outings to the beach, I didn't see as much of Ula after Aaron started attending a different school from her daughter. With my self-imposed work schedule in the mornings and room mother duties at Aaron's school, I didn't have a lot of free time. On top of that was the fact that Ula was often sick.

Most Europeans and Americans took malaria prophylaxis in that endemic region, but Ula and Detlef tried to avoid prescription meds and used herbal remedies instead. He had contracted malaria when he lived in Africa years earlier, and he believed it built up his resistance and toughened him against the disease. Ula tried to tough it out too, but beating malaria took more than positive thinking and bravado.

The first time she came down with it, her doctor treated her at home with a combination of medicines. She was listless and pale for weeks and quit attending her classes and meetings. I felt for her, having been sick a lot myself in our first year in Ivory Coast. Then Detlef got malaria too, and his arms and waist shrank to the size of Ula's. They returned to Germany early for the Christmas holidays and stayed for a month to recuperate.

Unlike Ula, I was healthy and thriving by my third year in Abidjan. My children were happy, and I was part of several friend networks that made me feel connected and at home there. Most birthdays and holidays we spent with the families of Stefan's colleagues.

When Ula and Detlef returned from Germany in January, they'd both gained weight and looked healthier. Ula started attending book group meetings and resumed her classes. But within a month of her return, she got sick again and had to miss meetings and classes for weeks. Everyone contracted colds and other ailments in Abidjan, yet Ula would develop symptoms that lingered. I called to check on her one day and was informed by her cook that she'd gone to the clinic with malaria again.

When she was feeling somewhat better, I drove to her house and sat on the terrace with her. Sipping citronella tea, she seemed pale and weak yet eager to visit with me. When I told her about a recent book group meeting, Ula started grilling me about Mona. Her questions made me feel awkward as I tried to figure out if she was jealous or hurt that we hadn't seen as much of each other recently. To satisfy her curiosity, I told her in broad outlines about Mona's work and family but was careful not to mention a trip we planned to take together in the spring.

At the end of our visit, I was caught unawares when Ula asked, "Do you have any travel plans in coming months?"

It was as if she'd read my mind or heard about the trip from someone. In a sheepish tone, I admitted, "Mona and I are thinking of going to Paris at the end of March."

Without missing a beat, Ula piped up, "I should go with you. It is exactly what I need."

I was too stunned and too much of a coward to tell her it wasn't a good idea. I also felt guilty about neglecting her and found it hard to refuse an ailing friend who gazed at me with imploring eyes. It was obvious that she wanted to be included, and I knew how that felt too, which is why I gave her a tentative okay.

I hoped that Mona would understand the difficult position I was in. But when I broke it to her that Ula had invited herself on the trip, she threatened to cancel. I tried to reassure her that Ula could go off on her own and we'd be able to write in parks and cafés as we'd planned. I even offered to book the hotel for us and carefully avoided discussing any more details with Mona.

One month later, I found myself sandwiched between two disgruntled friends on a night flight to Paris. Ula seemed anxious and kept asking me why Mona ignored her while the latter feigned sleep in the seat to my other side. I didn't get a wink of sleep myself through the long flight, stuck in the middle as I was and feeling like a spectator in my own life.

As soon as we touched down at Charles de Gaulle Airport, Mona turned to me and announced, "I won't be staying at the hotel with you after all." She didn't look at me as she continued. "I contacted a friend in Paris who offered to let me stay in her flat. You could have joined us, but three's too many."

I nodded and said nothing, too startled by her news.

After clearing immigration and retrieving our luggage, we took an escalator to the metro, and I watched with a heavy heart as Mona strode off to catch a different train from the one Ula and I would take to the city. Ula was excited about the hotel I'd booked in St. Germaine, the bohemian heart of Paris, while I was distraught over Mona's abrupt departure.

My spirits lifted when we found the hotel, which was situated on a cobblestone square overlooking the Church of St. Sulpice. The receptionist asked if we wanted to keep the two rooms I'd booked or if we preferred to share one. Ula said one room would be fine, but I shook my head and asked for a single room with a view of the square. I was determined to make my first trip away from Stefan and the children memorable despite Mona's absence.

It soon became memorable for all the wrong reasons. It was hard for me to enjoy the novelties of Paris when every time I turned around, it felt like I was bumping into Ula. She'd link her arm through mine and chatter in my ear whenever we went out walking, and in moments of silence, she'd sigh or hum. Ula's bubbly mood and parakeet tone grated on my nerves, especially since I missed Mona, who had intended to use that week as a writing retreat with me.

Mona turned out to be cold and elusive all week. I'd phone her in the mornings to arrange meetings, and sometimes we'd get our signals crossed and one of us would arrive late or in a huff. Sitting in cafés and restaurants together, she'd get irritated whenever Ula would sigh or say something. The tension between us was so thick that I was afraid to open my mouth and risk being pinioned by Mona's javelin glare.

One day, after visiting the Louvre together and hopping on and off city buses, I made the mistake of suggesting we go shopping in the Galleries Lafayette. Already tired and hungry, we plunged into the crowded corridors of the huge department store and trailed after each other from one floor to the next. Eventually we split up with a plan to meet in an hour on the ground floor. Ula and I managed to meet at the arranged time, but we couldn't find Mona. Since we didn't have cell phones, we wandered around for an hour searching for her until the store closed.

I called Mona as soon as we got to the hotel, and she answered the landline in her friend's apartment. "I was worried about you," I said, a little vexed. "We searched for you for an hour."

"I looked for you too," she said brusquely. "But my back hurt, and I was tired, and that store was an absolute zoo. I just decided to pack it in and go home."

"I guess it wasn't a good idea to tackle Galleries Lafayette at the end of the day," I conceded. "At least you made it home okay."

"Would you want to meet my friend and me for dinner?" she asked in an appeasing tone.

"How long would it take to get to her apartment?" I asked.

"A half hour by metro. Maybe less in a taxi, but it might be expensive."

I looked at the clock and sighed. "It's already eight, and I can't face another metro ride. Let's meet tomorrow in the Tuileries as planned so we can write. I'll send Ula off to a gallery."

"Fine," she said in a tired voice. "See you tomorrow."

As soon as we hung up, Ula knocked at my door and stepped into the room. "What did Mona say?" she asked in a testy tone. "Did she explain why she left without telling us?"

"She looked for us, but her back was hurting, and she had to leave," I responded vaguely.

Ula must have noticed my downcast expression. She pulled a chair to the bed where I was sitting and took my hand in hers, forcing me to look in her solemn eyes. "You should not be angry with me on account of Mona."

"I'm not angry with you. I know it's not your fault." I said this even though there was a grain of truth in what she said. She must have intuited that I was unhappy with myself and with her for ruining my plans with Mona.

"We should discuss this and tell each other our feelings," Ula insisted. "Let's go to dinner and discuss it over a glass of wine."

"I'm too tired from walking all day and just want to go to bed early," I grumbled. "Let's just eat the croissants we bought this morning and stay in."

Much later, I would regret not going for a glass of wine and having the heart-to-heart talk that Ula craved. She'd wanted to have an honest discussion about the dynamics between us, yet I couldn't voice my feelings and risk hurting her, nor could I admit that it was my fault for telling her she could go in the first place. Torn between a desire to make things up with her and needing time to myself, I ended up being curt and evasive as Mona had been with me that week. Having a hard conversation with Ula would have helped us resolve things and strengthen our bond, but I was exhausted and sought the easy way out.

The next morning I phoned Mona to fix a time to meet at the the Tuileries as we'd planned. "I've had a change of plans," she announced. "I'm taking a train to Strasbourg with my friend for a few days, and I'll return to Abidjan at the end of the weekend instead of tomorrow."

Stunned, I could only respond, "Okay, have a good trip, and I'll see you in Abidjan." I hung up the phone feeling more dejected than ever.

When Ula asked me what we should do on our last day in Paris, I suggested we visit a gallery and go to a matinee. I was emotionally depleted and didn't want to talk about anything of consequence. Tired of walking a tightrope between two demanding friends, I missed Stefan and the children and looked forward to going home.

My disappointment with the trip had less to do with Ula—who was always sweet and upbeat—and more to do with Mona's and my relationship. Instead of the trip we'd intended as a writing retreat, it had been tense whenever the three of us were together. Mona made the most of it by going off with her other friend, and Ula was happy to be in Paris with me. I was the only disgruntled one who hadn't known how to work things out with my friends and simply enjoy Paris in the spring.

I didn't see much of Ula after we returned from that trip. She contracted malaria again and so did Detlef. While it didn't keep him down for long, Ula fell out of the loop and stayed home for weeks on end. When I visited her one day, she reminisced about our time in Paris as if it had been a sublime experience for her. Then she surprised me with the news that they'd decided not to renew Detlef's three-year contract. They would leave Ivory Coast for good at summer's end. She seemed excited about the prospect of returning to her family and friends, though she said she was sorry to leave me there alone.

The thing is that I was far from alone. Besides Mona, I had friends at the international school, in expat groups, and among Stefan's colleagues. It was a big turnover year, and a handful of close friends would be leaving, including Jeane and my neighbor Marybeth along with Alan and Michele. In that summer of sad goodbyes, Aaron lost his best friend, Hana, along with other classmates. Yet new families were also arriving, and I would meet women with shared interests by hosting the book group at my house.

I was sad to see Ula go. She had so many endearing qualities that I valued in a friend and was a compassionate, vivacious individual who was interested in everyone and everything. She only wanted to connect, and to that end she labored to learn French and English so she could express herself with fluent candor. She tried to express her inner struggles and joys through creative dance and painting. I identified with her since I was trying to do the same through writing. When she left, I lost a kindred spirit who truly cared about me. We promised to stay in touch after we parted.

It would come as a happy surprise that Ula and I would continue to write and visit each other over the years—in Europe and the US—and that she would turn out to be one of my most faithful friends and correspondents.

Chapter 6

Entrenched in Our New Home

Trips and visitors often disrupted our work routines, though I didn't mind since we had concentrated family time with Stefan when he wasn't working. On one trip, we drove to Ghana to visit the former slave castles along the coast with friends from Germany.

We decamped for a couple of nights at a modest hotel at Biriwa Beach near the Cape Coast and Elmina Castles. Situated along the most picturesque beaches we'd seen in West Africa, both towns had been infamous slave-trading ports. The sea along that stretch of coast was turquoise green, and the surf lapped gently at the palm-lined shore, unlike the rough Atlantic off Ivory Coast. It was hard to square the stunning scene—of stark white castles against a coral sea—with the insidious history of the forts as holding pens for enslaved Africans before they were shipped overseas.

The narrow dungeons where tens of thousands of people had been shackled together for weeks and months were shocking. In the glistening sunlight framed by a white-sand beach, it was hard to conjure the desperation and terror of so many captives in crowded cells, the acrid stench as oppressive as the heat.

Apart from the picturesque setting, other contradictions were jarring. The castle had been sanitized to the point of appearing sterile, and the video describing the castle's history glossed over the horrors that took place within its confines. It focused instead on the talents of

West Africans and products they made while saying little about the torture that captives endured there.

I lingered outside the castle at the end of our visit while the others went off to find coconuts for the kids to drink. Ghanaian pupils trailed after our children, eager to speak English and peppering them with questions like "Where you from?" and "What's your name?"

Leaning against a fencepost, I was deep in thought when a guard came up and asked me, "What do you think of our castle?"

"It's horrifying to think about what went on there," I said with a grim expression.

"Well, you could look at it this way," he proposed. "Two hundred years ago, the people forced into slavery were among the poorest villagers in the land. Yet many of their descendants in America are better off today, and they are envied by those of us who remain in Africa."

I tipped my head and thought about it, not knowing how to respond—especially after interviewing a dozen African American expats who'd married West Africans and chose to live in Ivory Coast instead of the US. Most of them told me that racism had forced them to leave the US in the first place. My friend Debbie said, "I knew I would never survive in America and that I'd be just another angry Black woman. The role models were so few and far between. But in Abidjan, WE are the standard of beauty."

It was also why many expats said they would never move back— because they didn't want their children to face racism in the US. Sue, who was white, told me, "It was in the US that my son first learned he was Black, and he went through this big crisis where he didn't want to be Black. I prefer for them to grow up in Ivory Coast. The US is just too crazy—little kids on drugs and drive-by shootings. Life is simpler and slower here, and they can be kids longer." Carol, too, didn't want her daughters to have to choose between growing up white or Black in the US. "They'd be identified as Blacks in our polarized country and would have to leave me behind. A white mother can't help a child adapt to Black culture in America."

I'd understood the sting of racism in my country more acutely after interviewing these expats. Living in an African country where a huge majority of its citizens were Black allowed me to glimpse what it was like to be part of a minority. Yet Stefan and I were never profiled, nor did we experience the kind of discrimination that African Americans did in the US. We mixed easily with Africans and with our compatriots at social events in Abidjan, and we didn't have to worry about our partners and children being targeted by police or treated like second-class citizens.

Our third Christmas in Abidjan, the children and I flew to Uganda with Stefan where he and his team would present papers at the AIDS-Africa Conference in Kampala. When the conference was over, he took a much-needed break and traveled around Uganda with us.

The landscapes in East Africa seemed vaster than those in Ivory Coast, with sweeping expanses of savannah dotted by jacaranda and acacia trees and volcanic hills ringing crater lakes. We stayed in a lodge overlooking Lake Mburu where the children got to ride a camel and donkey. The scenery was also stunning in Queen Elizabeth National Park, although we only saw a small herd of elephants and a few waterbucks. A guide told us that most of the animals had been eaten during Idi Amin's vicious reign and in the ensuing decades of unrest in that country.

From Uganda, we flew to Ethiopia to spend Christmas with friends who lived in Addis. It was another lesson in contrasts, viewing a radically different country and culture from what we were used to in Ivory Coast. The landscapes were starker and more barren, and there were more destitute people roaming the streets of Addis than in Abidjan. I knew that the number of AIDS orphans in Ethiopia was staggering, yet seeing so many emaciated children tap on our car windows to ask for coins or pencils put faces on the abstract figures. It was utterly depressing.

We drove south to spend three days with our friends at a crater lake where exotic birds and flamingos roosted. Even there, as we drove through dusty villages, impoverished children ran beside our car pleading for handouts in choppy English. The refrain, "a coin or a pen, mother, give me," was heartrending. It was another harsh reminder that the AIDS epidemic had orphaned millions of children whose future prospects were dim.

The trip gave me a new appreciation for Stefan's work, and for the part he and his team were playing to slow the spread of AIDS. Though he had to work long hours and spend most days away from the family, given what was at stake, I supported him. It helped that he was able to compartmentalize and give us his undivided attention when he was with us.

After our trip to Paris, Mona and I continued to walk several times a week, and we sang together in the Abidjan Community Choir. I took on bigger jobs at the international school, like stepping into the role of coordinator for the annual UN day festivities. Happy news also came from home. Mike had fallen in love with a sweet Mexican woman, and they married and settled in the same city in Texas as our brother. A few months later, Tink called to tell me that she and her boyfriend Joe had eloped in Hawaii.

These events and relationships made me feel settled and connected in deeply satisfying ways. I'd also grown close to Gladys and Ousmane, whom I saw more than anyone else. Gladys sometimes advised me on tricky matters—like how to deal with Steve, the part-time cook who started showing up at our house with red eyes and smelling of alcohol. I tried to talk to him about his drinking and gave him several warnings over a period of months. Gladys talked to him too, and she sometimes prayed with him. Then one day his wife came to our door with bruises on her arms and face, and she complained that Steve spent all his earnings out drinking with friends. Gladys told me that he wouldn't stop drinking, and Stefan and I decided we had to let him go. A few months later, when Alan and his family left Ivory Coast, we hired their cook Gouba to replace Steve. Gouba was more adept at handling dinners and receptions since he'd been the cook for several CDC directors.

Ousmane was the guard who'd accompanied me to Adama's place when he was dying of AIDS. I grew closer to Ousmane after he became the day guard at our house. He was fit and thin, and his dark forehead was deeply lined with crow's feet since he smiled all the time. A modest man who spoke English and French along with several local languages, he was born in Burkina Faso, educated in Ghana, and worked most of his adult life in Abidjan.

One day Ousmane asked me to help him find a bicycle because it took him forty-five minutes to walk to our house each day from the crowded district where he lived. I scanned the Embassy newsletter for bike ads and found a used one for him in perfect condition. An all-terrain bike with eighteen speeds, it quickly became his pride and joy. He'd clean and lubricate it in our driveway and share it with other guards if they needed to go someplace.

We tried to make Ousmane's life easier in other ways, providing coffee, tea, and sugar as well as magazines and books to pass the time at our gate. An avid reader, he worked his way through the *Little House on the Prairie* series and Nelson Mandela's *Long Walk to Freedom*. The guard company contracted by the US Embassy paid him only one hundred dollars a month for twelve-hour workdays, six days a week. We supplemented his salary by paying him for odd jobs like raking leaves and washing the car.

He loved children and would chase Aaron and Elena around the yard with squirt guns and play hide and seek with them. He also grew attached to our dog, Bella, who followed him around the yard all day and kept the night guard company too.

Ousmane prayed five times a day on a prayer mat in our driveway. Every year he fasted during the month of Ramadan, refusing to eat or drink through long hot workdays. A year after we met him, he married a Muslim woman from the northern part of the country. He asked us to give him more jobs so he could earn money to buy wedding cloths and gifts for her family. Shortly after his wife gave birth to a daughter the following year, she became ill with what he thought was allergies or asthma. When Stefan advised her to go to a clinic for tests and x-rays, it was discovered that she had tuberculosis. She was put on medication and went to stay with her family in the dry northern region of Ivory Coast.

That summer, we flew to the US for vacation as usual. Upon our return, Ousmane told us his wife had a relapse and needed to go to the hospital for more tests and treatment. When it was time for him to leave at the end of his workday, he said goodbye to me and walked to our gate.

"Where's your bike, Ousmane?" I called after him.

With a sheepish expression, he replied, "I had to sell it to have money for my wife."

It took several months for me to find another bike for him, and the second one wasn't as nice as the first, but he was grateful because it drastically reduced his commute time.

It turned out to be a tough year for Ousmane. We'd chat most days when I was outside playing with the kids, and over time he told me more about his family. He said that his wife had become unbalanced after her bout of TB, and she was depressed that she couldn't have more children because of fibroids. A few months later, he told me that his wife left him and went to live with another man.

It was sad to see Ousmane drag his feet through the long workdays, knowing how hard it must be for him as a single father. Eventually he'd send his daughter to live with relatives in Burkina and attend school there, which meant that he only got to see her one month out of the year when he took annual leave. He knew some of our struggles too, and he got to meet family members like my sister Tink and Stefan's mother, who visited several times. Seeing his reassuring smile as he walked his rounds and exchanged news with me was like having my brother Mike around.

The bonds I formed with Gladys and Ousmane gave me a window into the daily lives of working people in Ivory Coast. I took their joys and struggles to heart and connected with them in ways I hadn't experienced before. It taught me that there were many kinds of friendship besides those with confidants like Mona and Carol. We saw each other through trying times, and those ties grounded me as expat friends came and went in our lives.

I also grew close to Martine, a massage therapist I was seeing weekly. She knew me better than my friends in a way—how the day's anxieties lodged in my shoulders and neck, and how carrying children made my back ache on account of my scoliosis. I knew her face and hands too—how strong and competent they were, and how they'd weaken if she was depressed or tired.

When Martine asked me to be godmother to her oldest daughter, I couldn't say no even though our time in Ivory Coast was limited and I couldn't be there for her long term. Martine wanted me to participate in her daughter's baptism, which was akin to a coming-of-age ceremony for girls in her age group (thirteen). I spent three hours with her at their Catholic church on a sweltering June day, and three more hours at a feast with Martine's relatives and friends. She'd stayed up most of the night cooking and preparing a reception for fifty guests while I baked a big cake. Under a rented tent outside her apartment building, she hosted a party that was like a wedding reception and an induction into her family that meant a lot to me.

Martine was one of the few Ivorians I got to know intimately. A few years younger than I, she was short and stout with a lovely round face and prominent cheek bones. Her dark eyes seemed all iris, and her husky voice was as soothing as her hands. Martine worked on clients in their homes since she didn't have a salon. We'd talk non-stop when she came to my house, mostly about our children's antics. Referring to her kids' skin color, she called her older son "the dark one" and her younger son "the light one."

I loved listening to Martine's stories about growing up in the western region of Ivory Coast. "There are no natural deaths in Africa," she told me before launching into a story about her first partner, a man from a neighboring village. The father of her daughters, he'd passed away at a young age after a brief illness, and Martine suspected a jealous cousin had poisoned him to get his fields.[11] After her partner's funeral, his relatives descended on her house and took away all the furniture, leaving her on her own with two daughters to support.

Martine had moved to Abidjan with her girls and found work with a French woman who trained her to be a masseuse. During the time I knew her, Martine had two sons with another partner in Abidjan. He asked her to move in with him, but Martine had refused because her teenage daughters didn't want to live with a man they hardly knew. Thus, she was forced to eke out a living for a family of five by herself.

Martine had undergone female circumcision at thirteen with other girls in her age group, as was the custom in her region. I begged her not to make her daughters undergo the ritual cutting. She said it would be up to them, but she steadfastly believed that men from her region considered uncircumcised women to be unclean.

Martine kept trying to improve her lot by doing odd jobs like selling ice on a street corner and taking adult literacy classes at a church-run school. She lived in a neighborhood where crime was rampant, and armed robbers broke into her apartment one night and stole everything she'd worked to provide for her kids—including a TV, camera, and radio. A few months after the burglary, her brother lost his job and brought his wife and five children to live with Martine. Her gait was slower after that, and she smiled less, worn down by fatigue. Her fondest wish was that someday one of her children would emigrate to America and have a better life there.

The words "familiar" and "family" come from the same Latin root meaning "closely personal and intimate" as well as "commonly heard and seen." I saw Gladys and Ousmane almost daily for six years and Martine weekly, and during that time we became familiar with each other's struggles and relatives. It was impossible to hide my sadness or joy from those constant companions or to ignore it when something was bothering them. They were there when I needed them and vice versa, and we felt seen and heard by each other. They helped me feel at home in a foreign country, and they were the ones I would miss the most when we would leave Ivory Coast for good, not knowing when and where we'd see each other again.

Chapter 7

The Arc of AIDS Work in Africa

In our fourth year, right after the AIDS conference in Uganda, Stefan asked me if I'd be willing to stay in Abidjan for two more years. He'd been offered the position of Project Director when Alan left, and it was a job he could easily assume. Knowing how much he wanted to take it, I didn't think it would be a huge sacrifice to let him extend his contract. I had good friends and was connected to several communities, and both children were happy at the international school. Plus, I knew that two years would pass quickly. As long as I could write, I'd be happy.

Since his early teens, Stefan knew he wanted to be a doctor and work in Africa someday. Born and raised in Belgian Congo, he had happy memories of growing up in central Africa. His father—a research veterinarian who lived and worked in Congo and Rwanda for thirteen years—had been the role model and inspiration for Stefan's career in public health overseas. During and after medical school, Stefan had worked at mission hospitals in Rwanda, Lesotho, and Zambia.

While he was doing his residency at Georgetown University, mutual friends had invited us to dinner, suspecting we'd be a good match. We hit it off immediately and dated each other exclusively after that, and three years later we were married. As newlyweds, we lived in Silver Spring, Maryland while Stefan was doing research at the National Institutes of Health.

One evening in the late 1980s, I got a rude surprise when I opened the refrigerator and found an insulated bag that I didn't recognize. Peeking inside, I was horrified to see a dozen vials of blood in test tubes. "What's this bag in our fridge?" I asked Stefan, who was in the next room.

"It's blood from some AIDS patients," he replied off-handedly. "I have to take it to the lab tomorrow."

"You put infected blood in our fridge?" I yelped, quickly shutting the door.

"The lab was closed by the time my flight got in. What was I supposed to do?"

I left the kitchen and refused to open the refrigerator for the rest of the night. There were no treatments for AIDS in the late 1980s and research was still in its infancy. When Stefan was working in the Viral Epidemiology Branch, he sometimes flew to New York to examine AIDS patients in a Manhattan clinic for one of his studies.

I had an inkling then of what might be in store for me, living with a man who hoped to work overseas and see patients with life-threatening diseases. Though he promised never to bring vials of infected blood home again, I knew he was looking for jobs that would put me and our future children in contact with people infected with HIV. Such contact was less scary when we moved to Abidjan in 1993. By then we knew it was rare to get HIV from casual contact, and that sexual intercourse, blood transfusions, and dirty needles were the main modes of transmission.

The timing was serendipitous for someone who wanted to work on life-threatening diseases in foreign countries. In a long career working with AIDS patients, Stefan would witness an impressive arc—from a sense of hopelessness about the disease in the 1980s and '90s to talk of ending AIDS by 2030 when the number of new HIV infections should become negligible. In the 1990s, the focus of his research at CDC was on better understanding the scale of the AIDS epidemic and on finding ways to prevent HIV infections and deaths. A decade later, when medications and funding were available, the focus shifted from research to expanding HIV prevention and treatment programs.

After he took over as Director of the CDC Project in 1997, demands on him intensified and kept him from home even more than before. He often traveled to clinics and hospitals around the country, and when he was in Abidjan, his time was taken up in meetings with staff and political leaders. His workload doubled when the staff had to prepare for a conference or a site visit from CDC and other government officials. As long as he blocked off Sundays to spend with the family, I didn't complain about his long hours at the office.

Being his partner meant that I would get to live in foreign countries and see the world. It also meant that my children and I would be exposed to diseases like AIDS, malaria, and TB, not to mention Ebola and other tropical diseases. Taking two small children to West Africa at the height of the AIDS epidemic had seemed like a risky venture, especially since AIDS was considered a death sentence as medications weren't available and little could be done to treat people infected with HIV.

It was gratifying to see how happy he was, and I was proud of him for doing critical work that was making a difference in people's lives. He was living his dream—doing research in an African country at the helm of a public health project—and he especially enjoyed working with Ivorians and other African colleagues.[12] For Stefan, the job in Ivory Coast would turn out to be the most engaging and rewarding of his long career. Two of his landmark studies would be cited for years to come: one demonstrating that the antibiotic Bactrim cut the mortality rate for AIDS patients in Africa by half, and the other showing that pregnant women in Ivory Coast who took AZT before delivery were less likely to pass HIV on to their babies.[13]

For me, after a difficult first year, Ivory Coast would be the place

where I'd learn the most challenging life lessons and make a dozen
enduring friendships. Like Stefan, I treasured the daily contact with
people of other cultures and was fundamentally changed by those
relationships. Pico Iyer, an American author and essayist of Indian
origin who lives in Japan, would encapsulate that experience in a TED
Talk he would give some years later. "Home isn't just a place where we
happened to be born. It's a place where we become ourselves." In Ivory
Coast, I became someone I hadn't foreseen in the process of finding
my place there. That process had also started for Aaron and Elena,
who considered Abidjan their "home."

When Stefan mentioned an upcoming conference in Togo, I asked
him if we could go and take Gladys along since I'd been wanting to
meet her family.

I often sought Gladys's opinion on events in Abidjan or issues with
my children. We'd laugh over little things that happened in the day, and
if one of us got irritated by something the other said or did, we'd go our
own ways and bide our time. There were never raised voices or angry
words between us, and irritations or snubs were quickly forgotten. I'd
come to rely on her in ways that I didn't rely on other friends.

Gladys had grown up in a village north of Lomé, Togo's capital.
She was delighted when I proposed that the children and I could meet
her in Togo while Stefan was at the conference. She went by bus a few
days before us to spend more time with her family.

The day after we flew to Lomé, I found a taxi driver who'd take me
and the children to Gladys's village an hour north of the capital. Along
the way, vast stretches of farmland were interspersed with coconut
palms, though there were few large trees remaining from the rain
forests that had once predominated in the region. Instead of the lush
growth we were used to seeing in southern Ivory Coast, Togo was a
land of baked red earth that was drought prone.

We turned off the highway and bumped along an unpaved ochre road to Gladys's village. Despite obvious signs of poverty, most of the houses were made of cinderblocks with tin roofs on top instead of thatch, and cement floors instead of bare earth. We were greeted warmly by Gladys's mother and grandparents as well as an uncle and two of her ten siblings.

With big smiles all around, everyone shook hands and the elders stroked Aaron's and Elena's blond heads. My kids were so comfortable with Gladys that they weren't bothered by the looks and comments—which we couldn't understand since they only spoke a local language. Gladys translated for us as Elena held her hand, jealously observing Gladys's daughters—who were six and nine—as they hovered nearby. Their simple dresses were dusty from playing outside, and Elena's quickly got dusty too after she started playing with the older girls.

Gladys told us that her family grew cassava, maize, and peanuts for their own use as well as for sale in the market. Her mother and grand-mother were short thin women who walked around bare breasted and with headwraps to protect them from the sun. When I asked if I could take a family photo, the women ran in the house to cover themselves with colorful cloths. The men draped bright *pagne* (African fabric) over their shoulders and a few more cousins and nephews wandered in to join the group photo.

Per Gladys's suggestion, we gave her mother a carton of soap that we'd bought at the market in Lomé along with colored pencils and paper that Aaron and Elena distributed to the children. One of the boys shimmied up a tree and knocked down a few coconuts for Aaron and Elena to drink.

After an hour of smiling and nodding, I could tell the children were getting tired, and so was Gladys after translating for us. We said our goodbyes and shook hands with everyone again, leaving Gladys there to spend a few more days with her family. We returned to Lomé

in the taxi, happy to have met Gladys's family and get a glimpse of her
home life.

To better grasp Stefan's work and see firsthand how people were
coping with HIV, I accompanied him on several site visits to prenatal
clinics and to a house for sex workers. I also went on home health
visits with his colleagues.[14] These visits put faces behind the statistics
that doctors at the project were collecting.

When we visited a shantytown on the outskirts of Abidjan, I listened as a home health worker counseled some of her clients. A family
of five from a neighboring country lived in a one-room shack that
was attached to others on both sides. It was a lot like the house of our
first guard, Adama, whom I'd visited before he died. Wood slats were
lined with discarded cardboard boxes and the shacks had tin sheets
for roofs. It was hot and crowded already at 9 a.m., and the sounds
of people in adjoining shacks and passersby resounded through the
rickety room.

The home health worker spoke softly to a young woman with
AIDS, who shivered on a thin mattress under a thread-worn blanket. The client's voice was barely audible as she answered the worker's questions about her eating habits. Speaking in French, I asked
her daughter who stood nearby how old she was and if she attended
school. She said she was thirteen, and that she had to drop out of
school to take care of her mother. The double tragedy was distressing—that the mother's disease had impacted the girl's life by curtailing
her education and future prospects.

At another family's quarters, a woman in her forties told the home
health worker that she was caring for three grandchildren while her
daughter lay dying inside. With an aching heart, I watched the sick
woman's children play outside and wondered what kind of future the
kids would have. They were wrenching scenes, softened only by the

kind and efficient ways in which the home health worker counseled her clients.

Another day I accompanied Stefan to a big house where sex workers were lodging. In 1997, the HIV infection rate among sex workers in Abidjan—many of them immigrants—was reportedly 55 percent. A stout older woman ran this particular house, and she told us that she gave out free condoms and required her sex workers to make customers use them. The workers were also required to have regular tests for HIV.

"What if a customer refuses to use condoms?" I asked the Madame.

The woman crossed her thick arms and snickered. "Then the girl will use a female condom, or the man will have to go someplace else."

Such rules must have been working, because the HIV infection rate among sex workers would plummet by the time Stefan left Ivory Coast in 1999. It was encouraging to know that the women were taking charge of their lives and protecting their health—if what the Madame said was true. Still, it was depressing to hear that many women were contracting HIV because of their partner's behavior. Home health workers said that most of their female clients blamed male partners for refusing to wear condoms or for going with other women and bringing the disease home to them. The fallout on children was doubly tragic, especially for girls who had to drop out of school to take care of an ailing parent and for the many kids orphaned by AIDS.

These visits reinforced my decision to let Stefan extend his contract for two more years, knowing that his work was making a real difference in people's lives.

The months leading up to two big annual AIDS conferences—the International AIDS Conference and the AIDS in Africa Conference—were always the most stressful at the project. For the first time, the

latter would be held in Abidjan at the end of Stefan's first year as director, in December 1997. In the weeks leading up to the conference, he'd
leave for work each day at 7 a.m. and return home at 10 p.m. It was
hard for an introvert like me to fathom how he could be around people
all day who needed his feedback on their research posters and presentations. Yet he always maintained his sense of humor and perspective
in stressful times. One night he came home at 10 p.m. and shook his
head when I asked him about his day. "It was nuts," he sighed. "We
think we're so important with our twenty-four presentations, and
because we're the biggest AIDS research project in Africa, but most of
it is BS." He wasn't referring to the actual work, but to the jockeying
for attention and ego-stroking that such conferences promoted.

On the last night of the AIDS-Africa Conference, we hosted a
dinner for forty guests—the largest number we'd ever had—under two
big tents in our yard. I did my best to talk to the Ivorian doctors on
Stefan's staff and to other guests, but it was hard for me after running
around all day prepping for the party and then having to interact with
so many people. I collapsed at the end of the evening as my exhilarated husband pronounced the conference to be a success.

Two days later, Stefan had to fly to Washington, DC and then to
Atlanta to defend his groundbreaking studies in front of a panel of
experts before the results could be published. Both of his studies—of
the positive effects for pregnant women who took AZT before delivery, and TB patients who lived longer after taking Bactrim—would be
cited for decades and used as guidelines for treatment of people with
HIV.

After Stefan returned from the weeklong trip to Atlanta, he was
utterly exhausted and jet lagged. Yet he still couldn't rest as another
deadline loomed. Abstracts for the International AIDS Conference—
to be held in Geneva the following June—were due, and he had only
four days to review and edit the abstracts for his staff.

By that point I had enough going on in my life that I didn't resent his absences and the many demands on his time. I was absorbed in writing my first novel, and I was also earning money by editing the annual report for the African Development Bank (thanks to a connection of Mona's). I sang in a community choir and still walked with Mona in the evenings. Hosting the book group and serving on the board of the Professional Women's Network also kept me busy. With caring people around us like Gladys and Ousmane, the children and I were very much at home and we had plenty of friends.

That year as in the past, the international school held a Christmas concert in which all the students participated. On a balmy evening in December, eager parents sat around a stage set up in the middle of the campus green, the palm trees ringing it strung with colored lights.

Elena's kindergarten class was the first to march onstage. She sang "Noel" in French along with her classmates, an earnest expression on her face as she enunciated each syllable of every word. When Aaron's class filed onstage, his blond head stood out among his classmates, most of them from African countries. The boys wore red and gold vests while the girls had skirts made from the same wax-print fabric. Their beloved music teacher, an Ivorian man, directed the children as they held hands and sang the South African national anthem first in Xhosa, then in English, and finally in French. It was three years since apartheid ended and Nelson Mandela became South Africa's President, and the sight of two dozen children holding hands and singing the national anthem moved me to tears. [15] It was deeply gratifying to know that our kids were growing up in an African country when South Africa was finally free. I treasured that moment as parents and children from sixty-some countries celebrated the holidays together.

The rest of Christmas week was a blur. I sang with the community choir at a reception hosted by the Ambassador, and we attended

several parties—including Angie's annual Christmas Eve bash—
before hosting Christmas dinner ourselves. Stefan pulled off his traditional Polish dinner by making most of the dishes himself, including
borscht, pierogies, a poached fish dish, and a chocolate log stuffed
with whipped cream. Several of his colleagues and their families
joined us and were duly impressed with his cooking.

On New Year's Eve, Mona hosted a dinner for Stefan and me to
meet her mother, her sister, and her brother's families. At the end of
the evening, she invited me to go to Lagos with her for the celebration
of her mother's seventieth birthday in February. I was excited by the
prospect of seeing Nigeria with a friend who knew the country intimately, and it meant a great deal that Mona wanted to include me. It
would be the high point of our friendship, and I was content to be
where I was.

Chapter 8
Last Acts in Abidjan

Even though it was an honor to be invited to Mona's mother's birthday, I had misgivings about going to Nigeria. The US State Department had issued travel warnings about Lagos, and I'd heard that Embassy personnel always rode from the airport to the city in convoys with armored vehicles since bandits sometimes attacked drivers along the road. Mona told me that her brother had been shot in Lagos by a burglar two years earlier. Though he was only wounded in the shoulder, his arm never functioned normally after that. But when I voiced my concern about security to Mona, she glared at me. "You know, sometimes I think about reevaluating our friendship," she said in an exasperated tone.

I swallowed my fears and trusted Mona to be my pilot and guide. She drove to Lagos a few days before me to prepare for her mother's party. The day I arrived, she picked me up at the airport and took me to a small hotel near her mother's place.

The birthday celebration was held the following evening in an upscale restaurant that had been reserved for the party. Mona was in the spotlight much of the night, sharing the role of emcee with her sister and brothers. Close to a hundred guests came, the men dressed in long robes and the women wearing elaborate head wraps that matched their colorful gowns. Mona seated me next to one of her friends, a hefty man in a powder blue boubou with a matching cap on his head. He escorted me to the buffet table and described the stews, vegetables, and fish dishes on display.

As dinner wound down, Mona and her brothers took the microphone and invited guests to share stories about their mother. Relatives and friends got up one by one to pay tribute to her, some of them wringing laughs from the audience while others brought tears to people's eyes. Mona capped the tributes by singing a song her mother loved, impressing me even more with her talents and courage before a crowd.

After the speeches, the band started playing and a dozen guests made their way to the dance floor. I danced with my dinner companion and Mona's brothers and didn't sit down until the band quit at 2 a.m. As the party broke up, her brothers invited Mona and me to a gathering at their house, and we agreed to join them. Giddy from unrelenting talk and exhaustion, I left them as the sun came up in the morning.

Mona showed me around Lagos later that day, and we got stuck in one of the city's legendary traffic jams. Knowing my keen interest in African art, she took me to a couple of galleries that showcased the work of her family friends. The paintings were reasonably priced, and I bought a few to take home with me.

Being with Mona's family gave me a deeper appreciation for her background and her devotion to her mother. I'd had nothing but good experiences in Nigeria.

Yet my relationship with Mona had always been difficult, and her moods were sometimes hard for me to comprehend. A few months after the trip to Nigeria, she stopped calling me to walk with her in the evenings. When we did meet up, I asked her why she didn't want to walk anymore. "I've started training for a marathon with my new French friend," she said casually.

Stung by her bluntness, I wrote in my journal, "After four years of friendship, it hits me in the face how utterly different we are and that I can't keep up with Mona. She's hard as nails at times, and she has little forgiveness in her heart. Though she's generous to a fault, she doesn't forgive weakness, and she's found plenty of it in me. For one thing, I'm not as gregarious and self-sufficient as she's always had to be. Maybe it's my turn to be dropped as she dropped other friends?" I knew this because Mona had told me about former friends she'd stopped seeing.

It was hard for me to take long walks anyway. I had developed hip bursitis from walking on the stone floors in our house for five years, and it was painful for me to walk even while wearing cushy running shoes. Swimming was the only exercise that didn't bother my hips, and it was a pastime Mona didn't share. We no longer saw each other at choir practice since the group had disbanded, and she rarely attended Professional Women's Network meetings. She seemed to be distancing herself for reasons I didn't understand.

Two months after my trip to Nigeria, Stefan took a week off at Easter and we flew to Senegal with our children. We spent a few days in the capital, Dakar—which we found to be cleaner and safer than Abidjan and with a more temperate climate——before hiring a taxi to take us to a beach town on the coast.

The drive through the dusty countryside took much longer than expected since we were held up multiple times by herds of goats spilling onto the road. Ahmed, the taxi driver, told us it was the feast of Tabaski—a Muslim version of our Thanksgiving—and that most of the goats and lambs would be slaughtered that day. After describing the Tabaski rituals as he drove, he spontaneously invited us to his family's feast and said he lived near the beach where we were going. We accepted his offer with some trepidation since we didn't know what Ahmed's family would think of four white foreigners crashing their holiday.

When we arrived at his home—a modest bungalow with a dirt

courtyard surrounded by high walls—a bleating goat was tethered in the yard, and Ahmed's brother and family were there waiting. Because the weather was hot and we'd thought we were just going to the beach, Stefan and I were dressed in T-shirts and shorts while our hosts were wearing long robes. I felt out of place at first, yet the family's warmth and friendly faces reassured me.

Ahmed sent one of his sons to buy soft drinks for everyone, and we stood around sipping Orangina as we watched him prepare to kill the goat. Ahmed dug a hole in the ground and sharpened an old butcher knife before pinning the goat down with its neck positioned over the hole. Quickly and efficiently, he sliced the goat's throat and let the blood drain into the ground. When he began to disembowel it, I watched Aaron and Elena anxiously to see if the slaughter might bother them. On the contrary, they watched in fascination at what turned out to be an anatomy lesson as Stefan identified the body parts when Ahmed removed the intestines, kidneys, liver, and heart.

While hunks of meat were roasting, Stefan spoke with the men in French and I watched the women tend the fire and roast the victuals. When they were ready, we sat on low wooden stools and ate our fill of rice and goatmeat as the children ran off to play with Ahmed's kids and other village children. We didn't see much of them in the ensuing hour—and I couldn't help worrying—as they ran around the village with Ahmed's children. Aaron and Elena had so much fun playing with the kids that they didn't want to leave when it was time to go to our hotel.

I wasn't alone in remembering that day as a singular experience. Years later, I would ask Aaron if he had mostly good memories of growing up overseas, and he'd tell me that his strongest memories of childhood revolved around play. He would cite that trip to Senegal as an example of how he could play with kids he'd never met before who didn't speak his language, though they did communicate in French. Few children in the US grew up playing games with foreigners and interacting with adults from other countries the way our kids did. As a result, they were flexible enough to adapt and feel at home almost anywhere.

At the end of our fifth year in Abidjan, Stefan and I agreed that we should move back to the US when his contract ended the following year. He said he'd be ready to leave Project Retro-CI after wrapping up his two major studies. He was already working with a newly formed UNAIDS group on a plan to deliver life-saving medications to AIDS patients. It would be the first time that HIV-infected people in Africa would have access to "combination therapy"—medications that would allow them to live longer and healthier lives. The Project's directives were about to shift, and Stefan was ready to pass the torch to a new director.

Family concerns were also pulling us home as his mother's health worsened and so did my hip bursitis. It was painful for me to live in a house with stone floors, and I needed intensive physical therapy. When we traveled to the US that summer, we told our families that we'd spend one more year in Ivory Coast.

Upon our return to Abidjan in August, I called Mona to tell her the news.

"Is this really going to be your last year?" she asked after pausing.

"Yes," I said with a lightness in my voice that must have betrayed my enthusiasm.

"You're really going to leave me here?" she asked in a solemn tone.

"I'm afraid so," I said without bothering to hide my excitement. I was being honest partly because our friendship had felt uneven for some time, and because I was physically and emotionally preparing to leave.

I didn't hear much from Mona after that phone call. My hip bursitis flared up again upon our return to Abidjan, and I was unable to walk or sit comfortably. The Embassy doctor sent me to London to consult an orthopedist, and he injected my hips with steroids. It kept the pain at bay for a while, but after several weeks of walking on stone floors, my bursitis flared up again.

Stefan made a plywood pallet for me that stood two feet off the floor, and we bought a thin foam mat to go on top of it. It enabled me to lie on my stomach during the day and work on my laptop while leaning over the edge. Though the pain was intense when I walked, I felt guilty about complaining when so many people around us were ill. Gouba and his wife were sick as was the neighbor's guard who had chronic pain that Stefan suspected might be stomach cancer.

I called Mona soon after my return from London, but she never came to visit or made time to see me. I assumed it was because she had little patience for someone with physical complaints. Then there was an unfortunate incident with her daughter, who was a year older than Aaron and had always enjoyed playing with my children.

Every Halloween, the US Embassy arranged a trick-or-treat route that dependents and their children could follow to the houses of other official Americans. For security reasons, only children of US Embassy personnel were allowed to trick-or-treat at designated houses, so when Mona's daughter asked me if she could trick-or-treat with Aaron and Elena, I had to say no. She told Mona that she thought we didn't want her parading around with us because she was Black. Realizing too late that I should have explained the rules better or arranged to do something else with her, I apologized to Mona for hurting her daughter. I tried to tell her that it wasn't about race since African American children affiliated with the Embassy trick-or-treated with the group.

I tried contacting Mona repeatedly after the incident, but she never responded to my phone calls or emails. I even wrote her a letter apologizing again for not including her daughter in some other way. After I drove the letter to her house and left it in the mailbox, she still didn't respond. When I finally did manage to reach her on the phone, I asked Mona why she was avoiding me.

"I'm sorry, but I feel like I have to protect my daughter," she said brusquely.

I was devastated and realized there was nothing I could say to change her mind.

With few close friends remaining in Abidjan, the last year was difficult for me. I still wrote most mornings, although I couldn't sit for long and had to use a standing desk or lie on the pallet while working. Some days I'd go to a friend's house and use her pool, standing waist-deep in the water while editing my work. It allowed me to be semi-weightless for a couple of hours and ease the pressure on my hips.

We still saw Angie and Peter and other close friends among Stefan's colleagues, but the political situation had become tense again with elections looming. I was fed up with living in a tense environment, which strengthened my resolve that it was time to leave.

The American community was on heightened alert for months after the US embassies in Kenya and Tanzania were bombed in August of 1998 and 224 people died. In retaliation, the US bombed military installations in Iraq, and the Embassy warned Americans to be on standby in case we had to be evacuated. During that tense time, Stefan had to travel to Senegal on business, and I worried that we might be evacuated to another country without him. When his return flight was cancelled several times, I became more anxious that something might happen to his plane.

The night he walked in the door unexpectedly and I beheld his tired face, it was like seeing the sun come out after a month of monsoon rains. Every time he went away for a week, I fell in love with him all over again.

It raised my spirits even more when my parents came to Abidjan for the holidays, as did Stefan's older brother with his wife and children. My parents got to visit Aaron's and Elena's classrooms for their holiday parties, and they attended Angie's annual Christmas Eve feast with us. Santa always paid a visit at the party, and that year they asked Stefan's older brother to play Santa since he looked the part. One week later, my parents were thrilled to spend New Year's Eve at Angie and Peter's place in Assini and watch the villagers ignite huge bonfires all along the beach at midnight.

Aaron and Elena escorted their grandparents on dog walks around the neighborhood and introduced them to the guards and street venders they knew. My parents were impressed that the kids could translate whatever people said to them in French. When we served a whole fish at dinner one night, Elena shocked them by plucking out the eyes and popping them in her mouth as Ivorian kids would do. My mother shrieked while my father's eyes widened. It was exactly the kind of response that Elena had wanted.

Their visit gave them glimpses of our lives in that special place along with the opportunity to meet Gladys, Ousmane, and Martine. Mona even stopped by to meet them, which meant a lot to me. My parents got to see things they'd never seen before—like craftsmen making shelves and clay pots on street corners and the way pineapples grow—and they were impressed with a visit to the world's biggest basilica in Yamoussoukro.

Gladys and Ousmane and other guards treated my parents like royal guests, honored that elderly people would travel all the way from America to visit their country. When I told Ousmane that my father was one of sixteen children, his jaw dropped, and he asked, "*Meme mere, meme pere?*" ("Same mother, same father?") since most African families only had that many children when a man had several wives.

It was the trip of a lifetime for my parents, who'd both grown up in poverty during the depression. My father told me as he was leaving,

"I'll never be the same after this." I felt that way too, and it meant a great deal that he understood how the country had changed us.

As the prospect of our departure loomed, I felt a heaviness about the people and places we'd leave behind. A few months before the holidays, Ousmane had announced that he would marry a woman from his home country, and he'd asked us to give him odd jobs around the yard to earn extra money for the bride price. He traveled to Burkina during his annual leave and brought his young wife back to Abidjan with him.

Then it was Gladys's turn to get married, and all of us were excited for her. Francis was a sweet man she'd met at her Assembly of God Church who clearly loved her, and Stefan and I were grateful that she'd found a partner. It eased my mind when I thought about leaving her and Ousmane in a couple of months—that they wouldn't be alone.

Despite the hard work that Stefan's team and others were doing, the ravages of AIDS went unabated and hundreds of thousands of people in African countries were still dying of the disease each year. It hit home again when our cook grew ill. Gouba was a Muslim man who, like Adama, had one wife back home in Burkina and a younger wife in Abidjan. A quiet, dignified man who didn't chat much when he worked, he always had time for the kids if they asked him for something. Short and wiry, he spoke French but not much English, and he observed things closely through his owl-like glasses.

The year we were preparing to leave, Gouba's first wife and the mother of his seven children passed away suddenly, most likely from AIDS. He took a month off and traveled to his village in Burkina for her burial and returned looking sick and emaciated himself. He had bronchitis and diarrhea and needed to take another month off to rest.

He had mostly recovered by the time a baby daughter was born to his young wife in Abidjan. The sickly infant was in and out of clinics during the three months of her short life. When she died, Gouba's wife fell ill too with throat and stomach pain and chronic fatigue. She was treated for TB, malaria, and worms, but nothing seemed to help.

Stefan urged Gouba and his wife to go to an AIDS clinic for tests. After doing so, the doctor gave him the results in a sealed envelope that he brought to our house to show Stefan. He opened it in front of them and was shocked at the results. Gouba and his wife were double positives for HIV 1 and 2. (HIV 2 was only prevalent in West African countries at the time.)

Stefan had the onerous duty of telling him the results and explaining what it meant for them. He knew that the stigma about HIV was so strong that they'd probably be shunned by family and friends. Gouba listened somberly and nodded as Stefan advised them to start taking Bactrim to ward off any opportunistic infections. Thanking him for his help, Gouba and his wife plodded slowly down our driveway.

Stefan murmured under his breath as he watched them go, "I should have known. It's so obvious, she didn't need a test."

Two days later, Gouba returned in a cheerful mood and said, "My wife is feeling better, and her diarrhea has cleared up."

"It's probably the Bactrim." Stefan nodded.

"Can I continue to work as long as I feel well?" Gouba asked in a respectful tone.

"Of course," Stefan said without hesitation. "But you must tell us if you feel sick."

Stefan didn't mind letting an AIDS-infected person work in our home since it was known by then that it was almost impossible to transmit HIV through food preparation and casual contact.

It broke my heart to see Gouba's jaunty spirits in subsequent days, and I cried quietly knowing what lay ahead of him and his wife. He was fifty-nine years old, and she was in her thirties. It would happen sooner than we guessed—only a few months after we'd leave the country—that Gouba would pass away and so would his wife. It would be an awful blow, knowing that he could have gotten life-saving medications if he'd survived for another year or so. His passing would leave two families bereft, one in his natal village in Burkina and the other in Abidjan, just as it would leave another hole in our hearts. Adama's death at the end of our first year and Gouba's in our last were like bookends around our sojourn in Ivory Coast and grim reminders of why we were there in the first place.

One of Stefan's Ivorian colleagues arranged a traditional ceremony in his honor before our departure. The doctor, from a prominent Bété family, hosted a weekend fête for Stefan and three other project doctors at his family's compound in Gagnoa, a major city in the center of the country. His brother happened to be the mayor of Gagnoa at the time.

On a Saturday in April, the welcome ceremony convened in the village square where the Chief and his elders received us under a big *paillote* (an open structure with a thatched roof) along with dozens of the host's family members and villagers. It was a blistering hot day in the sunbaked village, yet under the *paillote*, we didn't mind the heat.

After Stefan's Ivorian colleague introduced us, we shook hands with each elder and with the one woman who was there to represent all the other village women. We drank palm wine as a chorus of men stood in front of each guest and improvised a song about their apparent qualities. The song they sang about me went something like, "You look like a respectable woman and a valuable help to your husband. You're wearing a lovely skirt and shoes, and your children are a blessing to everyone. You are welcome in our village, and we wish to honor you."

When the singers finished welcoming us, the mayor of Gagnoa made a grand entrance and greeted the elders and visitors. He made a speech about Stefan's valuable role in educating his brother and thanked him for contributing to public health in Ivory Coast. He culminated the address by asking that our two families—Stefan's and the Ivorian doctor's—maintain the relationship after we left the country. It touched us deeply that the family valued the connection this doctor had made with Stefan. It was what Stefan loved most about his work: the opportunity to form close relationships with Ivorians while working on a life-threatening issue. When it was his turn, Stefan spoke glowingly about the young doctor's work at the project.

The welcome ceremony was followed by an elaborate feast that had been prepared by the women in the family. There was enough food to feed the entire village, with roasted chickens, goat, French fries, local dishes, and stews. Relatives and villagers drifted into the square and filled their plates at the buffet line after visitors were served. Masked dancers provided entertainment throughout the meal, and it was every bit as mesmerizing as the Ivorian dances we'd seen elsewhere. Traditional dance was one of the unique features of their cultures that we appreciated about Ivory Coast and would sorely miss.[16]

I hardly saw Aaron and Elena during the festivities as they ran around playing with the village children. By that point they were fluent in French, and I no longer worried about them. They could have fun and make themselves at home wherever they landed.

Years later I would wonder how different that last year might have been if I could have walked without pain and sat for hours while working. There were always interesting people to be around—in various embassies, at the international school, in the Professional Women's Network, and in the monthly book group. Yet needing relief from my hip pain made me long for home, and once the decision had been made, it was like flipping a switch in my mind as I started cataloguing all the reasons why it was time to move on.

Yet Ivory Coast had enriched us in so many ways, and I would miss things like swimming outdoors and writing outside on the terrace year-round. I'd miss the familiar voices of the guards bantering with each other outside our gate and the faint scents of frangipani and hibiscus in our yard. Most of all I'd miss Gladys, Ousmane, Nestor (the night guard), and Martine. Although I looked forward to the move, my excitement was tinged with sadness over leaving the people who made Abidjan feel like home.

It was easier for me to look forward to the move than it was for Aaron and Elena. Abidjan was the only home they knew, and people like Gladys and Ousmane made them feel safe and loved. Whenever he was bored, Aaron would walk down the driveway and sit outside chatting with Ousmane and the guard next door while Elena would draw chalk animals on the driveway with me or Gladys. For the children, leaving Abidjan meant losing their close friends and familiar environs. Only our dog, Bella, would be going with them.

On our last Sunday outing to the beach, I tried to commit ordinary scenes to memory: the waves pounding the shore as we ate lunch under palm trees, the batik and leather venders I'd come to know who called me from the beach with products to sell; Aaron and Elena playing for hours in the pool or the sand. The ocean was ferocious along that stretch of coast, and we'd learned early on that it could only be trusted at the margins. The currents were swift and unpredictable, and it made me anxious to let the children near the water. On one of our first visits to Grand Bassam, Stefan had tried to resuscitate a Canadian serviceman who'd been caught in a riptide, but they had pulled him from the ocean too late. Another Sunday we learned that a French woman had drowned at Assini in front of Angie and Peter's *paillote*.

Yet there were things about Ivory Coast that I wouldn't miss: the tense political climate and strikes that caused anxieties throughout our stay, the mildew that covered everything in our closets if we didn't keep air conditioners running. The climate sapped my strength as did the humidity, especially in hot season (i.e., March and April) when the torpor was debilitating.

I would also never forget the suffering and needs of the people around us. AIDS was a major cause of death in families like Adama's and Gouba's, yet sometimes people got sick and died from inexplicable causes. I worried about the guard next door who grew thinner each day with an unidentified illness, even after he'd been to clinics and had multiple tests. Having seen so much sickness and death, I felt like a wizened old soul as we prepared to leave.

As my heart turned homeward, I began to wonder where we'd spend Thanksgiving later that year and if I'd be able to play my old piano at Christmas again. Yet it was impossible to separate happy thoughts of home from concerns about those we'd leave behind. I couldn't help thinking of the guard who sat outside our gate one night and how he might fare in the coming months. He told us that he was a Liberian refugee who'd lost everything in the war, including his house, his livelihood, his siblings and parents. Would there ever be a happy home-going for him?

In our last weeks, there were more parties, including a reception in Stefan's honor at the Ambassador's residence and a farewell bash with the project's staff and Angie's family, who were also leaving. At each event, colleagues made speeches thanking Stefan for his work and the Ivorians gave us gifts that we would treasure for years to come. Members of the Professional Women's Network took me to lunch and gave me a twenty-two-karat gold pendant in the shape of Africa to thank me for serving on the board, and the new host of the book group had a goodbye lunch for me and other members who were leaving. Mona was conspicuously absent from such gatherings.

I dreaded the tasks that remained in our final week and the prospect of saying goodbye to everyone. It was a sad time for the children especially. Elena burst into tears whenever she thought about leaving her teachers, and Aaron was upset that he might never see the guards or Gladys again. At nine he was old enough to know what this move meant: that we'd say goodbye to people we loved and walk through a door without any possibility of keeping it open.

The morning of our departure, Aaron woke up in tears and cried on and off throughout the day. "I don't want to go," he'd moan intermittently. He was crying for all of us in a way since I was too busy and full of mixed emotions about leaving. Every time he went out to see one of the guards—Ousmane, Nestor, and David next door—he'd come inside and burst into tears again. Elena hugged the dog when she was sad, comforted by the thought that Bella was going with her.

My heart was heavy throughout the day as a stream of people came to say goodbye. Martine and her daughters sat in our living room with mournful faces all afternoon. I had to leave them while packing and directing traffic as other visitors came by. The children got to play with their friends one last time, while Martine and her daughters sat in our living room quietly crying.

When the CDC driver arrived and it was time to leave, Aaron, Elena, and I sobbed as we hugged Gladys and the others goodbye. "I lost one mother, and now I'm losing you," Martine cried. "I have no mother left in the world!" Nestor and Ousmane had tears in their eyes when they told me how much they'd miss us. David, the neighbor's guard, looked at me somberly and said, "We really love you, and we won't ever forget you when you're gone from here." Meanwhile, Gouba admonished them to be strong and stop crying since it was making it hard for us to leave.

As the driver closed the doors and the van pulled away, the kids were inconsolable. Both cried while looking out the windows for neighborhood landmarks after their house was no longer in sight. Stefan and I had to remain clear-eyed as we reviewed the documents we would need for the trip: passports, plane tickets, dog vaccination papers, and money. As the van sped along the lagoon and through downtown Abidjan, all of us grew quiet while taking in the vibrant street life one last time—brightly lit as always in the tropical night.

In the airport, the children hugged Bella and reassured her that they'd see her soon, coaxing her into her crate before an agent wheeled it away. Once we'd cleared immigration and found our gate, there was a palpable sense of relief after all the sadness that day. Mounting the steps to the plane, I collapsed in my seat between Aaron and Elena, all of us bleary-eyed from the emotional goodbyes.

Settling in for the long flight, I tried to console the kids by reminding them that Bella was resting in the hold below, and that she'd wag herself silly upon seeing them in the Amsterdam airport. Soon enough, both kids were distracted with the buttons on their chairs and watching movies. It was a rare treat to fly business class for a change—a courtesy that the US government extended to employees who were relocating.

Relieved that the trauma of packing and leave-taking was over, I leaned back in my seat and closed my eyes. I was looking forward to beginning a new chapter in our lives. Stefan and the kids would spend a week in Holland with his brother's family while I would fly to LA where Tink was about to have her first baby. The thought of our new home in Atlanta (I'd flown to the US in March with Aaron and found a house we really liked), the birth of my sister's baby, and the handful of close friends who'd be waiting lifted my spirits.

Aaron and Elena had no notion of what life in America would be like, and it would be up to me to help them adjust to their new surroundings and make themselves at home there. I could only hope that their adaptability—and mine—would see us through the many changes ahead.

Chapter 9
Atlanta Interlude

I made it to LA in time to witness the birth of Tink's baby. It had been a surreal trip, flying over the North Pole and Canada and along the spine of the Rocky Mountains. Grateful for a bird's eye view of the Great Salt Lake, the Wasatch Range, and the Grand Canyon from the air, I thought, *maybe there's life after Abidjan after all, with great expanses of wilderness to explore in the American west. Maybe we can fashion happy lives as a family here at home too.*

Equal parts jet-lagged and excited, I went straight to the hospital and was admitted to my sister's room minutes before the doctor told Tink to start pushing.

The infant's head emerged after the first few pushes, wet and gray and with a face that was a carbon copy of my sister's when she was a baby. I stayed with Tink and her husband for a week, cooking and cleaning and relishing any chance I got to hold baby Poetry. My sister and I made curtains for the baby's room with pillow shams to match. In a quiet moment, I was able to connect with Lorna—my dear friend from Abidjan—over lunch; a treat that we would repeat whenever I went to LA.

I treasured every moment with my sister and infant niece before it was time to return to my family.

Stefan and the kids picked me up at the Atlanta airport on a sweltering July day and drove us to our new house. The setting was a radical change from the home we'd left in Abidjan. Instead of high walls around a tropical garden with perpetually blooming bougainvillea and frangipani, our Atlanta house was set in a glen bordered by woods that belonged to Emory University. I knew already where I wanted to put my desk—in a room with a skylight and a bank of windows overlooking the sloped backyard and forest. The kitchen and sunroom also faced the woods, and there was a creek running along the edge of the property.

The children and I strolled down to the woods to look for crawfish in the creek. Growing up in Ivory Coast, Aaron and Elena had never played in woods like those, and they were amazed to have acres of wilderness behind the house instead of walls and guards. In subsequent days we would see all kinds of wildlife wander through our yard, including red foxes, deer, and wild turkeys.

The day after we moved in, several neighbors stopped by to welcome us—including a woman with a daughter Elena's age. Elena grabbed the girl's hand and led her on a tour of the house and yard. After the tour, she stood in the driveway with her new friend, listening to the girl's mother tell us about other kids in the neighborhood. Before Jane and her daughter left, Elena insisted on making a playdate the following day.

It would take Aaron longer to meet boys his age. At nine, he was having a harder time with the move than six-year-old Elena, and he told me repeatedly that he missed the guards and our house in Abidjan. I tried to find projects to keep him busy, like painting kitchen cabinets with me or working in the garden. Some days I'd drive the kids to Toys "R" Us so they could examine toys, books, and puzzles they hadn't seen before. Elena chose a bike for her birthday, which was coming up in August, and Aaron got to pick one too since he'd left his bike for Ousmane.

I had expected to let go of my anxieties about the children when we moved back to the US, not knowing that the return might be more traumatic for them than our move to a foreign country had been. They were at ages when friendships took on greater importance, and Aaron was feeling the loss of his closest friend, Jimmy, not knowing if and when he'd see him again.

I understood that sense of loss. For the first time in five years, we wouldn't be returning to Abidjan at summer's end. At odd moments, I'd catch myself wondering what Gladys and Ousmane might be doing and if they had easy transitions to their new jobs. Just before we left, I'd helped Gladys find a position as a cook and nanny for an expat family, and she was already working for them. Ousmane and Nestor had been reassigned to other houses, and I had no idea how they were faring. It would be several years before they'd get email addresses and start writing to me regularly.

Yet I immediately felt at home in our new place, and I hoped the children would feel it too. The house was configured like the house in Maryland where I grew up, though our new one was more spacious and open. It had a big front and backyard that would occupy me for hours with planting and tending. The city was familiar to us too since Stefan and I had lived in Atlanta together in the mid-1980s. It helped that everyone around us spoke English and we no longer stuck out as foreigners, nor did we have to be hyper alert whenever we left the house or worry about car jackings, burglaries, and civil unrest. Best of all, the new house had wood floors instead of stone, so my hip bursitis was improving.

Elena hit the ground running on her first day of school. The principal greeted parents and students in the foyer of the Friends School and directed us to the room for second graders. Elena ran ahead without waiting while I tried to follow and stood in the back of the room with other parents. The teacher and his assistant introduced themselves and gave a brief introduction to the class before parents slipped out. I drove home that day with a light heart, sure that she would find her way. When I returned to pick her up at the end of the day, Elena introduced me to her new friend Hannah and asked if she could come for a sleepover that weekend.

We'd enrolled Aaron in a different private school that had been recommended by Atlanta friends. When it started a few days later, Aaron found it harder to break into established groups since most of the kids in his fourth-grade class had known each other since preschool.

A couple of weeks into the term, when I went to pick him up at the end of the school day, his teacher asked to speak to me privately. "Aaron fell off the jungle gym during recess," she told me. "He said he wasn't hurt, and he didn't want you to come pick him up." My stomach clenched as she continued, "He sits at the top of the jungle gym every day during recess and just watches other kids play. I tried to get him to play four square or basketball with the boys, but he prefers to sit up there and watch instead of playing."

It saddened me to hear this. When we got home, I asked Aaron why he didn't try to play with the kids at recess. He shrugged and said with an impassive face that he didn't know them.

He was clearly going through culture shock in those early months in Atlanta. He didn't know the kinds of games American kids played, the music they listened to, or the TV shows they watched. Used to socializing with kids from other cultures and backgrounds, he had no idea how to be a "normal" American boy. He wasn't one who excelled at ball games or team sports, and he didn't care to watch football or baseball on TV; nor did his father for that matter. He was also dealing with the grief of separation from his best friend, his teachers, Gladys, and the guards.

As an adult, Aaron would look back on that first year in a US school as the hardest of his childhood. One of his classmates started calling him "Africa Boy" early on. We didn't identify it as bullying at the time, although Aaron hinted at other actions and name-calling that bothered him. I slept poorly and woke up early most mornings, full of worries yet hoping it was only a matter of time before both children were happy in Atlanta.

If only we had known about the budding literature on "Third Culture Kids" (TCKs), we might have been better equipped to help them adapt. A TCK is someone who spends a significant period in a culture other than that of their parents or country of origin, and they're forced to integrate elements of both in a unique third culture. It was a new field in the year 2000 when we moved back to the US, and the possibility of doing internet searches on culture shock for kids was still a few years away. Because our children didn't know any other TCKs in Atlanta, they were on their own.

After a couple of months, Aaron started playing with a boy in his class, and I was happy to arrange playdates for them after school. He also befriended a boy who was in the carpool I drove to Elena's school. Some days I'd invite the boy to come home with us in the carpool, and he and Aaron would explore the woods behind our house with Bella. But Aaron would never forget the loneliness of his first year back in the US. Only later did I realize that his culture shock was exacerbated by the "zeitgeist" or atmosphere at his school.

In Ivory Coast, children were treated warmly and with respect by the people around them—a practice that permeated Ivorian cultures in general. Groups were more fluid at the international school, with new students constantly arriving as others were leaving. The atmosphere was more open and accepting than at Aaron's private school in Atlanta, where new students from unfamiliar places were sometimes ridiculed—even if they looked like everyone else and had an American-sounding name. In contrast, the Friends School, which

Elena attended, was more diverse and welcoming to outsiders, and she was more of an extrovert than Aaron.

It was easy for me to make friends and adjust to life in Atlanta. Women in the neighborhood went out of the way to welcome us and invite us to events like Halloween and Christmas parties and a neighborhood book group. After the New Year, I started a writing group with my friend Kathryn, whom I'd known since we lived in Atlanta in the 1980s. We asked another writer to join us, and Anne and I instantly hit it off.

We were also happy to reconnect with old friends from Abidjan like Alan (Stefan's former boss) and Michele, who had relocated to Atlanta. We had dinners and barbecues at each other's houses and sometimes invited other families who'd lived in Ivory Coast. It was comforting to talk about the people and places we missed in Abidjan with friends who'd shared those experiences.

In April of 2000, nine months after we moved back to the US, I returned to Abidjan while Stefan stayed in Atlanta with the kids. He had traveled to Ivory Coast several times for his new job, and I was pining for the vibrant life and friends we knew there. I had been so preoccupied with details of our move and with my hip bursitis that I hadn't left with a sense of closure.

From the moment I landed in Abidjan, my body warmed to the familiar tropical setting and clammy heat, to the crowded city streets and the clamor of foreign horns. It was a welcome jolt this time, the lush foliage and humidity a far cry from the wintry woods behind our house and crisp air in Atlanta.

My friend Kristin—who started hosting the book group after I left—picked me up at the airport and had me stay with her family. She happened to live in the same house where my good friend Jeane had lived, and I was transported back in time to when Jeane and I used to visit while our children played.

The morning after I arrived, the first thing I did was call Gladys to let her know where I was staying. She said she'd visit me at the end of her workday, and in the meantime, Kristin and I would make the rounds of local markets. It was fun strolling among familiar venders and speaking French again. This time the heat didn't get to me as much as jet lag did, which made a midday nap mandatory.

That afternoon, Gladys strode up Kristin's front walk wearing eyeglasses that made her look like a professor. We laughed at the sight of each other, and our eyes swam with tears as we hugged. She settled beside me on the couch as we started talking about our families.

"My daughters are fine, thanks be to God." Gladys smiled. "The girls are as tall as me now. How are my kids, Aaron and Elena? I miss them so much. And my friend Bella."

I filled her in on how the children were doing and showed her some photos. With watery eyes she exclaimed, "He's so big! And Elena still dresses like a princess."

"How's your new job?" I asked. "Do you like your employer?"

"The lady is very nice. She is paying for me to go to cooking school, and I prefer cooking to cleaning. She doesn't have any children, and she hired another lady to do housekeeping."

At the end of our visit, we arranged to meet the next day for dinner at a maquis with a couple of our former guards. I was glad to be able to postpone our goodbyes one more time.

The following day, Kristin drove me through our old neighborhood to the house where we'd lived for six years. It pained me to see how much things had changed. It had a different gate, and extensive renovation work was going on inside. Ousmane and Nestor were no longer there, although David still guarded the house next door. He told me where to find Ousmane at an Embassy residence around the corner.

As soon as I saw Ousmane's familiar form standing outside the house, I had to choke back tears. I climbed out of the car to hug him, and he chuckled as I struggled to control my voice. "How are you Ousmane? How is your family?"

"I am very happy with my new wife, and my daughter is doing well at school in Burkina. What about Aaron and Elena?"

I pulled out photos, and he chuckled again when he saw them. "How is my friend Bella?" he asked. "And your mom and dad?"

I could have stood there talking with him for hours as we used to do, except that Kristin and her daughter were waiting in the car and three other workers who stood nearby were watching me dab at tears in my eyes. I confirmed the plan to meet him for dinner that night, and he promised to bring Nestor and the two other guards I knew, Isaaca and David.

Next, Kristin drove me to the house of Francoise, the mother of Elena's best friend whose pool I'd used when my hip bursitis was at its worst. I fell into her arms as soon as she opened the door and started crying all over again. She cried too and hugged me as Kristin and her daughter looked on. It was a relief to let tears flow and release my pent-up sadness over leaving—and to acknowledge the sense of loss over the intense experiences we'd had in that unique place.

"I've been depressed for months," Francoise sobbed. "Ever since you and my other friends left."

"I've been sad too," I nodded. "Life in the US is routine and boring after the life we had here."

"You wouldn't want to be here now." She shook her head sadly. "Everyone is anxious about the political situation since the coup. I can't wait to leave." She was referring to a coup that the army had staged six months after we left. A general had declared himself the new leader, and fighting had broken out in the northern part of the country, forcing many expats to leave.

"Do you know where you'll go?" I asked her.

"My husband requested a transfer, and we'll move to Budapest at the end of the school year. I wish it were sooner."

That night in the maquis, I couldn't stop smiling while looking around at the beaming faces of Gladys and the guards. It hit me again what the children and I had been missing in the months since we'd left; the daily contact with people we'd come to love and who cared about us. We'd greeted Ousmane and Nestor, Gladys and Gouba several times a day, and each time we were thrust out of our singular worlds in connecting with them. No matter how caught up we were with our own issues, we had to be attentive when interacting with individuals from other cultures and walks of life.

It comforted me to see Ousmane, Nestor, and Gladys happy and thriving. They were the people I'd missed the most after leaving Abidjan, and they were the ones I hated to leave again. Yet I knew that the vibrant life we'd shared with our kids in that place was over, and those times were now relegated to our memories. I was grateful to experience it one more time before letting it go. Aaron and Elena still had to find their ways after being forced from their coddled childhoods in that singularly beautiful place.

The final closure I sought was with Mona. She agreed to see me for lunch on my last day in Abidjan, and we met at a quiet restaurant along the lagoon where we'd dined in the past.

In the hour we spent together, we talked as if nothing had come between us the previous year. I described my life in Atlanta while Mona detailed her ups and downs in recent months. Her daughter had gone deaf in one ear after taking high doses of quinine for malaria, and doctors told her that nothing could be done about it. She'd decided to send her daughter to boarding school in Canada since she hoped to emigrate there herself one day. Mona was proud of having finished the New York marathon with her French friend, and she talked about her impending move to Tunisia where the African Development Bank was about to relocate because of the coup and fighting in Ivory Coast.

With a pit in my stomach, I ate mechanically as we carefully avoided the subject of our friendship. When the bill came and we were ready to leave, I worked up the nerve to ask, "Have you thought about why our relationship fell apart last year?"

She said reflexively, "It was mainly because I wanted to protect my daughter." Then she paused and added, "My mother told me I was silly to let our friendship go the way it did. She really liked you, you know."

With a lump in my throat, I waited for her to continue.

"I suppose I should have talked things over with you and let my daughter see how friends work things out. But I didn't know how to do that."

I nodded. "I understand why you felt you had to protect her. But that year was painful for me, emotionally and physically."

"I never meant to hurt you," she said with a sad expression, "and I'm really sorry about what happened between us."

It was a relief to clear the air with her, and my eyes filled with tears as we hugged goodbye. "Maybe we could pick up where we left off once you move to Canada," I said in parting.

Mona shook her head. "You'll never be able to trust me again."

Her statement stunned me. I hadn't considered that part of the equation and couldn't formulate a quick response. What came to mind later was that I had already mourned the loss of our friendship and moved on. We wouldn't live near enough to see each other on a regular basis, and I would never need her as much as I did when we lived in Abidjan. Perhaps that "need" had been too much, as had my emotional investment in her. Still, it broke my heart to lose a friend who once meant so much to me.

Over time, I would draw deeper lessons about friendships after losing Mona's. For one thing, many caring individuals would cross my path over the years, and I didn't need to run after the standouts to compensate for some perceived inadequacy in me. I had overvalued Mona's friendship partly because it appealed to my intellect and ego, and I'd undervalued the relationship with Ula, who was a more devoted friend in the end.

What had complicated our relationships were the disparities between us, cultural as well as situational; my freedom from financial pressure and reliance on a trusted partner, for example, and Mona's challenges as a single mother who worked full time. While it was a privilege to be able to stay home and write, appreciation for my situation was mixed with chagrin at being considered a "trailing spouse" who was less independent than wage-earning professionals like Mona and Carol. It was an issue I'd struggle with for years as a freelance writer who didn't earn much money. And yet, while I wasn't as bold and self-confident as Carol and Mona, I had certainly accomplished a lot and mustered courage when it was needed.

What complicates friendships in general are the expectations that we bring to them and the emotional investment each party puts in. It's one of the most important investments we make in life, particularly if we want to take a friendship to a deeper level. You make an unwritten contract to be there for each other, especially when one needs something that the other can give. On the other hand, you have to allow for hurts and disappointments since we all make mistakes and will invariably let each other down. Clear communication about needs and hurts is critical in building intimacy and trust.

Mona and I talked about everything and everyone except ourselves. Had we admitted how disappointed we were by certain actions or attitudes, it would have strengthened our bond. Such honesty would have deepened my friendship with Ula, too, as she'd wanted openness and candor from me. Had we known how to do it sensitively, Mona and I could have had a conversation with her daughter to understand why she'd felt slighted, and I could have apologized to her directly. Instead, we let issues between us simmer and tried to ignore them. Mona had been right about one thing, that we didn't know how to work things out.

Over the years, I would explore different modalities that teach communication skills, like Transactional Analysis (TA) and Non-Violent Communication (NVC). Back then, even in my forties, I still had a lot to learn. One of those things was that I could and would trust Mona again.

Upon my return to Atlanta, I wanted Aaron to have the same opportunity to visit Ivory Coast and say goodbye again. (It seemed less important for Elena, who was only six when she left and was already involved with her new school and friends.) A few months after my trip, Stefan had to go to Abidjan for work again, and this time he took Aaron. I emailed the director of the international school to ask his permission for Aaron to sit in on classes while Stefan was at work so Aaron would have a chance to visit with his former teachers and classmates.

Stefan and Aaron called me one evening when they took Ousmane, Nestor, and Gladys out to dinner. I could hear the excitement in Aaron's voice as he passed Stefan's cell phone to each of them. "Here's Ousmane, Mom," he said as he gave the phone to our former guard. After I spoke with Ousmane, Aaron passed the phone to Gladys. "It's Gladys's turn now," he announced as if chairing a meeting. I was happy for Aaron and missed being with them myself.

When Stefan and Aaron returned to Atlanta, the latter recounted all the things he did and the people he saw, including his teachers and classmates. He raved about the day he spent with Stefan at our favorite beach hotel in Grand Bassam, and how he'd bargained with venders for the souvenirs he brought back for Elena and me. Then he said something that stunned me: "It was fun, but I realized that I didn't belong there anymore. It wasn't my home."

It struck me that at age ten, Aaron had perceived something profound and was already grappling with issues like *Where is home?* and *Where do I belong?* Home was a fluid concept for all of us—as it is for many expats, immigrants, and military families—that would continue to evolve over the years. Every time we moved, we had to redefine what "home" meant; and each time my sense of home was less tethered to a physical place and more to those around me.

The fact that Atlanta felt like my home so quickly was partly a function of my familiarity with the city and because I had friends there and my parents nearby. Living in a house that had a yard to tend also grounded me, as did landing in a friendly neighborhood where I didn't feel like an outsider every time I left the house. For the children, it was more complicated. They were trying to fit into homogeneous schools at ages when many young people struggled to belong and to forge identities apart from their parents.

My children were forced to deal with complicated issues like *Where is home?* earlier than most kids. Though I didn't know how to soften their landing, I did find plenty of after-school activities to keep them busy. By the end of their first year in Atlanta, Aaron had joined a cub scout troop with boys in our neighborhood, and Elena was taking dance classes at an arts institute. Both did workshops at a local theatre and took part in several plays with kids from the neighborhood.

Several years later, I'd hear a clip from a Pico Iyer TED Talk that would seem even more apropos to them: "Where you're from is much less important than where you're going." He would also propose that "The age of movement brings liberating possibilities." It would be some years before my children felt that way. As preteens, they still defined home as the place where their parents lived. Someday they would be more future-oriented and not tethered to a place or to the past, and they would learn from moving around that their futures lay elsewhere. The process of forming their own identities and redefining "home" would be ongoing for years, and they would have to manage it on their own as they grew older.

Right before the new school year started, my parents came to stay with us for a week on their way to my sister's place in Ohio. Having them around made it seem more like home for all of us. My mother took the kids shopping and for ice cream while my father played checkers with them in the evenings. Over dinners, he would tell stories about his exploits in the Second World War—which was rare for him—and about growing up in a coal mining town in Pennsylvania.

My father preferred to work in the yard with me rather than go on outings. His favorite task was pulling the ivy off trees, and we had acres of woods behind our house to keep him busy. I enjoyed doing yardwork with him, though he tired easily and seemed more sluggish of late. Seeing him that way reaffirmed our choice to move back to the US despite missing more exciting lives in Ivory Coast.

I felt seen and understood by my father in ways that I didn't by my mother, much as I loved and respected her. She was an extrovert and effusive Catholic charismatic who got upset whenever I'd refuse to go to Mass with her on Sundays. She'd been telling me for years that her fondest wish was for me to return to the Catholic church. Although my father professed to being a charismatic Catholic too, he understood when I told him that I preferred to spend an hour in the woods communing with God instead of in a church. Though he wasn't much of a reader, he appreciated Emily Dickinson's sentiments when I quoted a line from one of her poems:

Some keep the Sabbath going to church;
I keep it staying at home,
With a bobolink for a chorister,
And an orchard for a dome.

In 2001, my father had a series of TIAs or minor strokes, and he was even more sluggish and confused. During that time, my mother had to have one of her knees replaced and needed a break from caring for my father. He came to stay with us for a couple of weeks while she was having surgery, and his comportment alarmed me. He was unable to remember simple things like the days of the week, and he remarked one day, "I can't believe how fast this happened to me. I feel like an old man already."

My siblings and I were planning a big reunion on the fifteenth of September to celebrate our parents' fiftieth wedding anniversary. All of us would convene in Rehoboth Beach, Delaware where we'd always had our family vacations, along with several of my father's sisters and some of their friends. I made my way to Rehoboth a week before the event to help organize the party and spend time with Tink's family. My brothers from Dallas and sister from Idaho arrived several days later with their children. Then 9/11 happened, and half the relatives who were supposed to come had flights cancelled or rerouted. Stefan had to drive from Atlanta with Aaron and Elena instead of flying, as did my siblings from Indiana and Ohio.

It was a bittersweet gathering on September 15 since thoughts of the many people who'd lost their lives that week were never far from our minds. It was also sad watching my father at the reunion dinner with his mouth hanging open and dribble on his chin, and listening to him stutter. The change in him after the latest TIA was alarming. He was only seventy-six, and he'd been so lively and intrigued by everything when he visited us in Abidjan two years earlier.

In subsequent months, my father started having panic attacks and was afraid to be left on his own, which was hard on my mother. His stutter grew so pronounced that it was difficult to understand him on the phone. I arranged for him to see a neurologist at Emory in Atlanta, and he also saw a urologist to get a second opinion on his prostate cancer. As we sat in the doctor's office together, the urologist asked him, "How many more years do you want to live, Pete? Would five be enough? Or would you want ten?"

My father responded with a sheepish grin, "Would ten be asking too much?"

Years later, my mother would say that God heard his prayer, because he would get what he asked for. The neurologist enrolled my father in one of his studies and inserted a stent in his carotid artery. My father had to return to Atlanta every six months for checkups, and each time he'd show marked improvements in his memory and movements. He went back to attacking the ivy on trees in our yard, and he took Aaron fishing when he visited us. My mother still worried about leaving him alone when she did errands in case he fell or needed something. One day an alligator chased him up the grassy bank at their place on the canal around Lake Okeechobee, and my mother decided it was time to pay someone to stay with him when she left the house.

It was touching to see how attentive and tender my mother had become with him. Growing up, my siblings and I had witnessed frequent arguments between them, with my mother sometimes threatening to leave him. Only God and her adherence to Catholic strictures could have kept them together for fifty-plus years. The rancor between them and chaos in our house were prime reasons why, as an adult, I tried to make a peaceful and orderly home for my children. It was important to me that my children grew up in a family where we communicated instead of argued.

Stefan's mother wasn't as fortunate as my father. Her dementia was progressing rapidly, and her gait became increasingly unsteady. She was incontinent and confused at times and would ask Stefan questions that alarmed him, like "Have I ever been to your house?" or "Have you finished your studies yet?" referring to college and medical school.

Every few months, Anna would come to stay with us in Atlanta, and I could see how much her dementia depressed Stefan. Whenever we took her for a walk, someone had to hold her hand, which was like holding the frail paw of a ghost. We toured a few assisted living places in Atlanta with her, but she didn't like any of them. "Too many old people," she'd say.

During our third year in Atlanta, I flew to LA for the birth of Tink's second child, a boy. I loved playing "My little pony" with her daughter, Poetry, and reading to her before naps and bedtime. My own kids had outgrown such pastimes, and Elena was growing more rebellious as a preteen. She seemed to do things earlier than most kids and with a passionate intensity. At ten, after she transferred to Aaron's private school, her teachers took me aside and told me what a leader she was even though she was the youngest in her fifth-grade class. She could be charming at school yet scornful to me at home.

Stefan had to travel frequently for work—mostly to west and southern African countries to monitor AIDS projects—but when he was home, Elena was all his. She'd chat with him for hours about movie stars, tennis pros, and fast cars while she'd make snide comments to me if I said anything. While her cutting remarks bothered me, I was glad she wasn't alienating herself from both of her parents. On the rare occasion when something bad happened to her at school, she would pour out her heart to me along with her tears. Such moments of intimacy between us had to suffice.

My writing group was a big comfort in those years. It was a boost to have friends read my work with discerning eyes and offer feedback on what I was writing. The novel I'd started in Abidjan had grown to six hundred pages and was turning into an exploration of mother-daughter relationships as the main character struggled with infertility; issues that I'd grappled with for years and was working out on paper. Having close friends in the writing group was an antidote to the lonely hours of introspective work I did each day, especially when Stefan was away.

Five years in Atlanta seemed to fly by. Elena excelled in her acting and dance workshops while Aaron was an avid hiker and camper who worked his way up to the rank of Eagle Scout by the end of ninth grade. Both kids seemed settled even though they had their ups and downs with friends at school.

With friends in my writing group, in the neighborhood and at the children's school, I wasn't looking to upend our lives again by moving overseas. I was glad to be able to spend time with our siblings and parents, particularly as Stefan's mother's health declined.

In our fourth year in Atlanta, he'd moved her to an assisted living place within walking distance of our house. We could take a path through the woods behind our house to the tree-lined complex where she had a one-bedroom apartment. I would visit her with Aaron after school, and Anna would spend most Sundays at our house. But her dementia had progressed to the point where she forgot people's names and couldn't take care of her personal needs. Within a year of her move to the assisted living place, the director said she'd need to transfer to nursing care.

In the spring of 2005, Stefan came home from work one day and surprised me with the question, "Would you consider moving to Tanzania?"

"You're kidding, right?" I replied. We hadn't discussed another move, and my first impulse was to say no because of our parents and ties to Atlanta. Plus, I didn't think the children would want to leave in the middle of junior high (for Elena) and high school (for Aaron).

But when Elena heard him mention Tanzania, her reaction was instantaneous. "You should do it, Dad! Go ahead and apply."

Upon his return to Atlanta five years earlier, Stefan had been excited about the newly formed Life Initiative (under President Bill Clinton) that funded AIDS prevention programs around the world. In 2003 the Life Initiative morphed into a much bigger inter-agency program called the President's Emergency Plan for AIDS Relief (PEPFAR) after President George W. Bush convinced Congress to allocate $15 billion over five years for AIDS prevention and treatment. PEPFAR was a game changer that would save millions of lives over the next decade.

Although Stefan felt fortunate to be at CDC headquarters at the inception of the Global AIDS Program, he yearned to get back in the field and work on the front lines. PEPFAR was allocating huge sums of money to fifteen countries, primarily in Africa where Stefan wanted to be. He had mentioned openings for directors at AIDS projects in Mozambique and South Africa, but I'd said no to Mozambique since it had just emerged from a brutal civil war and to South Africa because of Pretoria's violent crime rates. Tanzania, on the other hand, sounded intriguing when I thought about it. Like Stefan, I missed being around people from other cultures, and the idea of living in a country with legendary landscapes and a peaceful history sounded like a golden opportunity.

My biggest reservation about moving overseas was our children. I didn't think we should disrupt their lives even though Elena was unhappy at school. A group of girls in her seventh-grade class who'd once been friends had turned on her and were pointedly excluding her. She had started fantasizing about going to a different school in another country and living in a bigger house, which is why she urged Stefan to apply for the job.

Aaron wasn't crazy about his school either, although he had misgivings about moving in the middle of high school. We gave him the option of saying no to Tanzania if he had serious reservations about the move. But it didn't take him long to come around. "In three years, I'll be going to college and leaving my friends anyway," he said one day, "so why not do it sooner and have some adventures along the way?" His ability to step back and take a broader view of his life was inspiring.

Both kids had obviously inherited our love of travel. It was also evident that they had fond memories of growing up in Ivory Coast—so much so that they'd be willing to relocate at ages fifteen and thirteen. In some senses, they still felt like outsiders in Atlanta as Stefan did.

Our parents were another big concern for us. Stefan had grown increasingly depressed about his mother's condition, and he seemed to be mourning her loss already as her mental faculties faded. I didn't know how much longer he could stand to witness her decline. When his older brother in LA found a nursing home near him that took only five residents at a time, it sounded like a better situation for her.

My father had been doing much better after he had the stent put in, and it seemed as if a massive stroke or heart attack wouldn't fell him any time soon. Hedging my bets, I convinced myself that if we moved overseas, it would be enough to see my parents twice a year when we returned for Christmas and summer vacations.

Stefan and Elena were more eager to move than Aaron and me. For Elena it meant reinventing herself and meeting new people, while Stefan was keen to work in the field as AIDS treatment was scaling up. He was excited by the prospect of directing an AIDS program in one of PEPFAR's priority countries. With an annual budget ten times that of the program in Ivory Coast and a bigger staff, it would be a real challenge for him.

He applied for the position in Tanzania in March of 2005 and was offered the job a month later. He was asked to move quickly, and we decided to do it in early August when the school year would begin at the International School of Tanganyika in Dar es Salaam (IST). I was less conflicted about going abroad because Tanzania sounded fascinating. Unlike our first move overseas, I was ready to embrace the opportunity to live in Tanzania and learn about that part of Africa. Another world beckoned, and I wasn't content to sit and gaze out from an upper window as I'd been doing at my desk in Atlanta for the last six years. The timing felt right for all of us, and the country did too. Dar es Salaam was a safer city, and I wouldn't be as anxious as I was when we moved to Abidjan with small children.

I resolved to learn Swahili and be open to new experiences and travel—for my sake as well as for Aaron's and Elena's. More than anything, I looked forward to having a few last adventures with my family before the children were grown and gone.

Chapter 10

A New Page in East Africa

The sensory shock upon our arrival in Tanzania struck me just as it had when we'd arrived in Ivory Coast. Although it wasn't as humid in Dar es Salaam as in Abidjan, the air was hot and dusty when the CDC driver picked us up at the airport and deposited us in the driveway of our new home. Catching sight of the bougainvillea and hibiscus growing alongside the house and a flame tree in front, my first impressions upon entering the yard were positive ones.

It had high walls around it with metal gates like our house in Abidjan, and the guard wore the same uniform that Ousmane and Nestor had worn. There were bars on the windows and three bolts on outer doors as well as a house alarm. A deep sense of familiarity about the scene came over me even though we'd landed in a very different part of Africa, and I knew intuitively that it wouldn't take long to adapt to this place. All of us knew how to do it, including the children.

Our community sponsor had ensured that beds were made and the refrigerator stocked with enough food to last us several days. In my blurry state that first night, I noted some of the issues that would need to be addressed. Getting blackout curtains on the windows topped the list as the security lights outside shone directly into our bedroom.

The morning after we arrived, Stefan and I were required to attend a security briefing at the Embassy. While the city was supposed to be safer than Abidjan, the US Embassy in Dar had been bombed by terrorists seven years earlier and security was tight around the new Embassy compound. The RSO (the Embassy security officer) advised us not to walk alone at night even though our neighborhood was mostly inhabited by expats. The beaches lining the road from the Msasani Peninsula where we lived into downtown were unsafe even in daytime because of pickpockets and thieves. The RSO also warned us to drive carefully since mob justice was common in Tanzania. If someone hit a biker or pedestrian, for example, a mob might form to beat the driver.

I registered his warnings but didn't blow them up in my mind as I had upon our arrival in Abidjan. I knew it would become clear with time where we could or couldn't walk when we left the house. I'd regretted voicing my fears about safety around Mona when we lived in Abidjan and resolved to worry less about our security. Finding confidence inside myself would be key.

Within a few days, I could tell that the atmosphere was more relaxed on the Peninsula where we lived and in Dar es Salaam in general. I was an old hand at adapting and not a timid newcomer as I'd been in Ivory Coast.

One afternoon, a CDC driver dropped me and the kids at the IST a mile from our house. We liked the school as soon as we entered its guarded gates. The campus—shaded by baobab and palm trees—had an airy ambiance, and teachers passed us with welcoming smiles, some of them dressed like backpackers. A Dutch teacher stopped to greet Aaron and Elena and told them about all the fun activities they could do with school groups. As the kids went off to take the required placement tests, a woman with a German accent led me to the staff lounge and brought me a cup of tea.

When their hour-long tests were finished, Aaron and Elena met me at the school entrance. Our community sponsor had arranged to pick us up and take us to a small shopping center near our house to show me where to buy groceries. Stefan and I agreed to let the kids get cell phones, and our sponsor led us to a kiosk that had flip-top cell phones with prepaid plans (smart phones were still rare in 2005). I bought one for each of us at a surprisingly low price.

The biggest decision we faced was where to buy a car and what kind. We'd arrived too late to find a secondhand car sold by departing diplomats, and we ended up going to a dealer. Without a lot of choices, we settled on a car that seemed to fit the bill: a small SUV that was five years old and drove like a mini tank.

Since I'd be the one who would take the kids to school and do errands, I had to learn to drive with the stick shift in my left hand since Tanzanians drove on the left side of the road. This time around I wasn't afraid to drive on my own as I had been in Abidjan. After living in West Africa for six years, I thought I could handle almost anything. It helped that I was a decade older than when we'd moved to Ivory Coast, as were our children, and that I'd looked forward to the move instead of dreading it. Everything felt different—and better—this time.

The road in front of our house was unpaved, which made it impossible to keep dirt out—especially during the dry season when passing cars kicked up clouds of dust. Fortunately, a few days after we arrived, our community sponsor sent someone who could help me with housework.

Prudence was a hefty woman in her mid-thirties with a sunny, outgoing personality. She told me she was from Tanzania and had a husband and two children. We agreed that she would work for us three days a week and split her time with another family. She needed no directions when it came to housecleaning, tossing linens into the washing machine as soon as she arrived and moving from room to room with her dustmop. I asked her to wash the sheets and towels only once a week instead of every other day, and to let the kids pick up their own rooms. At lunchtime she'd prepare pungent sauces to go with her rice or ugali (a maize flour porridge). It didn't take an Einstein to figure out that Prudence liked to cook.

A week after she started working for us, the guard came to our door and announced that a Tanzanian woman wanted to see me. I asked him to let her in and waited as a short wiry woman approached, her hands clutched in front of her as she looked meekly up at me. She was barely five feet tall and thin as a cornstalk with a dark complexion and somber eyes. She must have been in her fifties, though she looked strong and spry.

"My name is Lucy," she said, offering me her hand. "I was the housekeeper for the former CDC Director, and I need a job."

"Didn't the director line up a job for you before she left?" I asked, as this was a courtesy most expat employers would extend.

Lucy shook her head sadly. "She didn't do anything for me, madame."

I realized she was talking about the same director who'd been forced to leave, and who had done nothing to help Stefan transition to his new job.

"We already have a part-time housekeeper," I said apologetically. "But I could put a notice in the Embassy newsletter for you."

"Yes, please." Lucy nodded.

During this exchange, I could hear Prudence rattling around the kitchen as she prepared her lunch, and an idea occurred to me. Stefan had asked people at the Embassy about cooks who might be available. As in Ivory Coast, we were expected to host dinners since Stefan held a representational post under the aegis of the US Embassy. But good cooks were hard to come by in Dar, and they were snapped up as soon as they became available. I'd resigned myself to being the chief cook and cleaner for the dinners we would host as well as for daily meals.

"Would you mind waiting a minute, Lucy?" I asked, motioning her to a chair in the living room. She perched on the edge of the chair while I went to the kitchen to speak with Prudence.

"Someone is here who's looking for work as a housekeeper, Prudence," I said quietly. "And I was wondering if you might be interested in switching jobs."

She eyed me warily as if she thought she was about to be fired.

I smiled and continued, "You seem to be a good cook, judging by the delicious lunches you make, and I was wondering if you'd prefer cooking for us instead of cleaning?"

Prudence's face lit up and she bobbed her head. "Oh, yes, madame, I want to be a cooker."

I walked back to the living room and said to Lucy, "Would you want to work for us part-time? I could try to find another family who could use your services the rest of the time."

Lucy's face lit up as Prudence's had, and she reached for my hand and held it. "Oh, yes, thank you." She beamed. "I can start tomorrow."

"Thanks, Lucy." I smiled, happy to have lit on something that would satisfy everyone.

The next time Prudence came to our house, I showed her a few recipes and explained how to make them. We also discussed Tanzanian dishes she could make, since Stefan and I were keen to try local dishes. I showed her how to clean fruits and vegetables as the Embassy recommended—in a bleach-and-water bath to kill amoebae and parasites—and told her what we liked to eat in salads.

She proved to be a fast learner. I'd heard through the Embassy grapevine that the Peace Corps Director had an excellent cook, and we asked if Prudence could learn from him. The Director agreed, and in the coming weeks, Prudence would spend several afternoons observing him. I would teach her how to bake breads and cakes and our favorite fish dishes while Stefan would show her how to make fresh ravioli and pierogies. She also made Tanzanian dishes for us, like fish curries and coconut chicken.

Lucy's presence was like an angel's hovering in the wings. She didn't sing out loud like Gladys, but I often heard her humming in other rooms when no one was around. Like Gladys, she walked around the house in bare feet while cleaning, yet she dressed elegantly when she was ready to leave. Given that she was close to my age, her strength and agility amazed me.

Lucy and Prudence called me by my first name as I'd insisted, whereas Wilfred—who guarded our gate five days a week for twelve hours a day—called me Mama. Stefan's CDC driver used that term for me too, saying that it was the respectful way Tanzanians addressed older women they saw frequently.

Wilfred was only five years older than Aaron, and he'd been a full-time guard for several years. Besides guarding the house, his main task was to open the gate when we went out and to screen visitors who wanted to see us. Like Ousmane and Nestor, he knew the guards next door and could tell us what was going on in the neighborhood.

Wilfred's English sounded fluent to me, but he said it hadn't been good enough to pass the national test for entry into secondary school. He aspired to learn a trade and be an electrician someday. To that end, he was taking evening classes and studying while he sat at our gate. He also read any books and magazines I'd give him.

The more I got to know Wilfred, the more it bothered me that by circumstance of birth, my son was attending a private school and could look forward to going to university while a young man of similar age sat outside our gate working for low wages. It was a daily reminder of the yawning gap between the privileged lives of expats and well-off Africans in comparison with low-income workers who did service jobs like housekeeping and guarding. Although I knew that the gap was deeply embedded in African countries, and that local people and migrants from other countries were desperate for work, it was hard to get used to the inequities around us again.

That Wilfred called me Mama and was close to my son's age troubled me. He wasn't my employee, and the presence of a guard outside our gate was mandated by the US Embassy. But it made my heart ache to know that this earnest young man who hoped to do something with his life was struggling against great odds to realize his dream. It seemed so wrong that young people like Wilfred would have fewer opportunities in life than my children. It was also wrong that the educational system barred children from furthering their education if they didn't master English, thus consigning them to low-wage jobs.

As in Ivory Coast, it was a shock to be confronted by signs of poverty around us every day. There were fewer panhandlers and beggars on city streets than in Abidjan, but the CDC driver explained that it was because the government shamed them into staying home and didn't let them congregate in the city.[17] When I asked him about salaries for service workers and guards, I was surprised to learn that they earned even less than their counterparts in Ivory Coast.

The Indian Ocean was a stone's throw from our house for someone with a strong arm. The closest beach, leased by the Dar Yacht Club, was only a block from our house, and Stefan and I walked over to see it a week after we arrived. The Yacht Club was a glamorous name for a rundown little outfit with prime beachfront real estate. We knew from our Embassy sponsor that few members owned yachts or sailboats at the small marina, and that most of the people who did own boats were South Africans who socialized together. Expats like us joined the

Yacht Club primarily to access the beach—the best one on the peninsula for swimming—and to socialize with other families. The club had a restaurant and bar that was popular on weekends, especially with teenagers since there were few other venues nearby for nightlife. I was surprised to learn that monthly dues were less than what we'd paid at the YMCA in Atlanta.

We picked up an application at the office before ambling down to the beach, which wasn't wide since the tide was high. Beyond the boats that were docked there was a large gazebo with round tables where members could pass the time. The beach was on a protected bay with an island at its mouth that blocked the waves, making the water perfect for swimming. I had an inkling when I took in the scene—of the beach with an island nearby and hills on the distant horizon—that it would anchor me in coming months when I needed a swim or nature break.

We couldn't access the beach while our application was pending, however, and I needed to find a place to swim after the stress of moving and setting up a new house. I'd heard about a nearby hotel that had a lap-length pool, and one day I stopped by after dropping the kids at school. A day pass was only five dollars, and I was able to do forty laps unimpeded with no one around on a weekday.

Shaded by palm trees, the hotel pool was perched on a rocky cliff overlooking the Indian Ocean. I could hear waves slap against the rocks below and watch graceful dhows (traditional wooden sailboats) glide by on the choppy sea. Finding an oasis like that was bliss to me.

Two days later, I found out that the pristine pool with a stellar view wasn't as clean as it had looked. I got sick with intestinal pain and diarrhea from some bacteria in the water. Over the next few days, I was reminded of my bouts of intestinal trouble during our first months in Abidjan. The health unit identified shigella as the cause, and the Embassy doctor prescribed an antibiotic that quickly cleared it up. But I hardly slept and had little energy for days. It was the big caveat to living in foreign countries—that one had to be careful while adjusting to new environs.

One week after we applied to the Yacht Club, our membership was accepted. I could swim in the bay and sit in the gazebo when reading and writing. Despite my illness and lack of sleep, it was easy to take the long view of the adjustment phase. When driving along the coastal road into town or to shopping centers, vistas of the Indian Ocean provided instant eye balm. Even more magical were frequent glimpses of white sails on the denim sea, the dhows slipping noiselessly by like fleeting dreams.

Our second Sunday in Dar, the Peace Corps Director invited our family to join hers at a small beach hotel that was located on a remote stretch of the coast south of Dar. We followed Christine and her family to South Beach in our Nissan Terrano, driving through downtown Dar to the port where a ferryboat carried cars and pedestrians across an inlet. The ferry ride was a mere fifteen minutes, but the trip involved a tedious loading and unloading process that took as much as an hour on weekends.

Our car inched forward onto the ferry amid a stream of pedestrians, some of them bearing baskets with mangos or bananas on their heads. We squeezed in beside a bicycle cart loaded with chickens and a boy leading a goat by a rope. We had to turn the engine off and keep the windows down because it was hot, which meant that we were prey to the many hawkers on the boat. Boys carrying boards loaded with sunglasses would start bargaining if we glanced their way, and men with a dozen Rolex knockoffs barked ridiculously low prices while others hawked music CDs. Aaron and Elena tried to ignore the staring faces while Stefan and I smiled and shook our heads no. At the end of the short ride, our car merged with other vehicles into a single lane, and I gritted my teeth as we inched along among the pedestrians, praying that our wheels wouldn't roll over someone's foot or crush a chicken.

Leaving the stream of pedestrians behind, we were soon cruising through undeveloped savannah dotted by a few rustic hotels behind scrubby bushes and palm trees. Christine pulled up to a single-story hotel with a thatched roof, and we staked a claim under a big banda (a thatched awning that provided shade on the beach).

Aaron and Elena hung out with Christine's kids while Stefan and I took a long walk with her along a deserted beach that stretched for miles. Upon our return, we plunged into the sea and swam before ordering lunch from the hotel restaurant. While waiting for our fish kebabs and French fries, Christine led us to a neighboring banda to meet a bearded American she recognized. She introduced him as a trailing spouse who co-owned a sailboat moored at the Yacht Club.

After shaking our hands, Jeffrey said to me tongue in cheek, "You need to meet my wife, Loren. As Christine can tell you, I'm kind of an asshole, but Loren's a lot of fun, and I'm sure you two would hit it off."

"I'm always open to making new friends," I said amiably.

When Christine mentioned that I was a writer, Jeff's eyes lit up. "I wonder if you'd be interested in writing a column for the magazine *Dar Guide*?"

I hesitated, having never written for a magazine and unsure about taking a job so soon after we arrived. He continued with his pitch. "I met the editor at a reception, and she corralled me into writing a monthly column about life in Dar. I've been doing it for a year, but I'm finding it hard to come up with ideas—especially since I'd rather be out sailing. You might enjoy it, and it's not much work."

"I'll think about it," I said slowly. "But if you can't come up with subjects to write about, I'm not sure I could."

"It's only once a month, and you can write about any aspect of life in Dar that interests you."

"I'll definitely consider it," I nodded. Jeff got my number and promised to invite us for dinner so I could meet his wife, Loren.

The meeting would turn out to be serendipitous, as did the excursion to South Beach. During our three years in Tanzania, we would spend many Sundays at that beach hotel with Jeff and Loren who had kids the same ages as ours; and writing the Dar Guide column would offer me a window and an entrée into spheres I would not have seen otherwise.

In contrast to our move to Atlanta, Aaron's and Elena's adjustments in Tanzania went smoothly. The first week of school, Elena had friends she could meet at the bowling alley on weekends or at the café in Sea Cliff Village, a small shopping court near our house. She started taking tennis lessons and played basketball at school.

Aaron seemed content too, although he spent much of his free time in those early weeks emailing friends back home and playing computer games. He biked to school every day and met a Norwegian boy from an adjacent neighborhood who also biked. Aaron joined the school's outdoor club, which organized hiking and camping trips on weekends. He also started playing Ultimate Frisbee with teachers after school since there was no student team.

Unlike our move to Ivory Coast, I was ready to join any group that might connect me with locals and expats. I attended a few weekly coffees for newcomers run by the Diplomatic Spouse Group (DSG) as well as their monthly meeting. Then I learned about the Corona Women's Society (CWS), which met every month at the Yacht Club around the corner from my house. The first meeting I attended struck me as casual and friendly, and I sensed it was a good fit for me.

That meeting featured representatives from local groups that were looking for volunteers. One woman stood out to me. Giselle was a stout Tanzanian in her mid-thirties who spoke English fluently, and she was flanked by a handful of teenage girls. Giselle had started an NGO called Kids on the Pitch for pre-teen and teenage girls who wanted to play soccer. Most of the girls were still in school, although some had dropped out after failing to pass the national English exam or because they were burdened with family responsibilities. Aside from playing soccer, Kids on the Pitch members took workshops on sex ed and AIDS awareness so the girls wouldn't become prey to older men who might try to cajole them into being their "fiancées"—a ploy some men used to get girls to sleep with them for gifts and money.

Giselle was seeking volunteers to work with her group one or two afternoons a week, tutoring them in English. My ears pricked up at the request since I'd taught English to Central American immigrants in Washington, DC. After the meeting ended, a British woman of Indian origin approached Giselle just as I did. We offered to be tutors even though neither of us were certified teachers for English Language Learners (ELL). Giselle drew a map to the local school where her group held soccer practices and classes, and the British woman and I agreed to start tutoring the following week.

I went home that day thinking how fortunate it was to have stumbled on volunteer work that suited me within a month of our arrival. I'd also landed a part-time gig writing for a magazine and joined the Corona Women's Society—activities that would connect me with expats as well as Tanzanians. Unlike my anxious early months in Ivory Coast, I'd jumped in with both feet and landed happily.

Chapter 11
Off and Running

For the long Labor Day weekend, Stefan wanted us to go on an Embassy-sponsored trip to a game park three hours from Dar. Neither Elena nor I were excited about the idea. I was trying to get the house in order, and Elena preferred to hang out with her new friends. But Stefan and Aaron were keen on going, and they talked us into it.

Once we left the city, the stark terrain framed by mountains reminded us of New Mexico's landscapes. As soon as we reached Mikumi National Park, Elena found other young people to hang out with, which was a relief since our one-room cabin would be tight for four of us. It had screens instead of glass in the windows and was open to the elements.

The cabin was a short walk from the lodge where guests gathered for meals. When we ambled over, we found the Embassy crowd milling around a roaring fire and nursing drinks while watching the watering hole below. All manner of game wandered to and from the small lake at dusk—elephants and various deer-like creatures that Aaron dubbed DLCs.

We sat down to eat and made small talk with other Americans who were affiliated with the Embassy. Seated beside me was the Community Liaison Officer (CLO) who also chaired the Corona Women's Group. Candy stood out with her orange hair, inquisitive smile, and sharp memory. When I mentioned my interest in learning

Swahili, she told me about the language instructor who gave free lessons at the Embassy.

"How do I get in touch with him?" I asked.

"Just call the Embassy and ask for Hamisi. He runs a Swahili language and culture trip to Zanzibar every year, and there's one coming up at the end of September."

"In three weeks?" I asked, perking up at the mention of Zanzibar. "Is there still time to sign up?"

"I think so," Candy nodded. "My husband and I did it when we got here two years ago, and we loved it."

When I told Candy that I'd agreed to write a monthly column for the Dar Guide, she was full of ideas for future topics. She was also a wealth of information about trips we might want to take as a family in the coming months.

At dawn the next morning, the deep stillness of the savannah was split by the occasional peal of birdsong, most of it new to my ears. Also new was the grinding of SUV wheels on gravel roads as animal seekers tore out at sunrise. We had to wake Aaron and Elena at 5 a.m. since we'd signed up to go with a guide who knew the best places to find animals.

The guide drove our group to a small lake where a dozen elephants were congregating. It was an anxious first sighting for me as a huge bull elephant stood in the middle of the dirt road and played cat and mouse with our open-sided vehicle. Every time the guide inched forward to try to pass, the bull would start to charge, and the guide would back up. I clung to the side of the vehicle even though it had no walls above my waist, was open on all sides, and had a canvas top. If the elephant actually charged, it wouldn't be much of a contest with the flimsy safari car. After a couple of females and babies crossed the road, the bull finally backed down and ambled after them into the bush. The kids found my frightened reactions hilarious, and they mimicked me for the rest of the morning.

We'd seen our fill of animals—lions, leopards, hippos, and scores of DLCs—and were heading back to the lodge when I happened to look over at Aaron and see a small green snake dangling from the canvas roof a foot away from his face. He was sitting directly across from me, and I tried to remain calm as I said to him, "Move away from the window, Aaron."

Turning his head to look, he leapt from his seat as soon as he saw the snake and landed on my side of the aisle. When the guide saw what was happening, he stopped the jeep and sauntered back to the spot where Aaron had been sitting. Hitting the canvas roof with his fist, he sent the snake flying off into the bush, and we all breathed a sigh of relief. I didn't dare ask him if it might have been a dreaded green mamba.

I went with the group to look for animals the morning of our second day too. But when Stefan proposed going out again that afternoon in our car, I elected to stay behind and enjoy the stillness of the savannah from the porch of our cabin. Elena complained less when I wasn't with them, and she didn't grouse around her father the way she did with me. Like the bull elephant we'd encountered on our first outing, she was combative if she felt restricted in any way. Since it wasn't expedient to antagonize both parents, and because I was more easily triggered than Stefan, she was harder on me than on him. I realized that my best strategy was to keep my head down and wait for the bull to back away.

The gift that afternoon was a private viewing of elephants and giraffes as they strolled past my porch on the way to the lodge's watering hole. I much preferred to watch the stately animals lope across the field rather than to chase them in a safari car. It was a rare treat to experience the stillness of the park from my porch, and I did it again the following morning when Stefan took the kids out for one last game drive. Instead of excited voices and the grinding noise of SUV tires on gravel, I reveled in the sounds of chittering birds and eerie silence.

After I signed up for Swahili lessons with Hamisi, he invited me on the language and culture trip to Zanzibar. It seemed rash to go away for four days when I was still setting up the house, but Zanzibar sounded intriguing as did the prospect of meeting other new arrivals. When Stefan said he could handle the kids without me, I told Hamisi I'd go.

The trip started with a nail-biting flight in a small prop plane that barely fit our group of twelve. Jeff's wife, Loren, was the only person I knew. She had been to Zanzibar several times and knew the hotel that Hamisi had reserved for our group. After we checked in, Hamisi sent us off for a walking tour of Stone Town with a superb watercolorist and historian, John Da Silva.

That evening, half the group decided to go to a restaurant nearby while the rest of us chose to try street food at the night market near the harbor. Loren knew the market and had few qualms about eating street food after living in a handful of African countries—as a Peace Corps volunteer as well as a staff member.

The night market was like a scene from a Fellini movie. Lit by gas lanterns, it was full of venders selling food on long portable tables while they stoked hibachis or grills behind them. I followed Loren from one table to the next, selecting skewers of fish that venders would grill for us. The array of fish was mind-boggling: tuna, marlin, red snapper, salmon, shark, shrimp, crab, and lobsters. At other tables we selected veggies, sweet potatoes, French fries, and plantains that venders had roasted on grills or cooked in deep fryers. Carnivores could choose from a variety of meats on skewers or in patties, and there were pizzas and crepes too. All sorts of beverages were available, including local brew (a malted beer), wine, juices, and smoothies.

After we filled our plates and doused the food with pili pili (a local hot sauce), Loren and I sat at a picnic table and ate mouth-watering meals that cost the equivalent of four dollars. In the hypnotic, fair-like atmosphere, Loren pointed out venders on the far side of the waterfront park who were selling clothes, jewelry, and other handmade products. Though I didn't have much energy after the exciting travel day, we decided to browse among the stalls anyway. Most of the venders were Masai men dressed in trademark maroon and purple garments, and they displayed the beaded earrings, necklaces, and bracelets that women had made in their villages. They also sold leather products and rubber sandals fashioned from used car tires.

Tired from the sensory overload that day, Loren and I made our way back to the hotel and slept soundly.

The next few days were a mix of intensive language study in the mornings and cultural excursions arranged by Hamisi in the afternoons— to a spice farm outside Stone Town and to a village shaman who went into a trance and did readings for us. We made great strides in speaking Swahili and could make ourselves understood at local markets.

On our last evening, Hamisi organized a party at the Embassy's residence in Stone Town. A local group played traditional taarab music with stringed instruments that looked like misshapen guitars, along with African drummers. After dancers performed, they coaxed us to get up and dance with them. Laughing at each other's efforts, one man in our group dared me to leap into his arms and let him toss me around at the end of a dance. I complied, to the surprise and delight of my companions.

As the musicians continued to play, we filed past a buffet table and loaded our plates with a variety of stews and sauces. At the end of the sumptuous meal, we toasted Hamisi and his team of teachers for their generous efforts.

I considered the trip to be a triumph and a propitious cap to my first month in Tanzania. I'd learned enough Swahili to converse in public places and made a few new friends—chief among them Loren, who was funny and great company. And though I'd had only glimpses of Zanzibari culture, those early impressions were intriguing.

A few weeks later, I had a very different four-day weekend with my family. The kids had a few days off for fall break, and we decided to take them to Mafia Island.

We were unprepared yet delighted by how rustic it was. The words "Mafia Airport" were painted in bold letters on the roof of a dilapidated terminal, and our Cessna prop plane—packed with a dozen passengers—had to circle the dirt runway until someone chased a cow from the airstrip. The plane skidded onto the runway and landed alongside village huts with goats and barefoot children scampering around them.

Inside the terminal, a driver from the hotel we'd reserved met us with a handwritten sign bearing Stefan's name. He smiled broadly and shook hands with each of us before leading the way to a rickety jeep that barely fit our luggage. With wires dangling from the dashboard and flowered wallpaper covering holes in the floor, the vehicle didn't look like it could go very far. We bounced along a narrow dirt road for twenty kilometers, at times swerving to avoid hitting bicycles or plodding women with loads of firewood on their heads.

Stefan and I had wanted to visit Mafia after hearing about its vibrant sea life and coral reefs, and Aaron was keen on diving since he planned to compile a guide to dive sites around Dar for his tenth grade IB (International Baccalaureate) project. But Elena wasn't happy to be on a remote island with her parents. Personality differences between us were becoming more pronounced since she turned thirteen, and everything I said seemed to exasperate her. Having been ornery and disrespectful towards my mother at that age, I held out hope that she'd outgrow it as I did.

Elena was a true extrovert who loved being with people and talked nonstop about movie stars, sports, and clothes. She'd pore over fashions on the internet and dream about what she would buy if she had money. I was the farthest thing from chic she could imagine, more interested in reading and hiking than in famous people and fashions. Fifth Avenue and Beverly Hills were her idea of paradise whereas Mafia Island was mine.

Yet even I was unprepared for how rustic the island was, from the airport and unpaved roads to the handful of small hotels dotting the coast. As our jeep pulled up to the Mafia Island Lodge, staff members greeted us with flowers and coconuts with straws. The activities coordinator—an enthusiastic young man named Ali—escorted us to the front desk and told us about activities we could do while staying at the lodge.

"Sign us up for everything," I chirped, earning a withering glance from Elena. Ali led her and Aaron off to play ping pong while Stefan and I checked in.

Our family room was a spacious though barebone two-bedroom bungalow that faced the sea. With a patio shaded by a cashew tree, it was an inviting setting that I would appreciate in the mornings when the others slept in.

We sat down to a late lunch that afternoon after a fun excursion to nearby Chole Island. Aaron was the only one who didn't eat with us. He'd decided to fast for the month of Ramadan as the Muslims around us were doing, and he went off for an afternoon dive with the dive master while the rest of us relaxed on the beach for a couple of hours.

In the late afternoon, Elena went off to play pool with Ali, and Stefan and I waded out to greet the dive boat as it motored in. "It was awesome," Aaron gushed as soon as he saw us. "We went over an underwater cliff and crawled along a wall where there were huge sea turtles and manta rays." Barely pausing to catch his breath, he barreled on, "Can I go out again tomorrow with Moise? He's doing a double dive in the morning."

We had to smile at Aaron's enthusiasm, which he rarely showed around his sister. "Sure," Stefan nodded. "I just wish I could go with you." He hadn't been able to get his dive certification because of his long workdays, and I preferred to snorkel instead of swimming with heavy equipment on my back.

The next day, Aaron went off to dive while Stefan and I took a dhow to go snorkeling at some coral gardens in the bay. Ali cajoled Elena into coming, and he got her to put on snorkeling gear and follow him into the water.

Plunging in behind Stefan, I was immediately captivated by the vibrant coral. Mustard-toned clumps that looked like mutant cabbages attracted scores of brilliant fish, as did violet finger coral and blue-veined boulders. I'd never seen such rainbow shades on parrot fish and lobsters. Mesmerized by the coral, I hovered above schools of fish that foraged along the ocean floor. Even Elena couldn't hide her excitement when Ali pointed out sea creatures to her.

A few hours later, we met up with Aaron who raved about his dive again. "We saw nurse sharks, octopus, manta rays, and fish I've never seen up close before. And I learned a lot from Moise about regulating my breathing and conserving oxygen."

"He is a dedicated student." Moise nodded, patting Aaron on the back. "I would be happy to take him out anytime."

Ali was equally impressed by Aaron's determination to fast during Ramadan. Ali's parents had sent dates and cashews so Aaron could break his fast in the evening the way they did. Stefan and I were touched by Ali's and Moise's efforts to connect with our kids and with us, an unexpected bonus on our family trip.

The long weekend on Mafia Island almost reassured me that moving our teenagers to the other side of the world had been a good choice for our family. Weekend outings to the beach and trips like this were leagues above anything we could do together in Atlanta. All of us had learned something about village life on a small island, and Elena had come out of her funk thanks to Ali. And I had enough time alone to experience a deep restorative peace.

Thus, it came as a surprise to hear Aaron's response to a question posed by Ali. "How do you feel about spending a few years in Tanzania and away from your friends at home?"

"I have mixed feelings about it." Aaron shrugged. "It's too soon to tell."

While his response sobered me, I understood how he felt. There was no doubt that the move had been right for Stefan, who was much happier doing critical work in foreign settings than he was in Atlanta; and he knew his work would help thousands of people with HIV live longer healthier lives. Elena, too, was a lot happier at her school in Dar than she'd been in Atlanta.

I'd assumed that we would face obstacles, and I already missed my friends and family at home. Yet thrilling experiences in places like Zanzibar and Mafia Island made it seem worth the sacrifice. Aaron and Elena could do community service projects and excursions that they could never do in the US, and I would seize such opportunities too.

Keenly aware of the trade-offs, I had mixed feelings like Aaron. It was too soon to tell whether one day we'd look back and say that moving to Tanzania had been the best choice for all of us.

Chapter 12
The Ambassador's Ear

I didn't know how much I wanted to go to Madagascar until I got there.

Four months after our family trip to Mafia Island, Candy convinced me to sign up for an Embassy-sponsored trip to Madagascar, an island the size of Texas off the east coast of Africa. She promised that I'd see plants and animals like nowhere else in the world: chameleons the length of a person's arm, for example, and lemurs. Though I found it hard to justify another trip after our family had just spent two weeks in Egypt at Christmas, the idea of being single and carefree in a new place was appealing. Stefan encouraged me to go, so I couldn't say no.

Candy failed to mention that February was rainy season in Madagascar and that the US Ambassador would be the only other unaccompanied person in the group. I learned both facts when I got to the airport and found myself sitting next to him on the airplane. With earphones in and an iPod in hand, the Ambassador was blasé about the whole thing and didn't pay much attention to me. He did offer me his window seat, which I readily accepted, eager to see maritime views from the air.

For most of the four-hour flight, I averted my face and drank in the sight of the turquoise sea dotted with tiny islands. Sitting next to the Ambassador—whom I knew by reputation only—made me antsy.

Stefan and I avoided him at Embassy functions, intimidated by the prospect of making conversation with a wealthy politico who'd been appointed to his post by President George W. Bush. He also had a reputation as a debonaire divorcee and was often seen around town with chic women from the Belgian and Italian Embassies.

Whenever I took my eyes off the scenery, I squirmed in my seat and pretended to read. As the Ambassador dozed, I stole glances at him and noted the taut skin around his eyes that belied expensive plastic surgery. His gray hair was slicked back in military fashion, and he had a narrow face with thin lips. Slender and somewhat tall, he was in his mid-sixties and wore tasseled loafers, khaki pants, and a polo shirt, which amplified my impression of him as an aging preppy.

People at the Embassy were stiff and formal around him, and they had to stand up when he walked into a meeting room and refer to him as Mr. Ambassador. Technically Stefan's boss, he had tried to exercise his right to oversee government agencies under his purview even though he knew nothing about AIDS or how CDC operated. Stefan wrote him off early on, convinced that he cared more about seeing the wildlife and sights in Africa than he did about programs for the sick and needy.

Peering through impenetrable clouds as rain pelted the windows, I tried to squelch my disappointment as the plane skidded to a stop on the runway. It was going to be a long week.

"Call me Mike," he told the group when we gathered in the hotel restaurant for dinner that night. But I couldn't bring myself to call him Mike. That name belonged to my brother, who was so different from the Ambassador, it would be too weird. Plus, I knew Candy had suggested to him that he travel on a first-name basis, and it wasn't his initiative.

As he pulled out the chair next to his and waited for me to sit down, his attention and flourish-y manners embarrassed me. He handed me a menu and asked me if I spoke French, so I put on my reading glasses to translate for him. Then I turned away and tried to converse with Candy and her husband, who also worked at the Embassy. Rounding out our group of eight were Candy's friends—a couple from Texas—and a Norwegian woman I knew from the Corona Women's Group. Bodil was accompanied by her adult son, and I knew she'd be fun company despite her shy demeanor around the Ambassador.

I used to be much more fun myself before my children morphed into surly teens. At graduate school in London in my mid-twenties, I'd danced to highlife music at parties hosted by my Ghanaian friends and had long discussions in smoky pubs with fellow students—not to mention a few relationships with foreign men. It was the kind of fun Elena wanted to have at age thirteen. Coaxing her to take things slowly was like trying to urge a bull elephant to stop charging.

It was bad luck to have a week away on my own and then be stuck with the Ambassador, who was acting like we were a couple. Everyone in the group was deferential and awkward around him, and I worried that his presence would put a damper on the trip for the rest of us. Fortunately, our guide—a lively, frizzy-haired woman from Madagascar—plunked herself down in the chair opposite me after we finished dinner. Colette passed out maps and timetables and showed pictures of the animals we'd see in the wild. As we pored over her maps and photos, an air of excitement infected us all.

When Collette finished speaking, the Ambassador started telling everyone about a walking safari he'd done with his wife twenty years earlier, and I couldn't help wondering what she must have been like. Then he related a joke about a disgruntled divorcee who refused to be trapped in marriage a second time, and his voice was full of sarcasm as if it hit close to home. When he started bragging about the many restaurants he owned, I did an inward eyeroll since I knew he was talking about McDonald's franchises. He also dropped names of his

White House cronies—chief among them Karl Rove—to remind us that he was a Big Man in the Republican Party.

As he talked about how his buddy Karl might manipulate the political machinery to pave the way for Bush's successor, it bothered me so much that I couldn't sit still any longer. I excused myself and went up to my room to read.

In the morning we boarded a van for a driving tour of Antananarivo (Tana), the capital of Madagascar. At first glance it resembled a quaint Italian town perched on a hilltop—San Gimignano came to mind—until I looked closer and noted signs of pervasive poverty. Tana was built on a handful of hills with shanties and shacks lining the ravines and lower slopes while villas of former colonial officials and French expats dominated the hillsides.

The van ferried us through twisting streets and up a steep hill to the ruins of the former queen's palace. From the top, we had panoramic views of distant hills and a big lake in the center of the city. We took advantage of photo ops before climbing back into the van to wind our way through Tana again.

When we reached a sprawling crafts market on the outskirts of town, the Ambassador asked me if I'd help him choose a few gifts for his daughter and a "lady friend." What he really wanted was someone to translate and help him haggle over prices. Being a seasoned bargainer, I didn't mind. I was also eager to peruse the stalls where venders displayed silk scarves and shawls, semi-precious gems and embroidered tablecloths.

While we were browsing at one stall, an old man with missing teeth approached us and extended a gnarly hand to solicit change. His unshaved face was deeply lined, and his tattered clothes barely shielded his stooping frame. My heart lurched as I looked in his eyes, figuring he was about my father's age. It startled me when the

Ambassador gave him a disgusted glance and barked at him, "Get a job," before darting into the safety of a shop.

Seeing the baffled look on the poor man's face, I dug in my purse and found a few coins for him. Then I went off to shop on my own, appalled and ashamed by the Ambassador's rude behavior.[18] I chalked it up to the knee-jerk reaction of a rich conservative and wanted nothing more to do with him.

That afternoon we boarded a flight to the northern tip of Madagascar. The airline pitched in gusting winds and rain, flying so low that I could see the coastline clearly. It was broken by beaches and coves and interspersed with velveteen cliffs and mesas. Huge red buttes covered with lush grass made for startling contrasts, as if the canyonlands of southern Utah had been transposed onto Irish soil.

Another van met us at the airport and deposited us at a lodge that was perched above a narrow bay with rolling green hills on the horizon. It was a perfect respite where we'd get to stay in one place for three nights. The balcony off my room overlooked a courtyard with manicured shrubs and scarlet bougainvillea, a swimming pool at the end of the lawn. The sight of that pool was all the incentive I needed to remain at the hotel while the others went off to do more shopping. A swim and a nap would be the best tonic after constant company and nonstop travel.

At breakfast on the deck of the restaurant the following morning, I was holding a book but not reading it since the view across the bay— of forested mountains jutting into the water—was more gripping than my novel.

The Ambassador appeared out of nowhere and startled me. "Mind if I join you?" he asked, pulling out a chair without waiting for a response.

"Not at all," I lied. No one else from the group was up yet, which meant that I'd be stuck with him again.

"Why's your hair wet?" he asked bluntly. "Couldn't you find a blow dryer?"

Bristling at his familiar tone, I said curtly, "I jumped in the pool and did a few laps."

"Oh, is that what you do for exercise?"

"Mostly, yes."

He shook his head disparagingly. "Not me. I like a full-service gym." He flagged a waiter over and asked in English for fruit salad. When the waiter gave him a puzzled look, the Ambassador repeated his request in a louder tone. Instead of telling him he should help himself at the breakfast bar, I asked the waiter in French if he'd bring a bowl of fruit to the table. He shrugged and went off to fulfill the request.

Meanwhile the Ambassador fussed with a napkin in his lap, taking care to cover his crisply pressed pink oxford shirt. When the waiter returned with his fruit, the Ambassador said without looking at him, "I'll have coffee with hot milk, please."

"I'll get your coffee for you," I sighed. "I was about to go to the breakfast bar anyway."

"Oh, thanks," he mumbled, not looking at me as he plunged his fork in the fruit bowl. "I'm vicious in the morning without a cup of coffee."

I took my time at the breakfast bar and returned to find him scanning the cover of my book.

"Who's this Coetzee fellow?" he asked, completely mispronouncing the author's name.

"A famous writer from South Africa. He's won all kinds of awards."

"Never heard of him." Pushing the book across the table, he added, "It looks depressing."

"It's a great book," I insisted. "The critics loved it."

"Why's it called *Disgrace*?"

"It's hard to explain." I hesitated, suspecting that he wasn't really interested in the answer anyway. And yes, I had to admit it *was* depressing.

"Personally, I'm a big fan of Danielle Steel," he remarked, picking at threads of mango between his teeth. "I dated Danielle some years ago. She's a real character."

Eyeing him, I was careful not to show my doubt about his claim. "I've never read any of her books, but my mother-in-law likes her."

"You wouldn't believe what a tough life she had. She grew up with an abusive mother before she struck out on her own and made something of herself."

"Really?" I asked, my interest growing.

"Oh, she's a character. She profiled me in one of her books after we stopped dating."

I couldn't help asking, "Which book was it?"

"I forget the name. But she made up some weird bedroom scene that was embarrassing."

Just when he had my attention, other members of the group filed in behind our guide and a noisy discussion about the day's activities ensued. Collette urged us to eat quickly and gather our things since safari cars were waiting to take us to a park to look for lemurs.

As we headed into the forest, everyone fanned out along the overgrown path and scanned the trees for lemurs. After a mile or so, Collette spotted a huge green chameleon squatting on a tree branch and we crowded around to marvel at its jade-flecked skin. When she asked if anyone wanted to hold it, the Ambassador stepped forward with his arm outstretched. Collette took a stick and nudged the chameleon onto his forearm, and he stood there beaming like a boy holding a 4-H prize. I couldn't help smiling as the others pulled out their cameras and took photos of him. When he held it out to me with a playful expression, I shook my head and backed away, too timid to touch it. He nestled his arm against a tree branch and urged the chameleon onto it.

Continuing along the path, the Ambassador started telling me about his childhood and how he used to spend days wandering in the Ozark Mountains by himself, tracking deer and raccoons in forests like these. He mentioned that his father was a military man who was rarely home, and I caught a glimpse of the young man behind his slick veneer. It saddened me to think of him as a boy who had to explore remote mountains on his own.

As light rain started falling, softly at first and slowly building, we gave up the search for lemurs and trudged up a steep path to the safari cars. Wearing running shoes instead of hiking boots, I slipped in the mud and fell to my knees. The Ambassador took my hand and helped me up the slippery path, only letting go of my hand when we reached the road. By then my face was burning, and I didn't look at him as we climbed into the jeep.

Forced to sit next to him again, I gazed at the passing scenery while he plugged into his iPod. The rest of us carried on a conversation with Collette mostly in French, which I didn't bother to translate for the Ambassador.

It startled me when he plucked out one of his earbuds and handed it to me. "Here, listen to this," he said earnestly. "I think you'll like it."

It was the prolog of an audiobook by Bill O'Reilly—whom I didn't normally read—about a fictional quest for the historical Jesus. The intimacy of it startled me—that the Ambassador assumed I'd be interested in anything he found intriguing and that he'd pass the bud directly from his ear to mine. I was squeamish when he offered it to me, and a little touched.

After another day of trekking through a forest without spotting any lemurs, our group gathered in the hotel restaurant for drinks in the evening. The Ambassador surprised us by toasting Candy's husband, who had a birthday, and I was moved by his remarks about Randy's modesty and the long hours he devoted to his Embassy colleagues. This time, when the Ambassador told a joke about a wizened divorcee, I caught hints of disappointment in his voice instead of rancor.

Later that night, I called Stefan to fill him in on the trip. "I'm glad you're having fun," he remarked, "but I'm also glad I'm not there. I'd hate to spend every day and night with the Ambassador as you're doing. I feel sorry for you."

"He's really not a bad guy," I tried to tell him.

"That's what they say at the Embassy," Stefan chuckled, "that he's a charmer."

"I'm not being snowed." I bristled, sensing he didn't believe me. Stefan's opinions had been set in stone after sitting through weekly meetings with other agency heads and the Ambassador, who believed in cutting government spending and wanted to curtail certain CDC programs. He had a thing against crows and reported every week on the number of birds felled by his eradication program. Stefan considered it petty when so many people were dying of malaria and AIDS. He was biding his time until the Ambassador got bored and left the country.

"How are you doing?" I asked, changing the subject. "Any fights with the kids?" I was referring to our family dinners, which were often rancorous as the kids argued with each other or with me—when they didn't ignore me, that is.

"Not really. In fact, both kids have been very pleasant. You wouldn't believe how peaceful dinners are these days."

The news was so disconcerting that I told him I had to go.

Alone in my hotel room, I didn't want to think it was my presence that made family dinners volatile. Nor did I want to admit that it humiliated and wounded me when Elena gave me scornful looks and only spoke to Stefan. I told myself that it was a phase, and that I had been disrespectful to my mother at that age. This was another situation—like the impasse with Mona—that I wasn't equipped to handle; nor was Stefan. We didn't know how to convince the kids to speak civilly and show respect to everyone around them, including myself.

By contrast, meals with the Ambassador and our companions were convivial and wholly reaffirming. Warming to the rest of the group, I slowly recovered my confidence and voice. The Ambassador asked me about articles I was writing for the Dar Guide, and the others asked follow-up questions too. It was a heady feeling knowing that they listened to every word I said.

The next day we piled into a van after breakfast for yet another excursion, this time to a beach in a protected bay. We had an idyllic setting to ourselves: a white-sand beach studded with palm trees and rust-toned boulders jutting up at the end of the bay. The Ambassador set off on a walk by himself while I made a beeline for the water. Bodil joined me and the two of us floated and swam for what seemed like hours. It was so delicious swimming in the pristine sea that when we spotted dolphins nearby, I felt like I was one of them.

When it was time to return to the van at the end of the day, Collette led the way along an unpaved road and through a hamlet of shack-like houses. Scrawny chickens and turkeys were darting around, and the Ambassador surprised us with a low-throated gobble that made the turkeys puff up their throats and gobble back at him. Time and again the turkeys responded to his call, and I laughed so hard that my stomach got a cramp.

The fun carried over into the evening when a troupe of acrobats showed up at our hotel. We stood around gaping as boys and men careened off each other's backs and shoulders. Then they launched oranges and soda bottles at each other, gyrating and spinning them off their hands, feet, and faces. Someone tossed a few oranges to the Ambassador, and he managed to juggle them for a minute before tossing them back. I caught myself grinning again, surprised at this playful side of him.

When we sat down to dinner, a full moon illuminated the peninsula and reflected off the silvery bay. The Ambassador leaned over my shoulder to read the menu and asked me what I'd recommend. By then I was content to sit next to him and translate. He ordered wine for everyone since it was Valentine's Day, which made the dinner conversations livelier than usual.

At the end of the evening, he walked around and gave each woman a goodnight kiss on the cheek. I blushed when the Ambassador planted a kiss on me, surprised and confused by my warm feelings toward him. It was a spontaneous gesture that left everyone smiling at the growing camaraderie in our group.

Later that night I couldn't help thinking about the contrasts between us that had seemed so stark a few days before. He read books by Danielle Steel and Bill O'Reilly while I preferred Toni Morrison and J. M. Coetzee, and he considered W to be the greatest President since Ronald Reagan whereas I disagreed so vehemently that I tuned him out when he started talking about him. Yet there I was, happy to be in his company and not minding that we were a couple. As both of us let down our guard, I saw the man behind his stiff persona and vice versa. In fact, the two of us, opposites though we seemed, were becoming friends.

Living abroad brought us in contact with individuals who weren't like us on a daily basis, and not just people of other cultures but wealthy Republican big shots. I was beginning to realize that given the right circumstances, you could always find the boy inside a Big Man; especially if you caught him gobbling at passing turkeys or juggling spontaneously.

The next day we flew back to Tana, hopped in a chartered bus, and drove for six hours through rainforests that cover the eastern side of the island. The rainy season—more pronounced in that part of Madagascar—was a heavy presence, like an overbearing in-law who wouldn't leave. The last five miles of the drive on a muddy dirt road were downright frightening as the bus fishtailed and chugged slowly up and over steep ridges. On one hill we had to get out and walk in the rain as the driver tried to pilot the bus up the muddy incline, sliding much of the way.

The rain let up when we reached the lakeside lodge where we were to spend the night. As the sky cleared, Collette herded us onto a boat that would ferry us across the lagoon to a wildlife reserve where lemurs roamed freely. It was a mesmerizing journey—plying the undulating waters in a wooden dhow full of grace and dignity. All of us were silent under the billowing sail as we took in the lush green scenery along the shoreline.

Once the boat docked at the nature reserve, we climbed out of the dhow with mounting excitement. Everyone seemed to feel it: an eagerness to finally see the objects of our weeklong quest. We trekked in silence as we followed Collette down a soggy path through tunnels of trees, the ferns as big as banana plants and the air as thick as the understory. Walking with eyes and ears focused on the dense canopy, my senses were acutely attuned as I listened for the sound of scampering paws in bushes and trees.

Suddenly Collette gave a shrill cry to summon the lemurs, and we lifted our faces like children scanning the sky for Santa's sleigh. Everyone saw them at once—a dozen lemurs with dark eyes and pointed snouts bounding through the branches toward us. Collette quickly handed out bananas to each of us and started waving one herself as she continued her curdling calls.

In no time at all, the koala-like creatures were upon us. They resembled big furry squirrels with raccoon tails, and I gaped as two of them climbed on Collette's and the Ambassador's backs. When a reddish-brown lemur jumped on my shoulder, I shoved my banana at him and begged the Ambassador to get the animal off me. He bolted to my side and lured the lemur onto his own shoulder while several others climbed on his back and head. Ashamed of being afraid, I watched in fascination as the Ambassador enjoyed every moment with them.

We gathered around him and aimed our cameras to record the spectacle. With a gray lemur perched on his head and two brown ones on his shoulders, the Ambassador offered them bits of banana and beamed like a prize-winning boy again. The animals were clearly as attracted to him as he was to them. In that moment he did remind me of my brother, the other Mike, who loved animals and would have given anything to have lemurs perched on his head and shoulders.

All too soon, a soft drizzle gathered momentum and forced us out of the woods before we were ready to leave the endearing creatures. The lemurs didn't like getting wet any more than we did, and they climbed high into the trees as we followed Collette through the saturated forest. All of us were soaked by the time we reached the shelter.

As I went off to find a restroom, the Ambassador saved a seat for me in front of a roaring fire, and he ordered drinks since he knew what I liked by then. Upon my return, he handed me my reading glasses and pulled out an article he'd been carrying that had photos and descriptions of every type of lemur. We scanned it together and tried to identify the species we'd seen.

When Collette announced that it was time to leave, we trooped back to the boat and took our places again. The slow pitch of the dhow as we drifted in the evening light and the sound of waves lapping in our wake lulled me into a deep peace. The sensory overload was so intense that I had to close my eyes—until a blazing sunset over the bay drew my attention that way.

After docking at the lodge, we went our separate ways to rest for an hour before the evening's activities. I was glad to have some time to myself and took a warm bath before a last supper in that magical place. There was even time to finish reading *Disgrace*, which I did as an escape from too much musing; and from kicking myself for being sad that we'd soon be heading home. I missed Stefan and the kids, of course, and I even resolved to bring them to Madagascar someday, although I knew it would never be the same.

Eventually I was drawn from my bungalow by the thrum of African drums and a harmony of voices singing along with stringed instruments. The rest of the group had already assembled in the lodge around a traditional dance troupe, with the Ambassador taking center stage as usual. One of the dancers shook her hips and shimmied around him as he attempted to imitate her, not caring that he was making a spectacle.

Then the song changed, and the dancers reached out to bystanders and drew them into a line dance. As the gyrating line passed in front of me, the Ambassador grabbed my hand and pulled me into the snaking line behind him. I followed reluctantly, only slowly catching the rhythm in my feet and the enthusiasm of the others. Yet it was contagious—the pulsating music, the drums, and the spirit of fun that infected everyone—and soon I was shaking my shoulders and hips along with the rest of the group. We laughed at each other as we tried to mimic the moves of the dancers, until the drumming slowed and a female singer intoned a softer tune.

As the others moved toward their partners, the Ambassador took my hand and pulled me close for a slow dance with him. I reached up and put my arms around his shoulders and let the slow flow of the dance envelop me, though my face grew warm and the close contact with him made me self-conscious and edgy. He must have sensed my awkwardness because as soon as the slow dance ended, we didn't look at each other as we parted.

Making my way to the table, I found my seat next to his as the drums started pounding and the band picked up the beat. Everyone else took their seats after me, and we fell into our old roles at dinner again. The Ambassador started telling us about his cronies and about a casino he owned with one of them, and it disturbed me to hear him talk about the shady business that went on in his casino. Then I recalled the baffled look on the old man's face after the Ambassador barked at him to get a job, and it reminded me that though he could be charming and fun, we viewed life through very different lenses.

I hardly looked his way during dinner, and no private words passed between us. He must have sensed my cold shoulder because he got up as soon as dinner was over and wandered off on his own. My eyes followed him down the path to the moonlit beach, and I began to imagine all sorts of things: that he was hurt and confused by my attitude, that he was lonely, that he wanted to be alone. I couldn't help feeling guilty for ignoring him and starting to judge him again.

Reluctant to return to my bungalow, I strolled the beach with Bodil and her son to gaze at the star-studded sky. Then I left them at their cottage and walked slowly back to mine, half-wishing that I'd bump into the Ambassador and have a chance to explain or apologize.

Sitting on my porch, I couldn't help mulling over animal attraction after what we'd witnessed in the forest, and how things can get muddled when a man and a woman connect on deeper levels. Why was it a strain to get my head and heart in sync and simply accept the guy for who he was?

Such reflections on the dark porch troubled me, yet it felt like a singular moment—to be alone and not alone and to wonder at the distances we'd come.

"Good night, Mike," I murmured in the still night air, hoping that he would hear it.

⚘

After that trip, the Ambassador started inviting me and Stefan to his private dinners as well as to official functions, and whenever we met, we'd greet each other like old friends. Later that year, I invited him to my birthday dinner along with Bodil and her husband, and the Ambassador brought his lady friend from the Belgian Embassy. As we reminisced about our trip, even Stefan warmed up to him. His respect for the Ambassador had grown since he seemed to take his job seriously and would ask how he could help his team overcome political barriers—to the point where he'd schedule meetings with ministers to facilitate his team's work.

As Stefan suspected, the Ambassador only remained in Tanzania for another year before returning to the US as the next presidential campaign got underway. I was sorry to see him go, knowing that our friendship was unlikely to continue outside of that extraordinary locale.

Yet I had learned that appreciating the values and customs of other cultures—like polygamy and shamanism—was no different from appreciating the alternative views of my compatriots. In Madagascar, we became companions and fellow adventurers who loved nature enough to put up with long slogs on buses in torrential rain and found lemurs and technicolor chameleons enchanting. We enjoyed the cultural idiosyncrasies of foreign places—the food, crafts, music, and dances—and were keen to see and do as much as possible. In essence, when we looked for things we had in common instead of judging each other, we were freer to experience the uniqueness of other people and places with "beginner's mind," as Buddhists might say. And in the absence of preconceptions and judgments, real connections formed.

Chapter 13:

Roaming Around East Africa

Two weeks after my trip to Madagascar, Stefan and I stepped into the lodge of a coffee plantation at the base of Kilimanjaro. He checked into the hotel while I walked outside to gape at the iconic mountain against a cerulean sky, two of its three peaks clearly visible. It was daunting to think that Aaron would soon be climbing Kilimanjaro with a group of schoolmates.

Only the buzz of cicadas and the occasional bleating of sheep on a nearby farm broke the stillness. It was a boon to be in the highlands and away from Dar during hot season when no one wanted to be outside and power outages were common—which meant no air conditioning or internet. At six thousand feet above sea level, a cool breeze made the temperature bearable.

Trips were turning out to be a big part of our sojourn in East Africa. Apart from family jaunts, the kids had regular school excursions and Stefan visited clinics around the country. That week, while Aaron and Elena were away on separate trips, Stefan had to go to Moshi for a conference, and I went with him. AIDS was the reason we were in Tanzania, and I wanted to witness what Stefan was doing. To that end, I would accompany him on a few home health visits with Pathfinder, a partner NGO serving thousands of patients with the help of volunteers.

The first visit took place that afternoon in a shantytown outside Moshi. The ten-foot square shack, connected on both sides to others like it, resembled houses I'd seen in Ivory Coast with walls made of mud or wattle and cardboard boxes lining them, topped by metal roofs. A five-year-old girl with HIV sat beside her grandmother, who was caring for the child after her parents died of AIDS.

Nyara was wan and sickly and seemed scared of Stefan and me. The home health worker asked her grandmother, "Is Nyara taking her medicine (ARVs) regularly?" The grandmother nodded, and the staffer asked, "Does she get enough food each day?" The grandmother nodded again and glanced at Nyara as if assessing her weight. "Is there anything we can do to help her?" the staffer asked the older woman— who may have been my age but looked decades older.

The grandmother mumbled something in a language I didn't recognize, and the staffer nodded before replying. "I will ask someone at an organization called CARE to help you find a school for Nyara." The grandmother dipped her head in thanks and stood up to shake our hands.

The second site was a slightly larger shack. It, too, had cardboard boxes lining the inside walls and a broken mirror tacked to one of them. The client, a thirty-five-year-old woman with AIDS, could barely lift her head from her shabby mattress. The woman's Kaposi's sarcoma was so bad that her legs were swollen to twice the normal size and her skin was brittle and scaley. The staffer had informed me before our visit that the woman's husband had recently died of AIDS, and she was only alive thanks to ARVs.

Her daughter stood nearby, and I turned to her and smiled. "How old are you?" I asked.

"Fourteen," she answered in English with a shy smile.

"Are you still in school?"

She shook her head. "I had to drop out to take care of my mother."

When the Pathfinder worker finished talking to her patient, she stood up to leave, and I took the girl's hand. "Thank you for taking care of your mother. I hope she will get better."

As we left the modest dwelling, it pained me to think about the girl's future without an education: selling fruit by the roadside or doing sex work? I asked the staffer if someone from CARE could help the girl return to school, and she shook her head. "She cannot leave her mother now, and with so many children out of school, CARE must focus on the younger ones."

The third place we visited was an actual house made of cinder blocks. With seven rooms, the owner was able to rent three of them to lodgers and earn a small income. She, too, was HIV positive and in her thirties, yet she looked quite healthy. The home health worker told me that this client had been taking ARVs for six months, and she was stout and fit enough to take care of her house and her children. One of them—a girl who was HIV positive—looked well since she was also taking ARVs. The woman's husband had died of AIDS one year before, yet she had been left with enough resources to maintain the home and feed her family.

These meetings with HIV-positive women and their daughters were wrenching. Yet I could see a silver lining to their situations because of the dramatic difference ARVs were making in people's lives. If only the medications had been available ten years earlier when we were living in Abidjan, we might not have lost our guard Adama and our cook Gouba.

In Ivory Coast, Stefan's work had mostly been focused on research and surveillance. Ten years later in Tanzania, the emphasis was on saving lives by getting as many infected people as possible on medi-cation.[19] By 2005, huge amounts of money were pouring into African countries thanks to the US Government's President's Emergency Preparedness Fund for AIDS Relief or PEPFAR. When Stefan stepped into the job as CDC director in Tanzania, he hired more staff to work with doctors from Tanzania's Health Ministry as well as counterparts in partner NGOs. By that point, two main government agencies were managing and distributing PEPFAR funds to implementing partners like Pathfinder.

Stefan's job in Tanzania was more stressful than it had been in Ivory Coast due to fierce competition between USAID staff and CDC for a bigger share of funds and high visibility. Some days he'd come home from work strung out after rancorous meetings between his staff and the team at USAID, and he was often forced to mediate since bitter infighting threatened to drive away his new employees. He found it easier and more gratifying to work with Tanzanian doctors in the Health Ministry and to travel around the country visiting labs and treatment centers.

While Stefan was spending long days at the office or traveling upcoun-try, I was undertaking new ventures myself. Several Corona mem-bers—Bodil included—asked me to teach a writing workshop, and I had convened the first class two weeks after the trip to Madagascar. An eclectic group of six women—all of them over forty—met in my house on Wednesdays with notebooks and pens in hand. I did little lecturing other than telling them what the writing process was like for me and dispensing bits of wisdom from my favorite writing guides at the time: Annie Lamott's *Bird by Bird* and Natalie Goldberg's *Writing Down the Bones*. I'd give prompts and timed writing exercises before asking each participant to read aloud when they finished.

In the writing workshop, I bonded with a handful of women—most of them Corona members—who were interested in writing and didn't mind sharing details about their inner lives. Forming such connections gave me the confidence to step into the role of Corona chair a few months later when Candy and Bodil asked me to take it on. Bodil and I had started walking together several times a week, and I treasured our growing friendship.

I had a lot to be grateful for after only six months in Tanzania. The amount of travel we'd done in that short span of time—and to some of the most idyllic settings in Africa—was mind-boggling. What meant even more were the relationships I was forming, not just with other expats but with Wilfred and Lucy and an artist I'd recently met named Salum Kambi. Just as in Abidjan, I valued the opportunity to interact with people who were unlike me and came from very different walks of life. It satisfied a deep need to step out of myself and connect when I could converse with the guards at our gate, artists, and venders at the local market; enlivening encounters that left me little time for brooding or worry.

One day when I returned from an errand and was waiting for Wilfred to open our gate, I happened to glance up the street and see a tall blond boy walking our dog, Bella. Next to him, I spotted Elena. Later, when I asked her about the boy, she told me that he was an IST student who lived in the neighborhood, and she'd happened to bump into him.

A week after that, a woman came up to me at a PTA meeting and said she knew the family of my daughter's boyfriend. She proceeded to tell me that the boy was a senior at IST and four years older than Elena. That evening, when I asked Elena about the boy again, she clipped, "He's just a friend from school."

"Is that why you're so willing to walk the dog in the evenings all of a sudden?" I grinned. "To meet up with your 'friend'?"

A tiny smile escaped before she clamped her jaws shut and scowled at me. "No!"

A month later Elena signed up for a school trip to Zanzibar to get her dive certification over spring break while Aaron was climbing Kilimanjaro with classmates. When she returned from Zanzibar, I asked her if she passed the test and got her certification.

"Yes, but I never want to go diving again. I don't like deep water. It's creepy and scary."

"I know what you mean," I said, trying to spark conversation. "That's why I prefer snorkeling. How many of your friends were there?"

"Just Melanie," she shrugged before leaving the room.

Stefan and I knew that the real draw of the diving course had been her friends. What we hadn't known in advance was that the boy she liked had also gone on the trip. It was one of our biggest issues with her—that she was secretive and didn't always tell us the truth about her doings. We constantly had to second guess and read between the lines to know where she was going and with whom. While I was glad to know she had friends and an active social life at her new school, it wasn't easy haggling with her over curfews and homework, which she hated doing. Academics didn't interest her as much as sports, particularly basketball and tennis.

Surprisingly, Elena didn't complain about doing community service, which was a requirement for all junior high and high school students. She came home in tears the first day she volunteered at a hospital for cancer patients after reading books to the children and drawing pictures with them. "You wouldn't believe how many kids had no hair," she told us that evening. "Some of them had bloody bandages on their heads, and their beds were all lined up in a crowded ward. I'm going to write to Vicki and tell her all about the hospital." (Vicki was a neighbor in Atlanta whose daughter was a cancer survivor.)

Aaron didn't mind doing community service after he got permission to tutor Tanzanian school kids with me. Bodil's son joined us too, which made it more fun for Aaron and a cultural immersion for all of us. The local primary school classroom where we tutored was crammed with dozens of wood desks and bare walls with only a blackboard at the front; a far cry from the big, airy classrooms at the international school that the boys were used to.

Toward the end of Aaron's and Elena's first academic year in Tanzania, the school board solicited parent volunteers to replace board members who were stepping down. I threw my name into the hat when board elections took place in May since it seemed a good way to contribute to the school and meet other parents. I was elected to the board at the end of the month and volunteered to take on the role of secretary. With the added tasks of chairing the Corona Women's meetings and writing a monthly column, I looked forward to a busy second year after we returned from summer vacation in the US. It felt good to be connected in so many ways and to have friends I looked forward to seeing in Dar.

Writing the monthly column got me out and about town and provided glimpses into Tanzanian life that I wouldn't have had otherwise. Several months after the home health visits with Stefan, I wrote two magazine columns about the AIDS scene in Tanzania. One article focused on women with HIV who became community volunteers in order to teach other women how to avoid getting the disease. The stigma against people with HIV/AIDS was so strong that it took a great deal of courage for these volunteers to reveal their status and speak out about the disease. I considered them to be unsung heroes in the struggle against AIDS and wanted to shed light on their efforts by profiling them.[20]

In another column that hit close to home, I profiled an American lawyer who ran her own adoption agency. Brooke knew the country's legal system well after working in Dar for a dozen years. She and her husband had adopted five Tanzanian children, and she facilitated twenty-plus adoptions by foreign parents annually.

"Adoption is not very accepted in Tanzania because breaking family ties and giving up the family name is frowned upon," Brooke told me. "Foster care is more acceptable, and it's widely practiced. But if a child has no living relatives or if the relatives can't take care of him or her, it's better for the child to be placed in a loving, permanent home than in an institution." Brooke and her husband had opened a children's home next to their own that housed thirteen orphans. In effect, they were raising eighteen children who considered them parents.

The visit with Brooke was uplifting and inspiring, but when I visited an orphanage as part of my research for another story, I had the opposite experience. Seeing dozens of children as young as two living in crowded dormitories was distressing. As an adoptive parent myself, I was acutely aware of two teenage girls about Elena's age who followed me around the entire time, hungry for attention. One girl named Rose told me that she'd been living there for five years after her parents died of AIDS. Her sweet voice and face would haunt me for weeks.

I went home that day with a heavy heart and asked Stefan, "Would you consider adopting another child?"

He shook his head slowly. "We already have enough on our plates."

Though I didn't want to admit it, I knew he was right.

That summer, we returned to the US to visit our families for a month. My father was in good spirits and walked the dog with me in the evenings. But he'd had another TIA while we were in Tanzania, and it was upsetting to watch his hands tremble when he reached for things. His drooping eyelids half obscured his Husky-blue eyes, and his fingers were unable to grasp the handle of a coffee mug since the last three fingers of each hand were stuck together due to nerve damage. His unhinged lower lip hung down and his tongue stuck out between his lips, allowing drool to escape. Old age sat heavily on him at eighty, and the changes in him after a year away were startling.

He told me one day about a dream he had about leaving my mother and finding himself alone in a strange place. I could tell he was afraid of dying and of the prospect of leaving my mother and all of us behind; of missing the things in this world that he held dear. He still had a twinkle in his eye whenever he was around Elena, the two of them fond of teasing each other.

I hated to say goodbye to him at the end of our stay, not knowing how I'd find him after another year abroad. I resolved to return at Christmas and not let so much time pass between our visits.

When we moved to Tanzania, we hadn't anticipated how early and easily our teenagers would be able to get alcohol and other substances. The drinking age was nominally eighteen (as in most European countries) although we knew that few establishments in Dar checked IDs. We also knew that Aaron and Elena would drink with friends at parties, and we let them have beer and wine at home on occasion to demystify alcohol.

When the new academic year started, school board members learned that kids as young as twelve and thirteen were getting mixed drinks at places they frequented. With just two small shopping centers on the peninsula, most kids met their friends at the bowling alley or in a burger joint and a café. We knew the burger joint was strict about carding people since it was part of a big chain.

Cathy, the board chair, and I decided to visit the other spots and speak with managers about underage kids getting alcohol. At the bowling alley, the manager told us, "Our waiters can't tell the ages of kids who come in. It's dark and crowded at night and hard for them to see. And local employees aren't comfortable asking white kids their ages."

"It's mainly the young kids we're concerned about," Cathy insisted. "Surely they can tell when kids are twelve and thirteen?"

The manager nodded. "I will instruct the waiters to look more closely and refuse to serve alcohol to younger kids."

We got a very different reception at the Java Lounge, where we talked to the manager who was sitting at the cashier's desk in a skimpy T-shirt and jeans. When we complained that underage kids were getting alcohol at her café, she snapped, "You parents give your kids too much money. You let them come out in public wearing revealing clothing, and you expect me to police them? If they say they're eighteen, what are my waiters supposed to do? Refuse to serve them?"

"Well, yes," I said sheepishly, stunned by her response.

It was odd to be confronted by a young woman who was herself dressed in revealing clothing and clearly from a privileged family. Yet there was no point in discussing it with her, as we suspected she was a relative of the owner.

Later that week, Aaron joined Stefan and me at the Yacht Club beach. He'd just left the Garden Bistro, where he sometimes met up with friends on weekends. He told us that he and a friend had seen two policemen interrogating a couple of IST students as they were leaving the bistro. The police didn't speak much English, and the boys didn't know Swahili, so Aaron's friend offered to translate for them. The policemen demanded a "fee" to let the boys go instead of arresting one of them for possession of marijuana. When the boy said he only had fifty dollars on him, the policemen offered to follow him home to get more money. After bargaining, the police settled on a sum of $200, which was what the boy said he could get at home. Aaron and his friend left them as the police followed the boy to his house to collect the money.

"You know marijuana is illegal in Tanzania," Stefan reminded Aaron. "And you need to be extra careful when you're dealing with police in foreign countries. We don't have diplomatic immunity, and you don't know enough Swahili to talk your way out of a situation like that."

"I know." Aaron nodded, visibly shaken. "I'd hate for that to happen to me."

As the three of us walked home from the Yacht Club together, we passed a tent that some Tanzanian men had erected out of plastic tarps. They'd set up shop at the end of our street a few weeks earlier, and every day they sat outside smoking joints and playing Reggae music while knitting hats that they hung on trees to sell. They were obviously selling more than hats, judging by the number of youths who stopped by the tent. As we passed them that evening, Aaron half-smiled when one of the men nodded at him. They'd obviously had some interactions, and it was clear that Elena wasn't our only offspring who was harboring secrets.

Aaron was a junior in high school at the time of the encounter with the police. He and Elena often met their friends at the Yacht Club, where bartenders were strict about carding teenagers. Only later did we learn that underage kids could easily get alcohol there by asking older schoolmates to buy drinks for them.

I'd been naïve to think that my kids wouldn't indulge in such things in a "provincial" place like Dar. All we could do was trust that our kids knew their limits and would respect our ground rules. We asked that they only go to parties and cafés on the Peninsula, and that they wouldn't drive with friends who'd been drinking. (Luckily, most IST students didn't drive since the legal age for a license in Tanzania was eighteen.)

Most weekends, Stefan was the one who waited up for our kids to come home since he was more of a night owl, whereas I kept my ear to the ground and networked with other parents at the school. Serving on the board gave me access to all kinds of info, especially after Cathy, the board chair, became a close friend. She had a daughter in Aaron's class and a son in Elena's.

I knew what it was like to test limits since I had done it in my teens. I'd gone to parties and started drinking in ninth grade, and I'd hosted parties at our house when my parents were away. I even snuck out at night to meet friends, and we'd play pranks on other kids. Some of my friends had experimented with marijuana, LSD, and quaaludes, but I only drank and in small quantities—partly because I had low tolerance for alcohol and would fall asleep after two drinks.

Knowing that I'd done some of the same things they were doing didn't make things easier. I was a worrier with a big imagination about the kinds of trouble our kids could encounter in a foreign country. Traffic accidents were my biggest nightmare since hospitals in Dar weren't as well-equipped to handle emergencies, and you didn't want to have a blood transfusion in an African country back then.

I couldn't help thinking of my parents at such times. They had raised seven children in the 1960s and '70s, and all of us had rebelled in various ways. They'd survived seven teenagers through faith and prayer. My mother worried less than I did because she believed we were in God's hands, and his were a lot bigger than hers. If only I could have believed that too, my mind would have been a lot freer.

During a weeklong vacation from school that fall, we convinced Aaron and Elena to join us on a trek up Mount Meru—the second highest mountain in Tanzania at fifteen thousand feet—with Loren and Jeff's family. Their daughter was in Aaron's class, and they had a son Elena's age who was in a rock band. The kids would bunk in a cabin together on the four-day trek and join us for dinners in a mess tent. It would be easier to deal with Elena with others around to act as buffers.

Elena grudgingly agreed to wear my old leather boots, which I'd bought twenty-some years earlier. After investing in lighter-weight boots, I gave my old ones to Elena since she wasn't a hiker and didn't care about getting new ones. Midway through our first day on Meru, the soles of both boots came unglued and flapped like camel's tongues every time Elena took a step. Those boots weren't going to get her up that mountain, and I was clearly the one to blame. Fortunately, one of the guides had brought along a second pair of athletic shoes that he offered to Elena. They were too big for her, but she soon got used to them. We ended up gaining three thousand feet in elevation that day, which was no small feat for any of us, especially Elena.

On the second day of the trek, the slope was super steep, and we had to climb two thousand steps that were built into the path. In a moment of inattention, I tripped, and my left hand came down hard on a patch of nettles. Within minutes, my fingers swelled and the burning sensation became unbearable. The wedding ring on my finger looked like it might burst with the pressure building up around it. I took Benadryl and put Vaseline around the ring to ease it from my finger. I got it off, but the burning sensation didn't stop. That night I hardly slept due to the pain in my swollen fingers.

I was giddy with relief when we reached base camp near the summit the following day. Despite my swollen hand and hip bursitis that had hobbled me six years earlier, I'd managed to climb another three thousand feet with the others. When the guides informed us that the approach to the summit would involve walking along a knife-edge ridge in the dark, and that they'd have to wake us up at 3 a.m. to reach it in time to see the sun rise over Kilimanjaro, I opted to sleep in and hike Little Meru instead. It was a lower peak with a gentler climb, and it too had stellar views.

Elena was full of bravado as she set off at 3 a.m. with the others. She returned several hours later with one of the guides just as I was waking up, her eyes wide as DVDs. She trembled when she told me, "It was so scary I thought I was going to die up there, and I had to turn around."

I wanted to put my arms around her and tell her how proud I was that she'd made it this far, but I didn't dare. We were a volatile pair in those days, her body flush with teenage hormones while mine were waning as I was going through menopause. If one of us got triggered, the other had to keep her head down.

"I know it must have been scary," I said quietly. "I hate narrow ridges where the path drops away on both sides. That's why I didn't even try it. But you're okay now. Maybe you could sleep for a while?"

She nodded dully as she headed for her cabin.

It was comforting to share these rare moments with her, and I felt a flood of warmth for her just as I had when we'd talked after a minor squabble a few days before. She'd told me in a moment of candor, "I'm going through a hard time and sorting out my feelings about being adopted. I feel really different from the rest of you, and I know I'll never have the kind of bond that you and Dad have with Aaron. I just want you guys to leave me alone and let me explore my own identity."

I had listened to her with a heavy heart, impressed by her maturity and insight. "We're happy to give you more space as you explore your identity," I had responded. "But it would be a lot easier if our communication was more open and you told us the truth about where you were going and with whom." She hadn't argued with me then. And now I knew it was time to leave her alone and let her make peace with her tired self.

It was clear and cold when I set off with a guide that morning, my hand no longer throbbing and no complaint of hip bursitis. I enjoyed the quiet hike and saw enough from the top of Little Meru to thrill me: the long narrow path to the summit stretching to the south and the distinctive shape of Kilimanjaro in the east rising above the Arusha plain.

As soon as the group returned, we packed up and headed down the trail toward the cabins where we'd stayed on our way up. All that day it felt like we were walking in paradise, the bald peak of Mount Meru behind us and the tantalizing outline of Kilimanjaro looming on the horizon. I could have hiked to the moon while feasting my eyes on that shimmering specter. I must have mentioned it to Loren—that it would be a dream to climb Kili as our kids had done—though I never expected her to take me seriously.

The Meru trek would cement our friendships with Loren and Jeff and give us allies in our effort to understand our teenagers. It helped to share our concerns with other parents and hear what was going on in our children's peer groups. It was equally reassuring to know that other adults were watching out for our kids.

We enjoyed listening to their stories and laughing together while playing cards in the evening, and I was glad that our kids enjoyed interacting with them too. One of the highlights of living overseas was that parents and children mingled more at cross-generational gatherings.

When I was growing up, we never went on vacation with other families. It was enough of a stretch for my father to take a week off each summer and do the three-hour drive to Rehoboth Beach, Delaware, with seven kids packed into his station wagon. My parents didn't entertain much either, especially after my mother started working full-time and my father was trying to hold down two and three jobs. They simply didn't have the time or resources to take us on trips; which was probably why, once I started traveling, I didn't want to stop.

Chapter 14

The Lure of Kilimanjaro

I was bitten by the Kili bug soon after we arrived in Tanzania. The infatuation deepened as I hiked down Mount Meru with Loren's family, my eyes riveted to the haunting massif as it hovered on the horizon. It felt like Kilimanjaro was drawing me inexorably towards it.

One year after that trip, Loren and I were preparing to climb Kili with a handful of women friends who'd signed up to go with us. Aaron had raved about his climb six months earlier, and he was coaching me on which exercise machines to use at the Embassy gym. I was also walking three to five miles a day—often with Loren—and swimming regularly.

All that physical activity came to a screeching halt when I picked up a heavy beach chair and wrenched a muscle in my lower back. For two days the pain was so intense I couldn't move. Lying on an air mat in our living room, I downed double doses of ibuprofen and wondered how to tell Loren that I might not be able to climb Kili with her—until someone gave me the name of a physical therapist who got me back on my feet in a couple of weeks.

I didn't give much thought to any dangers associated with the climb. Nor did I pay attention to the statistics I read—that over half of all climbers on Kili suffer from some form of Acute Mountain Sickness (AMS), and only 40 percent of those who attempt it reach the summit. I wasn't doing it for bragging rights even though it's considered the highest free-standing mountain in the world. I simply wanted to hike up Kilimanjaro as my son had done, and it was a trek that didn't require technical skills.

The daughter of a naval officer, Loren was more dedicated than I when it came to endurance training. She ran or walked every day and played tennis after putting in an eight-hour workday, and she carried weights when she sprinted several times a week to increase her lung capacity. She was a classic type A personality with a big heart who welcomed Peace Corps volunteers into her home when they needed help or support. She was also super-organized and took on the arrangements for our trip. If anyone could get me up the mountain, it was Loren.

We'd polled our women friends to see who might want to join us, and two of my Atlanta friends had signed on along with two of Loren's friends from Washington, DC. An Irish friend who lived in Dar, Irene, became the seventh member of our group. Loren collected money from each of us and paid the deposit two months before the trek.

One month later, Irene told us about a Finnish woman who wished to join us. Kaija told us she was ready to pay her deposit, but a week later she said she'd have to back out because her husband had to travel for his job, and she needed to stay home with their children. Then, two weeks before the start of our trek, Kaija said she was ready to commit again. Loren and I had reservations about letting her sign on so late, but we agreed to include her.

The two of us met Kaija at a coffee shop to discuss plans for the trip and get her deposit. As soon as we sat down, Kaija pushed an envelope with her money across the table to us and sat bolt upright as if she were interviewing for a job. Listening attentively as we described the gear and supplies we planned to take, she admitted that she had no hiking poles or gaiters and that she'd bought a pair of secondhand boots at a local market in Dar the week before. When we asked how much training she'd been doing, she said she'd done a few long walks in recent weeks. The rest of us had been walking for hours each day and working out in gyms for months.

"Hiking boots from Kariakoo Market and a few neighborhood walks?" Loren said after we left the café. "She thinks that's going to get her to the top?"

"She's fifteen years younger than we are." I shrugged. "That ought to give her a big advantage."

I was hardly one to judge another woman's ability to climb Kilimanjaro since I had nagging doubts about my own chances of making it to the top. Still nursing a sore back, I kept my hip bursitis in check by doing daily stretches; but the stress of hiking up steep slopes every day could cause a flare-up. Yet endurance on long hikes hadn't been a problem when we hiked up Mount Meru, nor had it been an issue on a recent four-day trek in the Ngorongoro Crater Highlands with my family. My personal goal was just to see how far I could get without focusing on summiting.

Three days before the start of the trip, I said goodbye to the kids before my flight to Arusha. Elena was unusually cheerful and even allowed me to kiss her cheek. She was clearly looking forward to a week without Mom.

In recent months, both kids had become more secretive about their social lives. Whenever I asked Aaron about his girlfriend, he'd assume a blank expression and shrug. Elena didn't even want us to know who her current boyfriend was. I tried to be philosophical about it by reminding myself of a Thomas Berry quote: "Humans have to move from being an intrusive to a benign presence in the world." I guessed it was time to assume that role in my children's lives.

After the short flight, I met the plane of my friends Patty and Jane from our old neighborhood in Atlanta. The three of us hopped in a taxi and drove to a mountain lodge where we would spend three days doing conditioning hikes at high altitude.

Overlooking the Ngorongoro Highlands, Gibbs Farm provided a total immersion for the senses. Stella and canna lilies, geraniums, and salvia grew waist-high in rich volcanic soil while fragrant fruit trees and Arabica coffee thrived on its slopes. Coffee beans were roasted on site, and organic vegetables from the garden were served at mealtimes.

At night we slept in the most luxurious suites I'd seen in Tanzania, and by day we hiked through the surrounding forest and up ridge trails. The effort it took to breathe while hiking at six thousand feet was alarming, given that all of us had been training for months. It meant that we'd have to work extra hard to get our middle-aged bodies up a mountain that rose over nineteen thousand feet.

The night before we were to start the climb, we met the rest of the group at a small hotel outside the gates of Kilimanjaro National Park. The dorm-style rooms at the Capricorn Hotel were like nun's chambers compared to the suites at Gibb's Farm, with a table and single bed in each room and bare walls speckled with squashed mosquitos. Yet the setting more than made up for it. In the late afternoon, all eight of us hiked to the park gate for a glimpse of Kilimanjaro in all its glory. We could make out the jagged spires of Mawenzi Peak to the east and the long sleek saddle connecting it to Kibo Dome, the highest and most prominent of Kili's three cones. It was utterly mesmerizing in the tangerine twilight.[21]

That night in the hotel restaurant, some of us voiced concerns about the challenges we might face in the coming days. Irene, who happened to be a nurse, admitted that she'd caught a cold and was taking antibiotics to ward off bronchitis and strep. Sally, Loren's friend from DC, worried that her cranky knees might prevent her from getting to the top. Her friend Cecille promised to stay by her side the entire time and help her up the mountain. Without mentioning the pulled muscle in my lower back, I told the group about grappling with hip bursitis in the past.

"What a crew," Loren sighed, listening to us vent.

Kaija seemed surprised by the amount of training the rest of us had done, and she looked puzzled when we aired our concerns—as if it hadn't crossed her mind that there were any dangers associated with the climb or that she might not make it to the summit. She had three young children at home while most of us had teenagers who were only too happy to be rid of us.

What struck me that evening was the disparity in our ages, physical condition, and motivations. Kaija and Cecille were in their late thirties while the rest of us were in our fifties. Sally admitted that she hadn't worked out as much as she'd intended, while Jane said she'd been training for months just as she did before she ran marathons. Patty was an exercise addict who excelled at weightlifting and spinning. Like Loren, both women were high achievers in their professions and left me with no doubt about their ability to make it to the top. Yet how much impact drive and focus would have on getting us to the summit was a big unknown.

For my part, keeping my expectations in check was a way of letting myself off the hook and steeling myself against disappointment if I didn't make it.

A fleet of porters shook hands with us before loading our gear on their heads and backs and sprinting off ahead of us. Thirty-five men attending eight women seemed like overkill to me, but there were strict limits on the weight (forty pounds) that each porter could take. We only had to carry small backpacks with our cameras and a day's worth of water and snacks.[22]

We set off in high spirits on a bright November afternoon. Walking at a leisurely pace, I hardly noticed the steady upward climb as we passed through farmland and pine groves. Juniper and scrub bushes obstructed the views early on, until the vegetation changed to rolling hills with less-dense foliage. Sweeping views of the surrounding countryside were so captivating that I was surprised when we reached the first campground after three hours of hiking.

The porters already had our tents up and the cook was preparing a hot chicken dinner as we shrugged off our daypacks and sat at a picnic table set with popcorn and lemonade. Everyone seemed to be in good moods with no complaints about aching muscles or joints. The setting contributed to the upbeat atmosphere as we gazed down on Kenya's Rift Valley with its dappled green-and-beige fields rimmed by mountains on the horizon.

At dinner that night, I talked about the Ngorongoro Highlands trek my family had done while Loren entertained everyone with stories of our Meru climb. She was the life of any party and knew how to spin a story even without the aid of alcohol. None of us were drinking since we'd started taking Diamox as most climbers do. (The drug tricks the brain into helping the body adjust to higher altitudes, but it also makes beer smell and taste like cat pee.)

After dinner was over and dishes were cleared away, someone suggested we play cards since it was still early. But when I glanced at Irene, who was sniffling and blowing her nose, I shook my head and said tentatively, "I hate to be a spoilsport, but playing cards is an efficient way to share viruses, and none of us want to catch the cold."

Patty, a public health doctor who worked for the CDC, agreed.

"Sorry, Irene," I apologized, not wanting her to feel singled out.

Equally leery of catching the cold, everyone else said goodnight and drifted off to read in their tents. It was reassuring to be among friends who knew that my motives were well intentioned. Super sensitive to group dynamics, I wanted everyone to get along and have a good experience on Kilimanjaro. If that happened, I would consider the trip a success whether all of us summitted or not.

We settled into our natural rhythms and paces on the second day. Irene was far from her usual lively self, as if it was taking all her strength to hike with a stuffy head at nine thousand feet. She and I were quiet hikers and walked solo at times, while Patty and Jane and Loren's DC friends never seemed to run out of things to say. Loren walked beside her friends or strode ahead, using the early hikes to prepare for her final push to the summit.

Kaija walked with her camera in hand instead of hiking poles, taking photos nonstop and chatting with two English-speaking guides. With white-blond hair and eyes the color of tanzanite, she was the standout and more of a blithe spirit in comparison with the rest of us. She had a lilting voice with a proper British accent even though she was from Finland. Her girlish mannerisms—she was constantly tossing her head to bob her wispy bangs out of her eyes—were a curious contrast to her sturdy trunk and legs. The guides vied to walk and talk with her while porters with heavy loads on their heads would turn and ogle her as they passed us.

The rest of us chatted with the guides too, although Brian—technically the trip leader—was mostly quiet due to his limited English. He'd nod when one of us said something to indicate he understood, only to ask a question later that showed he didn't get it.

Juniper and scrubby bushes had obstructed the views when we started out that morning, but after crossing hills that were studded with boulders, we could see all the way down to the Kenyan plains again. I found the rolling moors enchanting, filled as they were with heather and flora I hadn't seen before—like everlasting flowers and giant lobelia.

To my mind they resembled armless Saguaro cacti, whereas Kaija said they looked like big green phalluses to her.

The verdant moors eventually gave way to hillsides that were charred as far as the eye could see, and an acrid smell of smoke hung in the air. One of the guides told us that villagers sometimes set fires to smoke out bees and gather honey, and that a recent wildfire had raged out of control and forced rangers to close the Rongai Route for weeks.

It was a relief when we reached our second camp after hiking eight miles and gaining three thousand feet. Kikelewa campground was set in a broad open space that overlooked the distant valley where we'd started the trek two days earlier. Everyone's muscles and joints ached, although they were mostly minor complaints: sore hips and knees, stiff shoulders and calves. Thankfully, my hip bursitis hadn't posed a problem yet.

By the end of the second day, Kaija had developed hot spots on her feet and asked to borrow my medical tape to keep them from turning into blisters. She still bounded around with a buoyancy that amazed me as the rest of us collapsed in our tents. She was forever taking pictures of inanimate objects and searching for cell phone signals to check in with her family. I couldn't help envying her, having energy to spare and young kids at home who still wanted to hear from their mother.

Loren wasn't as taken with her as I was. She said to me privately, "That woman has no shame" after Kaija washed her panties and bras and hung them outside on her tent flaps to dry. And we all knew whom to blame when the bucket in our toilet tent overflowed by morning since Kaija insisted on carrying three liters of water in her day pack instead of one like the rest of us. Yet we were mostly a congenial group, lingering in the meal tent long after dinner, telling stories and laughing.

It was crisp and clear that night at zero degrees centigrade with a billion stars speckling the sky. On a last visit to the toilet tent, the enormity of the night sky made me realize what tiny figures we were, tiptoeing across the highest mountain on the continent in the inky dark. It was already enough to experience such moments even if I never reached the summit.

At dawn on our third day, the sun's rays bathed Kibo Dome and Mawenzi Peak in burnt amber tones. The outlines of both peaks were so stark that they appeared to be a short walk from the campsite. But such was not the case, as we would soon find out.

We started hiking in brilliant sunshine over rough and rocky terrain. The steady climb was tedious and exhausting as I tried to keep up with Loren, who set a brisk pace. Bothered by her knees, Sally lagged behind the rest of us with Cecille at her side, urging her on. Kaija took endless pictures of wildflowers and weeds, porters and guides. At times Patty broke into song and the rest of us tried to join in although it was hard to sing at high altitude while walking. Despite the hard work, everyone remained in good spirits, and we encouraged each other to maintain the pace if someone's energy flagged.

The trek that morning intensified as we approached the base of Mawenzi Peak, gaining two thousand feet in three hours. Upon reaching the campsite by lunch time, we were giddy with relief when Brian announced that we'd have the afternoon off to rest and acclimate to the higher altitude. We were lucky to have arrived early enough for the porters to pitch our tents on the upper side of a brackish pond known as Mawenzi Tarn. Hikers who arrived later and camped on the lower side of the tarn complained that scores of mice invaded their campsite.

We barely had time to eat lunch before a hailstorm forced us to retreat to our tents. Loren and I were tentmates, and we dove into our sleeping bags to stay warm as ice balls pelted the tent flaps. Resting with my eyes closed, it struck me as a bit bizarre that I was the one huddling in a tent at thirteen thousand feet instead of Stefan, who was the more serious mountaineer. But he got headaches at high altitudes and had no interest in climbing Kili.

Because the trek was more of a lark for me than it was for Loren, I wondered if my mindset made it less likely that I'd reach the top. Patty and Jane seemed likely to summit since they were more goal-oriented like Loren. But what about Kaija, who hadn't seemed as focused or prepared as the rest of us? I pondered these questions out of curiosity more than anything else, still hopeful that all of us would succeed. As absurd as it might seem, huddling at the base of Mawenzi Peak with hailstones pelting our tent made me feel more alive than ever. It was a thrill to be resting on the torso of that magnificent mountain and feeling like an integral part of it.

The stark beauty of that place would be emblazoned in my mind for years to come: the dense array of stars in the night sky, and the magenta clouds that flitted around Mawenzi's spires at sunrise. Though the temperature fell below freezing in the night, the sun lured us out early in the morning after a camp attendant delivered hot tea to our tents.

Kibo Dome loomed before us like a forbidding hulk that day as we crossed the Saddle, a narrow plain between Mawenzi Peak and Kibo Dome that resembled a moonscape. The wind gusted at times and whipped dust in our faces, yet a gentle sun and temperatures in the sixties made it pleasant hiking. In that alpine desert, with the earth bared to its essence, it felt like I was walking on air as we traversed the eight miles to Kibo basecamp. With the smell and taste of the wind filling my senses, I was high as a kite, knowing that I'd reached such heights on my own.

We walked into basecamp with plenty of time to rest before dinner, all of us relieved to have arrived without debilitating pain. My hip bursitis hadn't been a problem, and Sally's knees weren't bothering her too badly. Kaija had full-blown blisters that she had to keep taping, and Irene appeared to be having trouble breathing with her cold—but then all of us were panting at sixteen thousand feet.

Nobody had an appetite when we were presented with instant soup and pasta for the third night in a row, yet we had to force ourselves to down enough carbs to have strength for the hard work ahead of us. It was harder to force ourselves to sleep when Brian suggested we go to bed at 8 p.m. since we'd have only three hours to rest before the final ascent.

Sleep evaded me as rapture from the day's hike morphed into dread. My mind swirled with worries about the arduous trek ahead, knowing that we'd have to climb three thousand five hundred feet in four miles starting at midnight.

It was a nightmarish scene when Brian roused us: crawling out of sleeping bags without having slept and forcing ourselves to eat biscuits and tea even though we weren't hungry; pulling on thermal underwear before outer clothing and inserting warmers in boots and mittens.

It was cold but not bitter at basecamp, and the path was clear of snow. Despite a sense of foreboding, I was exhilarated as we started walking under a sliver of moon that provided little light. In the distance I could see dozens of tiny headlamps dotting a trail that snaked upwards, marking the trajectory of climbers who'd left before us.

Like a mirage, the dome we were attempting to scale never seemed to get any closer as we walked single file around endless switchbacks and up sets of steps. The thin air was so hard to breathe that I had to stop every few minutes to let my heart rate normalize.

An hour or two into the climb, Loren and Cecille said they wanted to press ahead without taking so many breaks since they were having less trouble breathing than the rest of us. Brian decided to lead them while an English-speaking guide named Clements would accompany Jane and me as we stopped at every switchback to rest. Irene struggled to keep up with us while Patty and Sally fell farther behind, plodding up the mountain at a snail's pace with other guides.

Faced with a choice between walking with me and Jane or forging ahead with Cecille and Loren, Kaija opted to go with the faster group. Though she said she felt okay, she might not have been thinking clearly on account of the altitude.

It was the steepest and hardest climb I'd ever attempted at an altitude I never expected to reach. By the time our trio got to the halfway point at Hans Meyer Cave, I was already exhausted and desperately short of breath. With the cold air bothering her sinuses, Irene could no longer keep up with us and one of the other guides said he'd accompany her at a slower pace.

Jane and I plodded on, struggling for breath but not stopping for long in the bitter cold. The hand and foot warmers in our gloves and boots kept the extremities warm, though my heart pounded furiously while my eyes were glued to the narrow path as we snaked up and around endless switchbacks. The thought of taking a wrong step on that sheer slope terrified me since I imagined tumbling all the way down the slippery scree to basecamp. I coaxed myself to keep going by saying "one foot in front of the other," and "ten more steps and you can take a break."

After four hours of grueling effort—concentrating on my breath and taking ten steps before pausing to rest—I started to think about turning around and going back down. When I discovered that the water in my bottle had frozen, it discouraged me even more. Yet fear of descending the hairpin switchbacks in the dark on that slippery slope was reason enough not to give up and head back down, not to mention the difficulty of getting around other hikers who were on their way up behind us.

Shifting my focus, I tried to imagine light and energy entering my body from some inner source and quietly chanted, "You have every-thing inside that you need to do this." Meanwhile Jane kept muttering behind me, "This is ten times harder than any marathon I've run." With aching muscles and shortness of breath, I promised myself that if we made it to Gillman's Point, I wouldn't force myself to push on to the ultimate summit at Uhuru.

The most uplifting sight I saw that night was a red rim of light on the horizon as dawn approached. At 5 a.m., the earth began to take shape around us, and the path ahead was clearly visible. With the jagged silhouette of Mawenzi Peak standing like a beacon in the distance, it came as a surprise when Clements announced, "Look, you are only ten minutes from the top."

We struggled up a series of steep rocky steps and scrambled over some boulders to reach Gillman's Point in time to see the sun rise behind Mawenzi. It was bitter cold at 18,600 feet as Jane and I hugged each other and took photos. Clements poured tea from a thermos and handed each of us a cup. When he held out a bar of chocolate, Jane accepted a piece, but I refused on account of my queasy stomach.

"What do you think," Jane asked as we sipped the hot drink. "Should we go on?"

I looked at her dubiously. "Uhuru is another mile and seven hundred feet higher. I don't know if I can push myself that far."

Jane turned to Clements and asked, "How long would it take us to get to Uhuru?"

"Two or three hours out and back," he responded, "and another three hours to get down to basecamp. Then you must walk ten miles to the next camp where you will spend the night."

The thought of another long hike that day was daunting, as was the sight of the snowy path to Uhuru that snaked along a precipitous ridge above a caldera. Tallying the five hours we'd spent hiking across the Saddle plus five to Gillman's, I calculated we'd be walking close to eighteen hours without sleep. Plus, my hip was starting to complain, and I was exhausted.

It startled us both when Jane suddenly started vomiting. "I feel awful," she murmured. "I shouldn't have eaten that chocolate."

Patting her back, I said quietly, "Maybe we should go down."

Jane nodded before turning to vomit again.

Loren, Cecille, and Kaija were nowhere in sight, and we figured they were already well on their way to Uhuru. Loren would tell me later that Kaija had started talking nonsensically by the time they reached Gillman's, indicating that she wasn't thinking clearly; but when Brian suggested she wait there for the guide with me and Jane instead of going on to Uhuru, she'd refused. Freezing in the sub-zero wind, Loren and Cecille wanted to push on to Uhuru, and Kaija went with them.

The wind pummeled them on the frigid crest, biting their hands and faces as they made for the ultimate summit. Kaija would say later that she hadn't wanted to continue because she was vomiting and her lungs were making gurgling sounds—hallmark signs of severe AMS. She said she was disoriented and scared and just wanted to get off the summit while she could still walk on her own.

Meanwhile, as Jane and I started down, we found the steep descent to be more punishing on our knees than the ascent had been. Walking the narrow path, I soon discovered that the sandy scree was thick as snow and not slippery in the least. Exhilarated, I hopped and boot-skied straight down instead of walking slowly around the endless switchbacks, kicking myself for being so scared of the narrow path on the way up.

We passed Irene along the way and later Patty and Sally, trudging slowly up switchbacks on the arms of their guides. They were determined to make it to Gillman's even though all of them were having trouble breathing.

Jane and I reached Kibo basecamp at 9 a.m., early enough to rest in our tents for a couple of hours before the others returned.

Kaija was pale and still vomiting when she staggered in sometime later, followed by Patty and Sally. But they had no time to rest since the porters needed to pack up their tents, and we still had to walk ten miles to the next camp, where we'd spend a last night on the mountain.

We descended by a more direct route than the one we'd taken on the way up. Though utterly exhausted and sleep-deprived, all of us were elated to have made it at least to Gillman's Point. We talked nonstop about our experiences the previous night as we trooped out of the alpine desert and into moorlands again; all except Kaija, who seemed dazed and subdued after her ordeal at the summit. Her symptoms continued to dissipate as she descended to lower altitudes.

The rest of us were grateful to our guides, who'd been solicitous and watchful throughout the night. Patty and Sally were particularly touched by the way their guides let them lean on them all the way to Gillman's and back, blotting the noses of the women from time to time.

We made it to Horombo Huts by late afternoon after four hours of walking. As usual the porters had our tents up and snacks waiting for us. It was pure pleasure to rinse the sweat and dust off my tired body in the portable shower one more time. Beyond that minor rush, I was numb with exhaustion and simply yearned for sleep.

After an early dinner, all of us collapsed in our tents and slept like stones that night.

The sun rose clear and strong as it had all week, spotlighting the austere spires of Mawenzi Peak and the massive cone of Kibo Dome. We could see part of a glacier clinging to one side of balding Kibo, although the guides told us that the snow mass was only a fraction of what it once had been.

That sixth day was bittersweet, and I was already filled with nostalgia as we hiked out of Kilimanjaro National Park in a state of euphoria. Still trying to absorb the enormity of our undertaking, I gazed at the majestic outline of Kibo with new eyes and recalled Hemingway's description of the mountain from the perspective of his dying protagonist: "There ahead, all he could see, as wide as all the world, great, high and unbelievably white in the sun, was the square top of Kilimanjaro."

The moorlands grew lusher as we passed through groves of giant lobelia once more. Subdued and no longer bounding down the path beside the guides, Kaija still stopped to photograph the towering cacti. The shifting terrain grew even more astounding as we left the moorlands and entered a tropical rainforest. It was crisp and dry instead of humid as I'd expected a rainforest to be, the ground covered with white and pink impatiens, mutant ferns, and strands of Spanish moss that clung to the trees. Black and white colobus monkeys cavorted overhead and watched us playfully, venturing close to see if we'd offer them something to eat.

The twelve-mile hike to the park gate was challenging at times, as we had to step carefully over tree roots and rocks or descend numerous sets of stairs with thigh and calf muscles aching. It would be days before any of us could walk down steps without wincing in pain.

When we finally reached the park gate, we sat down to a late lunch and ate in record time. After the meal, the tour organizer called us outside and handed out certificates with our names printed on them, certifying that everyone had reached the summit. With gratitude to our porters and guides, we took a few last photos and shook hands with the men before saying final goodbyes.

At the same bare-bones hotel in Marangu where we'd stayed before the climb, our dinner celebration was muted that night even though all of us had summitted at least at Gillman's. I could tell something was amiss, yet things only became clear when the tour organizer called me and Loren aside. "Kaija has lodged a formal complaint against Brian for pushing her to go on to Uhuru," he told us.

"She's the one who insisted on going with us," Loren objected. "And now she's blaming Brian?"

"She claims she was disoriented and vomiting and didn't want to go to Uhuru, but she felt pressured into going because Brian wouldn't let her wait at Gillman's for the next group."

Loren was furious that Kaija would blame her predicament at the summit on Brian, a complaint that could cost him his job. It had been Kaija's decision to go with the faster group in the first place, and she hadn't considered whether her decision might prevent her companions from reaching Uhuru—a goal that Loren and Cecille had worked hard to attain. Yet Kaija hadn't known how sick she would be when she reached Gillman's, and her thinking wasn't clear enough to make critical decisions.

Ultimately, Brian should have assessed the situation and determined whether she should go on, especially since she wasn't thinking clearly. His faltering English may have been one reason he couldn't assess Kaija's condition when Loren and Cecille left us to forge ahead, well before they reached Gillman's. Without cell phone service, he didn't know how far the next group was behind them. Another factor may have been his reluctance to challenge a foreigner who'd paid for the trip and seemed to have made up her mind. In any case, we would never know Brian's side of the story since the guides had gone home by then.

At that last dinner, the others didn't notice the rift between Kaija and Loren, preoccupied as they were with plans for their onward journeys the next day. Jane would return to Dar with me while Patty, Cecille, and Sally would fly back to the US.

It saddened me to say goodbye to everyone in the morning with tensions between Kaija and Loren unresolved. I'd often assumed the role of peacemaker in my family, and it had been important to me that everyone in the group got along. Being fond of both Loren and Kaija, I hoped to keep up with them.

In hindsight I would regret not pushing myself to go on to Uhuru, especially when Loren told me that the glaciers and icefields at the summit were a highlight for her, as was the view to the west of Mount Meru poking into the sky. I wondered whether it was fear that kept me from reaching the ultimate summit or if I'd been wise to turn around and head back down while I could walk without pain.

It had surprised me that Patty and Jane—exercise afficionados who'd trained diligently— didn't make it to Uhuru either. Like me, they had trouble breathing at high altitudes and couldn't push themselves further. It wasn't lack of motivation or focus that kept us from reaching the goal. Rather, it was external elements beyond our control—i.e., altitude sickness and exhaustion—that derailed us. You simply can't know in advance how your body will perform at high altitudes, just as you can't always end up with a genial group and mend rifts among friends.

Over the years, Loren and Kaija would maintain differing accounts of what happened at the summit. To my mind it reinforces the notion of subjectivity—that all of us perceive the world and "truth" differently. It also demonstrates recent thinking about memory—that it doesn't provide a literal retelling of past events. As psychologist Elizabeth Loftus wrote, "Our representation of the past takes on a living, shifting reality. It's not fixed and immutable, not a place that is preserved in stone, but a living thing that changes shape, expands, shrinks, and expands again."[23]

Loren and I would stay in touch and climb other mountains

together over the years, and I'd see Patty and Jane on my annual visits to Atlanta. In an email, Kaija would tell me that the Kili experience had been a turning point for her. It had opened a whole new dimension in her life after she discovered that walking led her to a state of exhilaration. Her love of mountains would grow when her family was stationed in Tibet, although she never wanted to undertake a serious climb again. In every country where her family was posted, she'd take photographs that would be exhibited in galleries and on her website. She clearly had an artist's eye, and there's an otherworldly quality to her photographs that borders on the transcendent; like basking in the afterglow of a mirage.

All of us agreed that we fell in love with Kilimanjaro somewhere along the way, an infatuation that deepened in time. With eyes wide open and steady steps over six long days, we walked the mountain's slopes, slept on its flanks, and marveled at the shifting landscapes in the stark light of high altitudes. Despite aching muscles and labored breathing, there were a thousand things that intrigued us each day; and in the vast reaches of that park, it was a privilege to walk in a state of wonder for a time.

Chapter 15
Adieu to Dar

Toward the end of our second year in Dar, my mother called from Florida one day and said in a jittery tone, "I don't want to worry you, but your father fell and hit his head in the middle of the night. He was bleeding so much I got scared and took him to the ER. After the doctors sewed up his head, they found he had a kidney infection and put him on IV antibiotics."

"How long will they keep him in the hospital?" I asked, trying to stay calm.

"Just a day or two if his condition improves," she said. "I'll keep you posted."

It was impossible not to worry even though Stefan assured me that kidney infections were easy to treat. My father had been in a fragile state after having several TIAs in the past year, and it had distressed me to see how poorly he was doing when I'd visited them at Christmas.

I called my mother back that night and asked how he was.

"He's getting worse instead of better," she said, unable to hide her distress. "His skin is yellow, and he's not coherent. A nurse took me aside and told me privately that I should get him to a better hospital. When I told that to your brother, he suggested having him evacuated to Dallas. He's going to call me back after he arranges a medevac."

"It's a good idea, Mom," I said with false calm. "Call me and let me know when you get there."

I hardly slept that night while waiting for news from home, hoping that I wouldn't get the call in the night that everyone dreads—especially expats living far from their families. At the end of the next day, my brother Nick called and said that our father was in intensive care in Dallas.

"Do you think I should come home?" I asked him.

"Wait a day and see how he's doing. He's got the best care possible, and I have faith they'll get him through this."

Nick called back the next day with encouraging news. "He's doing a lot better. They got him stabilized, and he knows where he is now." I asked him again if he thought I should fly home, and he said, "You could wait a few days. It's no longer an emergency."

I was on pins and needles all week, making daily phone calls to my mother and brothers to get updates about our father. It was a juggling act that many expats must face, guessing whether they'd have enough time to get home if a relative was in critical condition. What complicated the decision was that I already had tickets to go home in two weeks for summer vacation. If I waited, I could extend my stay in the US and spend more time with my parents and brothers. When Aaron and Elena got out of school, they would go to summer camps with friends while Stefan would fly to Los Angeles to join his mother and brothers.

The wait was excruciating. On the phone with my mother one day, I heard my father's voice in the background asking repeatedly, "When can I see the Skinny One?"—using the nickname he had called me since early childhood. I couldn't help lamenting the fact that we lived so far away, bereft at the thought of what the world would be like without my father in it.

Ultimately, my gamble paid off, and I was able to fly home as planned. By that point anywhere in the US seemed like "home" in comparison with the country in East Africa where we were living, and where my immediate family and possessions happened to be. At least in Texas, the language and country were familiar, and my parents would be waiting for me.

In June I flew straight to Dallas, and Nick picked me up at the airport. He briefed me before taking me to the rehab facility where my parents were staying. Even so, the sight of my father shocked me. He looked frail and shrunken in the hospital bed and deathly pale without his farmer's tan. My mother was spooning oatmeal in his mouth when he looked up and saw me.

"Skinny One's here," he announced, his face lighting up.

Tears welled in my eyes when he uttered my nickname, and I could tell he was going to be okay. He had tears in his eyes too as he ducked his head to let me kiss him.

"Hey, Skinny One," he said excitedly, gesturing at the windows. "Look outside and see if Cheerleader's there. He's been coming every day."

I feigned surprise. "They flew your favorite egret to Dallas with you?" My father was so fond of birds that he'd stand on his dock feeding egrets from his hand. He had nicknamed one that visited him every day.

My mother sighed when I bent to kiss her too. "He leaves a dinner roll on the windowsill for the birds every night."

"Let's go for a walk and see if we can find him," I said to my father. "Do you need permission to go outside?"

"Wait till I get him dressed and the nurse checks his vitals," my mother interjected. "You can take him out while I shower and put on my face."

When he was ready, my mother went to get a wheelchair. "I don't need that thing," he barked. "I can walk with the Skinny One."

"No, you can't," she snapped back. "You're not supposed to walk until the doctor gives you permission."

"Okay, okay." He threw up his hands. "But I'm gonna walk by myself before she leaves."

He was right on that score. While staying at my brother's place that week, I went to see my parents every day, and each time I returned to the rehab facility, my father looked stronger and could do more on his own. By the end of the week, he was eating by himself and walking with a cane, albeit slowly. With one hand on my arm and the other clutching his cane, he walked with me to inspect the garden and look for birds each day.

My mother wasn't keen on staying for long in the rehab place, nor would she consent to leave my father there on his own. After conferring with my siblings, my parents decided to leave Dallas at the end of the month and drive to Moscow, Idaho, where they'd stay with my older sister who was a nurse. She had a guest room with an ensuite bathroom on the main floor, and she'd planned to have our parents live with her when they could no longer be on their own.

It was hard to say goodbye at the end of my visit even though my father would be in good hands, and I would see them again when I returned for the Christmas holiday. I couldn't be sure of anything and would worry about my father's health after his close call. It was also hard to leave after the visit with my brothers and their families. I was glad to see that Mike—who'd remarried and had two more sons—was running an auto repair shop and had a healthy lifestyle.

It was a pivotal time for us, as Stefan had to decide whether to renew his contract and remain in Tanzania for one or two more years. The decision was less agonizing after we saw our parents that summer. I hated being so far away when my father was in precarious health, and Stefan's mother was declining rapidly. She was hardly aware of his presence when he visited her at the assisted living home in LA. We both decided that one more year abroad would have to suffice.

With three weeks left of our home leave, I flew to Atlanta and joined Stefan and the kids there. Aaron was a rising senior in high school, and we planned to visit colleges while Elena would attend a theatre camp in Atlanta. Aaron and I flew to Philadelphia and drove through Pennsylvania, New York, and several New England states touring colleges and visiting friends.

The fact that Aaron would be going to university in the US tipped the scales when we were deciding whether to move back in one year or two. We didn't want to be two long flights away from our parents or from Aaron as he was adjusting to college life. We also thought it would be better for Elena to finish high school in the US even though it meant she'd have to leave Dar after her sophomore year. A gifted singer and performer, she was bent on pursuing a career in theatre and music instead of going to college. But she had no interest in doing theatre at the international school since there wasn't much of a program, whereas the private school she'd attended in Atlanta was renowned for its musical productions. She would also have access to more voice teachers in Atlanta than in Dar.

While it seemed obvious to us that it would be better for Elena to return to her school in Atlanta, she didn't see it that way—even though her best friend at the international school had moved back to France by then. Elena was enjoying her social life and spent loads of time with friends or a boyfriend at the Yacht Club on weekends.

We hoped that in time she'd realize that moving back might be good for her, and that she'd make new friends once she got involved with the theatre crowd at her school in Atlanta. She was angry that she'd have to leave IST in the middle of high school, but she grudgingly accepted her fate.

That winter, after returning from spending Christmas in the US, Stefan and I found ourselves engulfed by a herd of wildebeests and zebras, some of them so pregnant they could barely walk. The driver of our safari jeep pulled off the road and inched through the grassland, parting the ranks of hairy wildebeests as we merged with the herd.

"What if they get mad?" I asked nervously. "Is this even legal?"

Clearly the driver had done this before, because he never blinked as big animals surged around our jeep. It was calving season in the Serengeti when as many as eight thousand baby wildebeests were born each day along with zebras too numerous to count. We passed a few newborn wildebeests rocking along on wobbly legs and a gazelle that was just seeing the light of day as its mother licked placental fluid from its face.

With a handful of months remaining before we'd leave Tanzania for good, Stefan and I were ticking off our wish list with a safari in the Serengeti. Seeing the great migration was the experience of a lifetime for us and a fitting way to say goodbye to a country we didn't want to leave. (Our kids were doing separate excursions with their classmates and had to miss this spectacle.)

Stefan had loved living and working overseas again. And he disliked the thought of being stuck in an office in Atlanta, driving to work on freeways instead of glimpsing the Indian Ocean from the shoreline road on his daily commute. I didn't want to leave Tanzania either, but the decision had been made, and we were determined to make the best of the remaining months there.

On our last afternoon in the Serengeti, when I'd had enough of bouncing over unpaved roads in a safari jeep, I opted to stay at the hotel while Stefan joined the embassy group for one more wildlife drive. I settled into a lounge chair beside the pool with my notebook and pen along with binoculars. The lodge sat on a low hill in a copse of trees, an excellent prospect from which to view animals on the surrounding plain. A couple of giraffes were grazing fifty yards away, nibbling on the leaves of an acacia tree. I watched them through my binoculars before picking up a pen to write my last column for Dar Guide.

"How do you say goodbye to a place that offered you a glimpse of Eden and a portal of peace, which is what Dar Es Salaam means?" I wrote. A second line quickly followed the first: "Leaving Tanzania is hard to contemplate while gazing at a family of giraffes from a hillock in the Serengeti, or while picnicking under a *banda* at the beach with my family."

I started listing the things I'd miss about Tanzania, chief among them being proximity to the ocean and to stunning landscapes that never failed to raise my perspective, and being able to walk and swim outdoors year-round. Within a day's drive of Dar were mountains like Meru and Kilimanjaro as well as game parks in the Serengeti and Selous. Most of all I'd miss the many people we'd come to know and the range of interactions we were able to have each day.

I put down my pen with a heavy heart, realizing how hard it would be to write about leaving that extraordinary country. To balance things, I'd have to consider the negative aspects of life in Dar along with the positive. But for now, I simply wanted to enjoy the few remaining hours in the Serengeti. Closing my notebook, I picked up my binoculars and was surprised to see the giraffes still munching on leaves a stone's throw away (if you had a good arm).

On the fourth day of our trip, Stefan and I opted to do a Highlands walk with a guide near Lake Manyara. The trek started at a Rift Valley cliff wall from which we could peer down into Lake Manyara National Park and watch the animals watering there. Hiking down a steep path to the river gorge below, I worried that one of us might step on a scorpion or snake hiding in the tall grass, or that we'd surprise the water buffalo whose skat our guide had identified. But the only animals we came across were baboons and blue monkeys as we crossed and recrossed the river several times.

After walking for three hours, we reached the town of Mosquito

Creek, which was situated on a busy road. The guide told us that the town was famous for its multiple tribes living peacefully side by side for many decades. It also had one of the highest HIV rates in the country because of its location on a major trucking route and on account of the tourist trade. The guide had parked his jeep in the lot of the regional hospital, and before we got in to leave, Stefan asked if we could duck inside the hospital.

The nurse on call said she'd be glad to show us around after Stefan introduced himself. Most of the beds in the HIV ward were occupied by young Masai men. One of them was curled up in a fetal position with an IV in his arm, and he was moaning piteously. The nurse told us that he'd been carried in by his father and wife the previous day. We nodded at a young woman sitting by his bedside who couldn't have been more than eighteen. She was cradling a skeletal baby in her arms.

A doctor from Minnesota came over to greet us, and he seemed happy to tell Stefan about his patients and the activities at the regional hospital. The doctor said that the young Masai man would probably survive since he'd started receiving medication in time. "Once people get on ARVs, about 80 percent of them make remarkable recoveries. We only lose 15 to 20 percent of our patients to AIDS, and it's usually because they come in too late."

The HIV infection rate in that part of the country, particularly among the Masai, was extremely high since many men migrated to cities for work and brought the disease back home with them. Thanks to social media and sex education in the schools, fewer young people were getting infected with HIV. The doctor said he'd seen a remarkable shift in behavior since he'd started working there three years earlier, and that more people asked questions about HIV.

This was what Stefan loved most about his work—visiting sites in the field and learning about AIDS treatment. For me, the hospital visit was a grim reminder of why we'd come to Tanzania in the first place. I was proud of the work Stefan was doing and the enormous contribution that he and others—like the doctor from Minnesota—were making to alleviate the suffering of people like the young Masai family; work that was saving tens of thousands of lives.[24] On the flip side, it saddened me to realize that our move back to the US would deprive Stefan of such person-to-person contact in the field. He wouldn't have opportunities like this—trekking through the Ngoro Ngoro Highlands and visiting regional clinics—after we returned to Atlanta.

In early spring, a few months before we were to leave, the Corona Women's Society was to hold an annual luncheon to bring women from numerous countries together for a feast. As chair, I was nominally in charge of the affair and expected to preside. Fortunately, a Tanzanian woman who'd been a member for twenty-some years—another Irene—took it upon herself to organize the luncheon with me at her side. It was a learning experience that I would come to regard as a one-day crash course in Tanzanian culture.

The day before the event, I spent hours with Irene at the home of the former prime minister, whose wife had offered to host it on the lawn of their mansion. A huge tent had been erected for the occasion, and dozens of round tables and folding chairs were in place. Irene and I decorated the tables and strung lights and bunting around the tent to make it look like a Turkish harem, with flower bowls on the tables and mini palm trees at the door flaps.

The next day, when women started arriving, African drummers and dancers greeted them with glasses of punch and tiny sachets that they could attach to their wrists or lapels. Wine bottles in coolers were waiting at each table along with dates and nuts in colorful dishes. Waiters took drink orders and deposited samosas on tables as the tent filled up. I played hostess and greeted Corona members and guests while Irene directed waiters at the buffet tables. She made sure that the music never stopped, with a Masai singer crooning to the guests while they ate.

Buffet tables groaned under the heated dishes that Irene had ordered from a Turkish restaurant, including savory goat and spinach stews, cashew chicken in coconut milk, whole red snapper adorned with olives and tomatoes, and a dozen vegetable dishes and curries—enough to feed two hundred attendees along with the wait staff. Strolling from one table to the next to chat with guests and make sure the wine was plentiful, I didn't sit down until everyone had a turn at the buffet table. Even then I was unable to relax or eat much as my eyes were attuned to nearby tables to make sure everything was going smoothly.

I needn't have worried. Irene had arranged a fashion show to keep guests engaged after lunch plates were cleared away and dessert and coffee were served. A stately Tanzanian woman emceed the event and described each outfit as five young models strutted around the tent in different sets of clothing. After the fashion show, one of the models donned a bridal gown and the emcee explained a Tanzanian bride-rite ceremony, demonstrating how brides were instructed, perfumed, and massaged by their ladies in waiting (played by the models). It was entertaining as well as educational for many expats who were unfamiliar with local customs. An older woman who was a friend of Irene grabbed the mic after the bride-rite ceremony and did a stand-up comedy routine that was hilarious.

Once the entertainment wound down, Irene and I made the rounds one last time, saying goodbye to everyone before they left. Both of us had put in an eight-hour day, yet we were elated that so many women thanked us and said they had a marvelous time.

That luncheon—the first in years to draw two hundred participants and the first one I'd chaired—was another bittersweet moment before our departure. I cherished such interactions with Tanzanians like Irene and Giselle, who ran Kids on the Pitch where I was tutoring;

caring individuals who were determined to help those around them. I would miss gatherings like these with women of other nationalities and backgrounds. The luncheon that day allowed me "To see a world in a grain of sand and a heaven in a wildflower, hold infinity in the palm of your hand and eternity in an hour," as William Blake wrote long ago.

Another unexpected pleasure that I'd miss about Tanzania was the opportunity to mingle with local artists. I'd frequented art shows and galleries and had come to know a handful of artists during our time there. One of them, a carver named Ruben, made intricate mahogany towers of figures climbing on each other's shoulders and heads in circular patterns. The distinctive wood sculptures were called "family trees," and I'd sent friends to Ruben's stall in the Mwenge Crafts Market whenever we had visitors.

The artist I came to know best was a self-taught painter who lived in Dar. I'd attended an exhibition of Salum Kambi's work at a local gallery soon after we arrived in the country and was captivated by his colorful canvases. He'd caught the unvarnished light in East Africa through his impressionistic renderings of wildebeests, fishermen, and Masai families. Kambi's face had lit up when I told him how much I liked his paintings, and he'd invited me to visit his studio in his parents' compound on the outskirts of Dar, which I did within days of our meeting.

His family compound was a few blocks from the big crafts market at Mwenge that drew throngs of tourists and crafts afficionados. A self-effacing Tanzanian in his late thirties, Kambi no longer lived in the compound where his parents and sister had tiny houses around an earthen courtyard, but the location allowed him to paint in an open courtyard near the crafts market.

There were only a handful of galleries in Dar at the time, and he was one of a dozen artists whose work they exhibited. He had a small fan base in the diplomatic community, including the Norwegian ambassador who'd liked his paintings so much that he arranged an exhibition for Kambi at a gallery in Oslo and invited him to attend the show. Over the years, I took many visitors to Kambi's compound so they could watch a local artist at work. It helped him sell paintings by word of mouth, and I loved watching him paint with an array of palette knives.

Right before the movers came to pack up our house, Kambi strolled up the front walk with a dozen canvases rolled up under his arm. I had offered to take some of his paintings to Atlanta in hopes of finding a gallery that would exhibit and sell them. I'd already purchased six paintings for us and another four to give as gifts.

"What did you bring?" I asked him.

"I want you to take more paintings to Atlanta," he said with an earnest expression. "If you can arrange a show for me, I could sell a lot."

"I'll do my best," I promised even though I wasn't sure of how to go about arranging a show. "If I find a gallery for your work, maybe you could come to Atlanta for the opening and bring more paintings with you."

"That is my wish too," he beamed. Kambi draped the canvases over my living room chairs and sofa so I could select the paintings to take with me.

"This is a feast for the eyes," I sighed. "It's a privilege to be able to choose paintings to take with me."

"Please," he implored me, "take all of them if you can."

Kambi's friendship had enriched my time in Dar and deepened my appreciation for artists there. Seeing his evocative paintings of the people, animals and landscapes in Tanzania helped me view my surroundings in a new light, as did hearing about his struggles to support a wife and daughters despite a fickle art market and fluctuating tourism. Helping Kambi sell his work was one way to support him and his family, and his paintings would always remind me of the special places my family had known and loved.

In the months leading up to our departure, Elena became attached to a Tanzanian boy in her class. I knew it was a relationship that meant a lot to her since she wanted us to meet him. When Jameel stepped into our front hall and offered me his hand, Stefan and I greeted him warmly and asked questions to try and engage him. But he was shy and gave only cursory responses. Unlike the guys Elena had been attracted to in the past—including the boy next door who was a hunky basketball star—this boy had the temperament of a forlorn poet who had yet to find his voice. He was like a deer in headlights that evening as he stood in our front hall, his thick hair swooped from one side of his face to the other like an old man's combover.

Elena spent all her time with Jameel instead of her friends during our last month in Dar. As we prepared for the move, she grew resistant and begged us to let her stay with friends and finish high school at the IST. When we insisted that she had to go with us, she asked if she could go to boarding school instead of returning to Atlanta. But we told her it was too late to consider that option. In response, Elena waged a sit-down strike and refused to pack her things or lift a finger for the move, nor did she leave the house except to go to school or to her boyfriend's.

I understood her anger and sorrow. We would all miss Tanzania, especially Stefan, who loved working there. Aaron would miss living near the beach and the people he'd come to know, Wilfred among them. The hardest part for all of us was knowing that we might never see the people and places we loved again. As we knew from experience, those doors were almost impossible to reopen once you returned to your country on the other side of the globe.

All of us were sad about leaving, but Elena was the only one who was moving against her will. Her spirits plummeted—not just on account of the move but because she was having issues with some friends. School ended several weeks before our departure, and she'd started sleeping until noon each day. We agreed to let her spend as much time at her boyfriend's house as his parents would allow.

A week before we were to leave Tanzania, I walked to the Yacht Club beach with Stefan and Aaron. The two of them were going sailing one last time while Elena was spending the day with her boyfriend. I didn't particularly like going out in Stefan's fiberglass dingy since it pitched and bobbed when the water was choppy. One time the boat had capsized in rough waves, and Stefan and Aaron had to be towed in by a rescue boat. After that incident, whenever they went sailing, I'd gulp and say, "Have fun" while praying that nothing bad would happen.

As their boat drifted across the bay, I sat in the gazebo and tried to finish my last column for the Dar Guide—the one I'd started writing while in the Serengeti. Picking up where I left off, I described the things I loved most about living in Dar. The country was a model of ethnic tolerance and interfaith cooperation, as evidenced by Muslim, Hindu, and Christian leaders who were working together to teach their congregations about the dangers of HIV. It was inspiring to see Tanzanians and expats work together to help sick and less fortunate people improve their lives. In the column I also mentioned individuals who had enriched my understanding of the country and culture—like Kambi and Giselle—as well as the people who worked with us like Wilfred and Lucy.

What I didn't mention were things I wouldn't miss—foremost

among them the air and noise pollution that plagued us daily. A neighbor in the house behind ours burned trash in his yard every week, and the smoke from his toxic fire would fill our house. Another house behind ours was abandoned, and a squatter family had taken up residence. They kept chickens and a noisy rooster who couldn't tell time, since it crowed at 3 and 4 a.m., waking me well before the imam at a nearby mosque broadcast his call to prayer at 5. Then there was the day care center in our next-door neighbor's house from which screams of toddlers and wailing babies would erupt from 8 a.m. to 5 p.m., forcing me to keep our windows shut most of the time.

I closed my notebook to drink in the fading light as Stefan and Aaron sailed back across the bay. In another month I'd long for evenings like this, and for the chance to sit on a beach and gaze at a marine-scape that always raised my spirits. Stefan, too, would sorely miss the sunsets and sailing, while Elena would be crying for her boyfriend. I presumed that Aaron would be spared since he'd be preoccupied with college life. A week before our departure, he left Tanzania to meet up with his Atlanta friends and travel around Europe with them.

Our last days in Dar were filled with goodbyes, including a champagne lunch at the Yacht Club beach with Cathy and dinner at Loren and Jeff's. On the day of our departure, Jameel's mother invited me to have coffee with her. She told me about her Muslim background and hopes for her son. Toward the end of our visit, she asked me, "Would you mind if we invited Elena to spend the holidays with us in Dar? I don't know if it means a lot to you to have her with you at Christmas."

I thought about it for a moment before responding. "It does mean a lot to us, but I know she'll miss Jameel and her friends so much that she'd rather spend the holidays here than in Atlanta." I refrained from voicing my other thought: that I hoped Elena would think hard about her relationship and whether it was worth pursuing it long distance.

After I got home, a steady stream of visitors came to our door. Kambi came to pick up the laptop and camera we'd promised to leave for him, and he dropped off more paintings for me to take to Atlanta. Ruben came with a mahogany "family tree" that I'd commissioned for a friend at home. In between visitors, Lucy helped me dispose of the remaining food in the fridge and pantry, stuffing some of it in the suitcases that we gave her along with sheets, towels, and rugs we'd decided to leave. I paid her final salary and gave her a letter of recommendation as two taxis pulled into the driveway to take Lucy and Wilfred home with their belongings. Prudence had said goodbye the previous day.

Wilfred took my hand, and his eyes grew red when he said shyly, "I think this must be the saddest day of my life."

Lucy and I didn't look at each other as we hugged goodbye, both of us crying quietly. It was every bit as hard to leave her and Wilfred as it had been to leave Gladys and Ousmane a decade earlier, knowing that we'd have few meetings in the future.

At 8 p.m. I made my way downstairs with my bags as the CDC van pulled into the driveway. The driver loaded our suitcases into the van while Elena climbed in the back and sat there sobbing for her boyfriend. I coaxed the dog into the van and let her climb on the seat beside me as Stefan slid into the front seat. When the driver shut the doors, Bella rested her head on my lap, submitting to her fate as the rest of us did.

We would wake up in Amsterdam after a nine-hour flight and escort Elena to her gate for a connecting flight to Atlanta. She had offered to take the dog there and stay with my friend Kathryn—whose son she was close to—while Stefan and I would fly to Norway and spend a week with Bodil and Cam.

We'd made the Norway plan to give ourselves a respite after the tumultuous process of packing and sad goodbyes in Dar. Bodil and Cam would understand what we'd just gone through since they'd moved back from Tanzania one year prior. Staying with dear friends would help us transition as an exciting chapter of our lives came to an end, and it would help us get our bearings before the return to Atlanta.

Chapter 16

Atlanta Again

A aron's excitement was palpable as he hurried across campus, looking for international students who were gathering for an orientation. The grass was lush in mid-September, though the ivy on Gothic buildings was already turning yellow, auguring an early fall. I was intimidated by the place and still surprised that Aaron had chosen to go to Princeton. In my mind, it was a preppy college for the country's elite—a class my family had never been part of. Yet among the East Coast colleges that Aaron had toured, it had a strong engineering school, and he'd immediately felt at home there. His decision seemed as much intuitive as it was reasoned.

We had flown to Philadelphia the previous day and spent the night with friends who lived nearby. Creeping across campus in a rental car, we'd managed to find his dorm in a Harry Potter-style hall that looked nothing like the faceless concrete buildings where I'd resided at a small college in Ohio. He'd been assigned to a four-person suite with a common living area and two small bedrooms, a set of bunk beds in each. The rooms were so atmospheric that I could almost smell the dusky air of Princetonians who'd smoked pipes by the fireplace a hundred years earlier.

As soon as he caught sight of a dozen students milling in the quad, Aaron strode off without saying goodbye or looking back at me. My heart lurched as I watched him go, knowing he wouldn't want me to follow.

Looking for something to do, I strolled through campus, admiring the mix of modern and Gothic architecture. The international students would spend the afternoon and evening together before freshman orientation officially started the following day. Then freshmen would split off for trips to various destinations. Aaron had signed up for a long weekend in the Appalachians, eager to meet other students who liked hiking and camping.

After an hour or so, I walked back to see what Aaron's group was doing. Two folding tables had been set up with trays of deli foods and coolers beside them. A handful of parents joined students in the food line and held paper plates while chatting with each other. Unlike me, they were clearly from other countries and fit the bill as international parents. Feeling out of place, I walked over to Aaron and asked him if he wanted me to stay.

"You don't have to," he shrugged. "We'll do a campus tour and meet people in our departments after lunch, and there's a group dinner tonight."

"I should say goodbye then." I half-smiled, determined not to make our parting harder for him or me. Saying goodbye around a bunch of strangers was far from satisfying, yet there was no other way.

He hugged me briefly before turning away.

"Are you sure you don't want me to do any errands for you while I have a car?" I asked.

"It's okay, Mom. I'll be fine."

I squeezed his arm and turned to go, not wanting him to see me cry as he grabbed a plate and got in line. Ambling across the lawn to the rental car, I told myself to be brave. I was leaving him in a bucolic place where he would have extraordinary opportunities in the coming years. I wanted to remember the sound of young people chattering and the slanting sun on Gothic buildings instead of a backward glance at my son's distracted face. At least I'd get to see him in six weeks when Stefan and I flew up for Parents' Weekend.

I drove to the airport and boarded a plane to Atlanta with a hollow heart. On the return flight, my eyes kept leaking against my will every time I thought about Aaron.

Later that night, when he was absent from the dinner table and his voice no longer resounded in the house, I broke down and wept in Stefan's arms.

"He's going to have a great college experience and make lots of friends," he said gently. "And what a perfect way to start the school year, by hiking and camping with kids his age. You should be happy for him."

"I am," I sobbed. "It's just hard to get used to not having him around."

I could tell by the way Stefan sighed that he felt the loss himself.

As hard as it was to leave Aaron in another state, I was grateful to be only six hundred miles away from him instead of six thousand as we would be if we'd stayed in Tanzania.

The next few days were filled with duties that distracted me. Elena was eager to paint her basement bedroom and buy new furniture for her lair. She also wanted to replace her old flip-top cell with a smart phone so she could skype with her boyfriend.

Somehow everything got done, including a visit to the vet with Bella. Elena and I painted her bedroom and shopped before her school year began. With Aaron gone, our relations seemed more congenial than they'd been in several years. She was more often in a good mood than not, and when school started, she was pleasant at dinner and talked about the students in her classes.

"If I'm not mistaken," I said to her one evening, "you almost seem glad to be the only kid in the house."

"At least I don't have to compete with Aaron for the TV or computer," she shrugged.

"How's school going anyway? Do you think you'll like it?"

"I don't like how white the school is. A lot of kids seem close-minded, and no one knows where Tanzania is. They couldn't care less about other countries."

"Who are you hanging out with? Anyone from your old group?"

She shook her head, frowning slightly as if it were a sore subject. "I signed up for hip hop dance with some African American girls. We're also in chorus together."

Sensing she was getting annoyed with my line of questioning, I switched subjects. "What's the news from Jameel?"

"He's coming to the US with his mother in October," she said, suppressing a grin. "Dad said I could meet them in Miami for a long weekend."

I wasn't surprised that Stefan had given in to Elena's request as he often did. I fully concurred with this one since it gave her something to look forward to. She talked to Jameel every day, and we'd received an astronomical phone bill at the end of the month. We gave her an ultimatum and told her that she needed to use Skype instead of her cell phone.

Aaron called later that week and reported that he was doing fine. When I asked him if he was homesick, he said, "I'm homesick for Dar. Aren't we all?" I had to admit that we were.

That night, while sitting on our back deck by myself in the twilight, I couldn't help crying for that place and those days. It seemed like it was already part of the distant past, our time together in Tanzania. Now Aaron would live apart from us for years to come, and Elena would keep pining for her boyfriend. Both kids were feeling the loss as intensely as I did, and Stefan didn't like being back in Atlanta and working in an office complex overlooking the freeway.

It was one of those hard choices that we'd had to make, leaving Tanzania and returning to more mundane lives in Atlanta again. Yet living far from our parents when they were ailing and from Aaron as he was embarking on a new chapter in his life wasn't a better option. It was a matter of weighing trade-offs instead of judging them as right or wrong.

Three months after our return, I was back at the airport anxiously awaiting the arrival of Salum Kambi. I'd managed to arrange an exhibition for him in a small Atlanta gallery, and he'd secured a visa to come for the opening. He planned to stay with us for two weeks.

An hour after his plane landed, I was still waiting in the terminal and growing increasingly worried. For security reasons, the airline wouldn't confirm that he had boarded the flight from Dar to Amsterdam and another one to Atlanta. After waiting two hours, I asked an airline rep if it was possible to call Immigration, and she directed me to a wall phone.

Upon reaching Customs and Immigration, I explained the reason for Kambi's visit and told the agent that I'd been waiting for him for two hours. The agent took my cell number and said he'd call me back.

An hour later, another agent called me and asked if I could verify the passenger's name and purpose of his visit. When I did so, he asked if I was Kambi's sponsor and could guarantee that he'd leave the US before his visa expired.

"Of course he'll leave," I said, trying to stay calm. "The man's a famous artist with a wife and two kids at home, and he has no intention of staying in our country."

Three hours after his plane landed, Kambi finally walked through the security checkpoint looking desperately around for me. Relief spread over his face as soon as he saw me. His shirt was soaked with sweat, and he grasped my hand in both of his. "They did not want to let me in," he murmured, visibly upset.

"Were they interrogating you this whole time?" I said, incensed.

He nodded. "They kept asking me the same questions and didn't believe me."

"Let's get out of here," I said, taking his arm and steering him to the baggage carousel to retrieve his luggage. "I'm so sorry you had a bad experience your first time here." I tried to remain calm even though I was furious at the way Immigration treated foreign visitors, especially those from African countries.

"They wanted to send me back," he murmured, his voice shaky.

"Well, you're here now, and we'll be home in no time."

Kambi was so upset by his experience at the airport that he couldn't eat dinner when we reached the house. He asked if he could take a shower, and I showed him to the guest bathroom. Afterwards, he went straight to his room and locked the bedroom door. He didn't come out for the rest of the night.

Kambi looked more rested when he appeared for breakfast, although he still seemed anxious as I was showing him around. Everything about our house and the wooded neighborhood was strange to him, and a world away from his environs in Dar.

He listened attentively as I told him the plan for the day. "On our way to the art gallery where your show will open tonight, we'll stop by Elena's school so I can introduce you to the head of the art department. His name is Henry, and he was very interested in meeting you when I told him about the exhibition."

"Okay." Kambi nodded, smiling for the first time since he arrived.

The meeting with Henry exceeded my expectations. He invited Kambi to teach some workshops for high school students and offered to pay him a visiting artist's stipend. I gladly agreed to drive Kambi to the school the following week, and he was delighted at the prospect of teaching students and earning money.

Kambi was even happier when he saw his paintings on display in a gallery in the Cabbage Town section of Atlanta. We helped the owner set out wine and hors d'oeuvres before the opening reception and then stood around as dozens of people wandered into the gallery, many of them eager to meet Kambi. He stayed by my side the entire time, too timid and embarrassed about his English to converse freely. I felt for him, remembering how shy I was about my French early on when we moved to Abidjan. What made matters worse was that Kambi was anxious around African Americans because of the negative impressions he'd formed from watching crime shows on TV. Too many shows portrayed African Americans as criminals and drug users.

Kambi was overjoyed by the end of the evening, having sold close to a dozen paintings. He was won over by the kindness of Terence (the gallery owner) and Henry (the art teacher), who helped dispel his negative images of African Americans. What really brought him out of his shell and eased his anxieties—to the point where he stopped locking his bedroom door at night—were his interactions with my father.

Two days after Kambi's arrival, my mother called and said that a water pipe had burst in their mobile home and damaged kitchen cabinets and floors. Repairs would take a month, and during that time they would have to stay in a hotel. My father hated hotels, and she wanted him to stay with me while she remained in Florida to oversee the work.

Instead of an empty nest, I suddenly had my hands full and was cooking and cleaning and arranging activities for two male visitors. My father was happy to be in a house with a big backyard and a dog that followed him everywhere. He was an easy guest in that he didn't want to go anywhere, preferring to do yardwork or sit on our back deck. His health was much better, although he wasn't as spry as he used to be. I gave him projects like pulling the ivy off trees and weeding with me. With an acre of land and woods behind our house, it was easy to keep him busy.

Kambi had initially been shy around my father, and they didn't have much to say to each other. But my dad won him over with his easy-going manner, ambling around the house and yard in a tank top and shorts. Struggling to remember Kambi's name, he asked him one day, "Can I just call you Steve?"

"Of course," Kambi smiled broadly. I asked him later if he minded being called Steve, and Kambi shook his head. "I like to have an American name," he beamed. "Your father reminds me of my father before he passed away."

Whenever he saw my father working in the yard, Kambi would carry the easel I'd borrowed for him to the patio and paint outdoors. Working quickly with his pallet knives, he painted images of the woods around him and of ostriches and wildebeests that he saw in his mind's eye. He gave one of these paintings to my father when the latter asked him what a wildebeest looked like.

It was a pleasure watching the two men work outside, though I had little time for my own work when they were there. It required an inordinate amount of patience and attention to walk the dog slowly around the block with my father each day and take him to the YMCA to do the exercises his doctor had recommended. I also wanted Kambi to see as many galleries and historic sites as possible during his stay. When Stefan or Elena could stay with my father, I took Kambi to the aquarium, the Martin Luther King Center, the High Museum of Art, CNN, and art supply stores to buy materials he couldn't get at home.

It turned out to be serendipitous that his visit overlapped with my father's. My dad had treasured his visit to Ivory Coast ten years earlier, but he hadn't been well enough to travel to East Africa when we lived there. In a sense, Tanzania came to him, and he got a flavor of our lives there in meeting Kambi. It was sweet to see both worlds blend for a couple of weeks as two men I cared about found respite in my house and bonded with each other.

Both men thanked me profusely and said they were sorry to leave when I drove them to the airport for their separate flights home. I asked Kambi to let me know when he arrived in Dar, and he sent me an email the following day. "Thank you for everything," he wrote, "and tell your father Steve says hello."

Six months later, in the spring of 2009, Stefan and I were sitting in a huge Atlanta theatre at an awards ceremony for high school musicals across Georgia. Elena sat several rows away with her theatre friends, laughing with them and oblivious of our presence. The ceremony was being broadcast on local TV, and a famous newscaster was the emcee. Elena had been nominated for Best Supporting Actress for her role as Eveline in "The Wiz," and we were anxiously awaiting the results.

I'd gone to her school to watch her perform in all three productions before sold-out audiences. Mesmerized by her transformation when she stepped onstage, I'd teared up every time she started singing her lines; and when the audience gave the actors a standing ovation at the end, I'd blushed with pride. The role had helped her get over her sadness at leaving Jameel after she spent Christmas break with him in Dar.

While waiting for the award for Best Supporting Actress to be announced, I worried about how she would take it if she wasn't chosen.

"And the winner of Best Supporting Actress for her role in a high school musical is . . ."

I gripped Stefan's hand and closed my eyes. When we heard her name announced, I looked at him in disbelief. "She did it!" I cried.

Elena's mouth formed a perfect oval as she gaped at her friends. Pulling herself together, she hoisted a corner of her gown and strode to the front of the theatre and onto the stage. After shaking hands with the emcee, she walked to the podium and took the mic. The exact words of her speech escape me, but she reiterated several times, "This award isn't just for me, it's for all of you who performed in musicals this year. Everyone did a great job."

It was hard to sit still for the rest of the ceremony, and even harder to get close to Elena in the vestibule once it was over as other parents, friends, and strangers crowded around her. When we finally had a chance to give her a bouquet of flowers, Elena was glowing.

"We're so proud of you," I said in the moment we had with her. "I just wish your grandparents could have been here. They would have loved seeing you up there."

"Yeah, it's too bad," she said distractedly. "I have to call Jameel and tell him the news."

"Do you need a ride home?" I asked as she turned away with her cell phone.

"I'm good," she clipped over her shoulder.

I couldn't have been happier for her. Our move to Atlanta had been hardest on her since she'd had to leave her boyfriend in the middle of high school, and I knew she felt like an outsider in Atlanta, which didn't feel like "home" to her.

My relationship with Elena had deteriorated since the honeymoon period after Aaron left for college. Whenever Stefan traveled, she'd hole up in her basement bedroom or stay out with friends, and she'd spend hours on the phone with her boyfriend. When Stefan was around, she spoke civilly and addressed all her comments to him at the dinner table without looking at me. Stefan rarely called her on it since he walked on eggshells around her too, and he hated confrontations.

She begged us to let her return to Dar again that summer. I had an inkling that we'd already lost Elena when we were living in Dar, eager as she was to separate from us and be with her boyfriend. I just hoped that we'd be able to establish a new relationship after she got the independence she craved and was no longer living under our roof. It seemed that we had to let her go in order to get her back.

❀

It was a relief to have Aaron at home when he took a summer job at Georgia Tech. He worked in a lab by day and played Ultimate with a club team several nights a week. Toward the end of the summer, he and Stefan went on a backpacking trip before Aaron returned to college.

While Stefan never minded traveling for his job, it took him awhile to work up the courage to visit his mother at the long-term care home near his brother. Her dementia had advanced to the point where she was unresponsive as she lay in a fetal position on her bed. Stefan and I flew to LA to see her in August, and she didn't appear to recognize me. She fixed Stefan with a penetrating stare when he held her hand and spoke to her. I left the room to give them time alone as he told her about his work and life in Atlanta. Then he managed to say what he thought she'd want to hear even as it broke his heart to say it: that she could go when she was ready, and that he and his brothers would be fine.

Her three sons agreed with the head nurse that it was time for hospice to be called in. Anna's five-year decline into dementia ended one day in December with her oldest son at her bedside.

Stefan wasn't surprised when he got the news of his mother's passing. He'd been losing her gradually for years, and it was obvious that the shell of her body no longer contained her essence or former effervescence. The adventurous Polish exile who'd traveled to Congo in 1948 to be with her fiancé and ended up staying in Africa for thirteen years had already faded away.

In March of our second year in Atlanta, while Stefan was in Haiti for a month doing relief work after the earthquake, my father again came to stay for a couple of weeks. His memory had started slipping since his last visit, which worried me. Sometimes when he woke up, it would take him a while to recognize his surroundings. After napping in our sunroom one day, he looked at me with a puzzled expression and asked, "Who are you?" My heart clutched as I reminded him that I was the Skinny One, and recognition slowly dawned in his face.

Another day I had to go to a writers group meeting and leave him alone for several hours. The writing group had become my touchstone and the place where I invested my best energies. I'd rejoined the group as soon as we moved back to Atlanta in 2008, grateful to have feedback after working in isolation for years. We met monthly at my friend Kathryn's house, each member submitting a chapter from a work in progress and discussing it. Kathryn and Anne had started the group with me when I moved to Atlanta in 1999, and they were still among my closest friends.

The morning of my writers group meeting, I had asked Elena to come home after school so someone would be there when my father woke up from his nap, and she'd promised to do so. I told my father that my meeting would end at 5 p.m., but it ran over since one of the members arrived late. Worried about my father, I was distracted and anxious and close to tears when I got a critique of my work that stung me. I left the meeting early and raced home.

It was 6:15 by the time I got there, and my father was waiting at the door.

"Where were you?" he asked, his voice accusing and angry.

"I had a writers group meeting. Isn't Elena here?"

"No one is here, and I didn't know how to get in touch with you," he groused. "I was about to go next door to ask the neighbor if they knew how to find you."

It was the last straw at the end of an anxiety-filled afternoon, and I was unable to hold things in any longer. "Just leave me alone for five minutes," I barked.

Tossing my shoulder bag on the kitchen table, I ran to my bedroom and burst into tears. I shook with rage as I lay on the bed, feeling guilty about yelling at my father when I was actually angry at Elena. Now I'd have to walk the dog for her AND make dinner for my father.

Paralyzed with guilt and anger, I lay curled on my bed when my father knocked at my door a few minutes later. "Hey, Skinny One," he called in a chastened voice, "come out and give me a hug. It'll make it all better." Obeying him reflexively, I opened the door to hug him, and he was right; it cleared the air and made us both feel better.

After I made dinner, we ate together on the back deck in the twilight. Then we went inside to watch a movie that touched us both deeply. *God Grew Tired of Us*, about the Lost Boys of Sudan, made our own issues seem petty.

When Elena came home that night, my father greeted her in his usual teasing tone. "I missed you this afternoon."

"Oh, yeah?" She could see that I was seething and responded more to me than to him. "We got permission to perform at graduation, and I had to meet with my backup group."

This was news to me, though it hardly excused the way she'd shirked her duties.

"Your grandfather was upset when you didn't come home," I said sternly. "He was all alone because I had to stay late at writers group. And the dog didn't get walked, by the way."

"She's so old, she doesn't need a walk." Elena shrugged. "You are too," she joked with my father, making light of the situation.

"I'm not happy about what you did," I persisted, "and that you didn't let me know you wouldn't be home."

"Sorry," she clipped, not sounding the least bit sorry. She left the kitchen and went down to her lair, stooping to scratch Bella's ears and apologizing to her on the way.

After we went to bed that night, I had a hard time falling asleep. I was frustrated with Elena for her flippant remarks and surly presence—or absence—while Stefan was away for a month, and I felt guilty for leaving my father and for blowing up at him. I didn't want him to feel unwelcome or like a burden in any way.

For as long as I could remember, I'd always had a special affinity with him, or a kind of intuitive camaraderie. As a child, I could always tell when he was going through his occasional bouts of depression by the way he'd drag his feet after a long workday. Without being asked, I would join him on the sofa in the living room and sit beside him while he read the newspaper or stared into space. We didn't need to talk, and I didn't know how to ask him about his day or how he was feeling. We'd simply sit beside each other as commotion swirled around us, my siblings running in and out of the house and my mother preparing dinner.

I had a similar affinity with Stefan and Aaron, the three of us content to sit in a room while reading or going hiking together. Elena was more of an extrovert with her outsized presence that commanded attention, and she spurned introspection over nonstop activity. She felt the differences between us acutely, and I'm sure she felt judged for her choices—for preferring shopping over hiking, or watching TV over reading, and always wanting to be with friends instead of on her own. It had little to do with the fact that she was adopted—which I hoped she understood—and more with fundamental personality traits, much like the differences between my mother and me. I empathized with her since I'd grown up feeling like an odd duck in my own family. But over time, I had learned that all of us were more closely linked than we realized and connected in deeper and more profound ways than the superficial personality traits we exhibited.

I had also learned and grown a lot more in relating with Elena than I had to with Aaron. She challenged me more, and Elena was strong enough to revel in her differences and do exactly as she pleased. In her teens, she already showed an emotional acuity beyond her years. She could size people up and intuit things about them that were generally accurate, which would serve her well in her career someday. I hoped it would be something we'd appreciate about each other one day; but we were far from it during her last year at home.

A year after Elena won the award for Best Supporting Actress, we were on the edge of our seats again in an Atlanta theatre while waiting for her to perform. It was graduation day, and hundreds of family members had been sitting in the auditorium for hours watching the seniors receive diplomas from the headmaster, who always said something personal about each student. The audience was obviously restless and ready for the ceremony to end.

Elena and her friends had been chosen as the closing act, and she strutted onstage in a sequined blue dress and stiletto heels. She was accompanied by two African American friends in tight black dresses and five boys who took up instruments behind them, one at a grand piano.

The fact that Elena had made it to graduation was nothing short of a miracle. She'd spent much of her senior year in her basement bedroom, on the phone with Jameel or on her laptop. Her closest theatre friends had graduated a year before, and few visitors had come to the house to draw her out of her funk over her boyfriend. She rarely spoke to me, especially if I complained about a big phone bill or that it was her turn to walk the dog in the evening.

Elena couldn't get out of our house fast enough, eager as she was to start her new life with Jameel in LA where she planned to enroll in acting school. Stefan and I had agreed to send her to Dar after her own graduation so she could watch Jameel and her old friends graduate at IST. The two of them would then travel in Europe for a couple of weeks before moving to LA. Elena was pinning all her hopes on him, believing that he was the key to her future. I hoped that she'd be happy with Jameel even though I often heard her arguing with him on the phone.

At her graduation ceremony, the band played a short intro
before Elena lifted her mic and crooned the first few lines of "Proud
Mary" in a pitch-perfect southern drawl. She started slow, her voice
unusually deep and low for a girl of seventeen. It was mesmerizing,
watching her strut across the stage with the mic at her mouth and
stare at the crowd as the tune grew in volume and filled the hall.
Though we knew what was coming, it was still a surprise when the
band picked up the pace and she launched into the fast rendition of
the song. Elena hit the notes hard, belting out a version of "Proud
Mary" like Tina Turner's as the backup singers shimmied behind her
and the band rocked—all of them owning the stage until the last bars
echoed through Atlanta's Symphony Hall. At the end of the song, the
audience leapt to their feet and gave them the only standing ovation
of the night.

It was a proud moment for Stefan and me as we watched our
daughter take bows with her friends onstage. People came up to con-
gratulate her and us, shaking their heads in astonishment. Men like
Clyde, our neighborhood doctor, and Kathryn's husband talked about
Elena's performance with tears in their eyes, marveling over her moxy
when she stepped onstage.

Soon she'd be on her own in LA, where people's dreams sometimes came true . . . but more often not. Whether she'd be able to mar-
shal her talents and succeed was a big unknown, driven as she was by
two main goals: to live independently from us, and to be with Jameel.

"He's gone and I want to go too," my mother wailed into the phone. "I
just want to go with him!"

Her call came midmorning on a hot July day. My mother was
crying so hard that she had to give the phone to a friend. Jean told me
that my father had just passed away in my mother's arms, and though
she'd called 911, they were unable to revive him.

Putting down the phone, I dropped to my knees beside Bella and buried my face in her fur, hugging her since she was the only breathing being in the house. She must have sensed my sorrow since she closed her eyes and allowed me to weep on her neck. Though I'd known it could happen any time, the shock of his passing was impossible to process. I couldn't fathom a world without my father in it.

He'd had another TIA six months before, over the Christmas holidays, and his confusion had been more marked of late. He had even tried to prepare me for this event in a subtle way. Three days earlier, he'd called me when my mother was out running errands and he was alone. "Skinny One, I think I'm dying," he said quietly.

Instead of asking him if he was afraid or how he felt about it, my stomach had clutched, and I'd stammered, "Why do you think so, Dad? What are your symptoms?"

He listed complaints I'd heard before—that he didn't have any energy and couldn't feel much sensation in his legs.

"Just sit tight," I told him. "I'll call Mom and ask her to take you to the ER."

I'd reached my mother on her cell phone and asked her to hurry home, but by the time she got there, he was already feeling better. He had an appointment with his regular doctor the next day, and they decided to wait instead of going to the ER on a Sunday night. The doctor did an EKG in his office the following morning and took his blood pressure before sending him home. Despite these precautions, there was no prolonging the inevitable. My father's health had deteriorated as had his brain cells. At least he got to go in his own bed and in his wife's arms.

My rational self immediately took over. I called Stefan to tell him what happened and asked him to let Aaron and Elena know since I needed to book a flight and get to my mother as soon as possible.

One of my brothers happened to arrive in Florida around the same time, and we rented a car and drove together to Okeechobee.

When we got to the house, my mother started wailing as she hugged us. Just as she was calming down, one of my sisters walked in, and she fell apart all over again. This happened four more times when each of my siblings arrived.

Still in a state of semi-shock, I tried to hold it together for my mother's sake and went on autopilot, arranging dinner for everyone and scheduling a meeting with the funeral director for the following morning. By then my mother was calm enough to make decisions about which songs she wanted for the funeral mass and which urn to buy for his cremains. She wanted to have an open casket viewing so people could say goodbye to him one last time. My sisters and I chose photos of him to use in a slide show at the viewing, and her friends arranged the funeral mass and lunch in the church hall afterwards.

Stefan drove Aaron and Elena to Okeechobee the day after I got there. It all went by quickly—the church service, the luncheon afterwards, the dispensing of his cremains in several urns. My mother had ordered a large urn to keep in her living room while three of my siblings requested smaller urns to take with them. I didn't want one, preferring to hold on to my memories of him and not the remains of a corpse that wasn't my father.

The most important person and focus of our attentions that weekend was my mother. We hugged her whenever she cried and tiptoed around her when she needed quiet. One of my sisters planned to stay with her in Florida for a week while Nick and I would file insurance claims and take care of business with the estate.

I tried to lift my mother's spirits by promising to take her to Paris in the fall. After they'd retired, she and my father had traveled to holy sites in Rome, Jerusalem, and Medjugorje (a town in Yugoslavia where Jesus's mother had appeared to some children), but she'd never been to Paris and had always dreamed of going.

Grieving for my father would stretch from months to years as my practical side remained in gear. Just back from her trip to Europe with her boyfriend, Elena had opened up one night and told Stefan and me that she'd been reading spiritual books with Jameel, a Muslim. It made her think more about God and reincarnation, and she'd decided that she didn't like who she was when she was partying with her friends. She and I talked about how we fell into bad habits whenever we interacted with each other, and I admitted how hurtful the last couple of years had been. I apologized for reacting in anger too often and tried to make excuses for my behavior. It was a relief to speak frankly with her as she appeared to take it all in.

Following up on our discussion about spiritual books, I tried to tell her about Thich Nhat Hanh's work on forgiveness and compassion and said I hoped we could muster more of both in the future. I cherished the moments of connection we'd had and trusted that it would transcend the phase she was in.

After losing my father, the only way I could get through each day was to remind myself to "chop wood, carry water"—a Zen proverb about engaging in daily tasks instead of dwelling on negative thoughts. I missed hearing my father's voice on the phone, asking me about some medical issue or how the stock market was doing. It was like losing a limb or part of myself that would never grow back, which meant that I'd never feel whole again. I dragged my heavy feet around the house, numb inside while putting on a cheerful face with the many guests who came to stay with us that summer. Each day I'd try to finagle an hour to myself when I could fall apart and cry in my pillow. Then I'd collect myself by getting into my favorite yoga pose with legs up the wall.

I kept reminding myself how lucky he was to have lived as fully as he did to age eighty-five and leave this world the way he wanted to, in my mother's arms; and how fortunate I was to have returned to Atlanta in time to spend the last two years of his life near him. When he'd stayed at my house, I had him all to myself and didn't have to share him with six siblings. We had quietly connected with each other, working in the yard for hours each day and listening to the afternoon news before eating dinner on my deck; and scanning the woods behind our house for owls. He'd told me he was relieved not to be in my shoes and have to worry about upkeep on a house or deal with a teenage daughter, and I was relieved to see that he was happy in his old age.

Kambi messaged me on Facebook one day to ask about the sale of his paintings. When I wrote that my father had just passed away, he immediately wrote back, "I can't talk anymore; I'm crying too hard." It touched me deeply to know that a faraway friend shared my pain.

I was freer to vent my sorrow and process the loss of my father in sleep. Sometimes he'd show up in a dream and his presence would comfort me, except one dream in which I spotted him standing on a street corner in his favorite blue suit and ran over to talk to him. I was about to throw my arms around him when I looked at him closely. He wouldn't open his eyes, and it was then that I realized he was dead. I cried inconsolably in my dream and woke up with tears soaking my pillow, the sense of loss more devastating than ever.

Two months after my father passed, when Aaron was back at college and Elena had started acting school in LA, I flew to Florida and met my mother in the Miami airport. I had booked two round-trip tickets from Miami to Paris since she didn't want to fly alone. It was a good thing I was there since she had a panic attack on the plane.

"I can't breathe," she gasped, gripping my arm and looking at me wide-eyed at takeoff.

"Close your eyes and try to take deep breaths," I told her, clutching her hand. "Count to five as you inhale, then count to five as you slowly breathe out." I scrolled through movies on the screen in front of me and chanced upon some oldies that I thought she'd like. "Hey, Mom, do you want to watch *Philadelphia Story* or *Rear Window* to keep your mind occupied?"

She pointed to *Rear Window* as I plugged her earphones into the armrest. Once it started, she was fine for the rest of the flight. She even fell asleep for a few hours, though there was no sleep for me as usual on a long-haul flight.

After we landed, I managed to get my mother and our luggage to a taxi stand and then to the apartment I'd rented in central Paris. It was a stone's throw from the Musee D'Orsay and just across the Seine from the Jardin de Tuileries. We were lucky to have an elevator to the fourth-floor apartment, although only one of us could fit in it with the luggage.

My mother found the apartment utterly charming. The small sitting area had a half-size dining table and two chairs in front of a window overlooking a central courtyard ringed by other apartment buildings. It faced south and let in plenty of light. We could sit at the table and gaze across the courtyard at the windows of a dozen apartments just like in the movie *Rear Window*.

She sat at the table with her diary and spiritual books while I went off to look for a store to stock up on groceries. In a bakery at the end of our street, I bought a couple of individual quiches and a baguette for supper. Farther on I found a shop that had coffee, milk, and other essentials that would last a few days. After unpacking and settling in, we ate together in front of the window and went to bed early, she in the bedroom and I in a nook with a curtain partitioning it from the sitting room.

Waking early the next morning while my mother slept in, I slipped out of the apartment as soon as it was light and walked to the Seine, crossing a bridge that had little traffic in the early morning. The

Tuileries was the perfect place to stretch my legs, its tree-lined paths and fountains in the middle of a huge metropolis soothing. Gazing at the ivory statues while wandering the empty paths, I let my mind go blank and listened to the sounds of the city waking up. Being alone in nature was my favorite form of quiet time, and the neatly manicured park was the best one could get in central Paris. It was also essential to give my mother a couple of hours to collect herself in the morning by praying and reading her devotionals.

I stopped at the bakery and bought fresh croissants and raisin pastries on my way back to the flat. My mother was sitting at the table with her eyes closed in prayer. With the window open, I could observe a handful of tenants across the courtyard sitting down to breakfast like us.

As soon as my mother saw me, she burst into tears. "What is it, Mom?" I asked, already knowing the answer.

"I miss your father." She wept noisily, her shoulders shaking.

"I know," I soothed, hugging her and getting teary-eyed. "I do too."

This would be our morning routine for the next week—both of us gathering ourselves for the day in our own ways, and my mother venting her sorrow. As soon as we left the apartment, she would become immersed in Paris street life, which captivated her. She especially liked sitting in outdoor cafés and watching passersby while writing postcards.

She was able to handle only one tourist site per day before returning to the apartment to rest. We visited the Musee d'Orsay one day and the Louvre the next; and on a boat trip along the Seine, she was bowled over when we rounded a bend and the Eiffel Tower loomed before us. A bus tour of the inner city was the only way she could see other sites since she couldn't walk far.

Her favorite site was the Notre Dame Cathedral where we attended Mass one day and took a guided tour of the interior and exterior doors and statues. Another day we stumbled on a convent that held the relics of some obscure saint, tucked away in a side street in Saint Germaine. My mother was able to communicate with a nun in broken French, her favorite subject in high school. She jumped at the chance to speak French with taxi drivers, waiters, and people we passed on the street, always ending an encounter with the blessing, "Dieu vous benisse." It caught many French people by surprise since few Americans bestowed blessings on them in their language.

I had to summon a supreme amount of patience to spend so much concentrated time with my mother. She'd often embarrassed me when I was young by dressing in flashy clothes, speaking or laughing loudly, and saying the wrong things. Unlike my father, my mother was an only child who seemed to like being the center of attention. She was like Elena in some ways—an extrovert who'd rather be with people than read a book or garden.

I loved walking the streets and neighborhoods of Paris, which I knew well after a half-dozen visits. But with my mother, I had to amble slowly at her side and let her lean heavily on me. At seventy-eight, she had trouble catching her breath when she walked, probably due to the serious case of tuberculosis she'd had when she was thirty.

It was hard watching her break down in tears every day, although I was glad to be able to comfort her after all she'd done for my father in his last decade. I couldn't mourn him myself when I had to figure out how to get her from one place to the next without pushing her too far, and I needed to be strong since breaking down in front of her might tip her into a crying jag.

At a young age, I had assumed big responsibilities and worries about my parents and siblings. Even in my teens, my mother often came to me for advice and support instead of vice versa. In the past I had resented this role reversal—"parentification" as it's called—and always having to be the stalwart in charge. But now she was truly alone without her husband of sixty years, whereas I had a partner who would walk to the moon and back for me. She was one of the most loving and generous human beings in the world, and I credited her with making each one of her children feel so special that we all thought we were her favorites.

We found a different kind of affinity with each other in Paris—my mother spending several hours every morning in prayer while I did a kind of walking meditation outdoors. She recorded her daily activities and insights in her diary while I found an outlet in poetry and wrote about my father in cryptic verses.

In the end, I couldn't decide whether it was the best of times or the worst of times to take my mother to Paris so soon after his passing. She was fragile and prone to tears and completely dependent on me on foreign soil, without the support of her many friends at church and in her neighborhood. At least the trip knocked her out of her routine, and it fulfilled a lifelong dream.

Things didn't go as Elena had hoped when she moved to LA to be with her boyfriend. Jameel wasn't happy in LA, and he didn't like the college he'd planned on attending. The day after Elena met up with him, he told her he preferred to go to the college his brother had attended in Florida. The two of them fought, and he promptly broke up with her.

Elena took refuge at my sister Tink's house for a couple of weeks, crying herself out before picking herself up and moving on. Tink and her husband were on the verge of separating, and Elena spent much of her time with Joe and the kids.

I flew to LA to help her find an apartment since someone would have to co-sign a lease with her. She agreed to look for a roommate to share the expenses. Our relationship hadn't improved in the short time she'd been away, and she seemed to resent having to rely on me again when she longed for independence. Though I knew the source of her unhappiness was the breakup with Jameel, I was the one in her immediate line of fire, and she'd always found me to be a safe target since I would love her no matter what.

It was a depressing trip, given Elena's attitude and my helplessness as Tink's marriage unraveled. Hoping that their paths would become clear in time, I flew home and plunged into writing. A member of our writing group had suggested that a short story I'd penned, which was set in Zanzibar, could easily stretch into a novel. His suggestion sent me off and running.

Thoughts of my father often caught me unawares. Some days I'd wake up with a malaise that was impossible to shake, only to realize after a while what the source was. Then his loss would come rushing back, and I'd long to hear his voice on the phone or see him pulling the ivy off trees in my yard; find him napping on the sofa in our sunroom or listening to the evening news on NPR. Where had all that lifeforce gone, and how soon would my memories fade?

Stefan still traveled often for his job, and with an empty nest, I was able to accompany him on some of his trips. In February, two and a half years after we moved back to Atlanta, he was asked to go to Tanzania to work for a month. I jumped at the chance to revisit our old stomping grounds and the few friends who remained there.

We stayed in a hotel next to the Yacht Club, where I could wake up and see the bay each day—a scene that had always raised my sights when we were living in Dar. Stefan sat across from me at breakfast one morning after an early swim. "How will you spend your day?" he asked, cutting into his papaya.

"I'm taking our Danish friends to Kambi's studio this afternoon. They want to buy a painting before they move back to Copenhagen, and Kambi asked me to take some paintings to the gallery in Atlanta."

"No more Kambi paintings, please," he protested. "We have enough already."

"They aren't for us. They sold so well last year that the gallery owner wants a few more."

"Anything else on your agenda? No swimming?"

"Maybe when the tide comes in this evening. This morning I'd like to walk to the house where Wilfred is posted."

"How'd you find him?" Stefan asked, mildly surprised.

"I asked someone who works at the same guard company. What about you? A day full of meetings?"

He pulled a long face. "Unfortunately, yes—with our colleagues at USAID." I knew he was referring to the same people who'd made his job difficult when Stefan worked there.

He kissed me goodbye, and I followed him outside to greet the CDC driver who'd just arrived. After they left, I went back to the breakfast table overlooking the beach and opened my notebook. With several hours to myself, I welcomed the chance to write about our return to Dar.

Later that morning, I walked to the house where Wilfred was on duty, and my eyes welled up as soon as I saw him. The look on his face was one of pure astonishment, and he beamed as I moved closer to hug him.

"I am honored that you took the time to find me," he said, his face flushing. "Look, here is the bicycle you gave me! It's still in fine shape."

In fact, the bike looked newer than it had when we got it for him.

When I asked Wilfred about his studies, he told me that he still hadn't passed the test to become an electrician. I was sad for him, knowing how much he wanted to find another trade besides guarding. It was unclear whether he simply wasn't cut out to be an electrician or if working twelve-hour shifts left him too little time to study.

I handed him the books I'd brought for him, knowing how much he loved to read, and we chatted for a while about his family and mine.

"I miss you so much," he said as we parted, "and also Aaron and Elena and Bella."

A sad smile and hearty hug were all I could manage with the lump in my throat.

I met Lucy and her daughter for a late lunch the following day after she got off work. When I asked her how she liked her current employer, she nodded. "She's very nice, and she lets me leave early if I get my work done. Then I have time to watch my grandbaby." She beamed at her grandson who was sitting quietly in her lap.

"Have you started building your house yet?" I asked, recalling that she'd planned to use the severance pay we gave her to buy land on the outskirts of the city.

Lucy shook her head with a downcast expression. "The landowner cheated me. He falsified documents and didn't put my name on the deed."

"Oh, Lucy," I groaned. "Did you try to get a lawyer to help you sort it out?"

"The landowner told me he had a lawyer, and it would be expensive for me to accuse him. I didn't have money to do anything about it."

"I wish you'd told me," I said, though I realized it would have been useless for me to try to help her from far away. I held my tongue while railing inside at wealthy people who cheated the poor out of their meagre savings. No wonder most people found it impossible to get ahead no matter how hard they worked. "So you won't retire anytime soon?"

She shook her head slowly. "Thank God I am in good health and can work."

Later that day I went to the international school to visit the campus and greet teachers. The director invited me and Stefan to dinner at his place, and he invited board members I knew. There were other dinners that week with Stefan's former colleagues as well as lunch dates with Corona members and women who'd attended my writing workshop.

It was a thrill to swim at the Yacht Club beach and walk the streets of our neighborhood again. But old friends like Bodil, Cathy, and Loren were no longer there, and seeing our house made me miss Aaron and Elena even more. It hurt, too, that I couldn't call my father to tell him about the trip and my visit with Kambi.

It hit me then how much we'd lost since leaving Tanzania: a life that we had enjoyed as a family, Stefan's beloved mother and my father, and our children living at home with us. I had to remind myself that our return to Atlanta had been well-timed since it had allowed me to spend my father's remaining years with him, and that it was healthier to love without holding on to people and places too long. It was time to move on and not keep yearning for our time in Tanzania as a family; to treasure the memories of that place without longing for the past.

Chapter 17

The Lure of the Alps

"Would you consider moving overseas again?" Stefan asked me at dinner one evening.

Four years had passed since we'd moved back from Tanzania, and both of us were growing antsy in Atlanta. With no kids at home, the house was too big for us and the yard too much work for me. Most Americans downsized by looking for smaller houses, but Stefan didn't operate that way. In his view, if we were going to move, why not go to another country?

"I'd consider it if we were only one flight away from the kids," I said guardedly. "But not two long flights like we were in Dar." I waited, sensing he had more to say.

"There's a position open in Geneva that I'd like to apply for," he said wistfully.

"Switzerland?" I asked, my mouth dropping. "You'd leave CDC after all these years?"

"I'd be seconded by CDC to the World Health Organization, to lead the hepatitis team."

I sucked in my breath and let it out slowly. "Wow. That would be a game changer."

"I know," he said, his eyes shining. "It sounds exciting."

Geneva sounded exciting to me too. I'd had a similar reaction when he first mentioned moving to Tanzania—an intuition that it might be a leap I was willing to take. While I had never considered living in Geneva before, the thought was tantalizing.

My associations with Switzerland went back to early childhood when *Heidi* (based on a novel by Johanna Spyri) was first dramatized on TV in the 1960s. Images of snowcapped mountains, cows with big bells around their necks, and cabins tucked into precipitous slopes had enchanted me as a child. At age twenty I was just as beguiled when I crossed Switzerland by train, winding through mountains and valleys enroute to Luzern and Lugano. I spent a summer studying German at a language institute in Salzburg, Austria, and my friend Beth and I bought Eurail Passes to travel to neighboring countries. Salzburg was an idyllic town in the Alps made famous by the movie *Sound of Music*. I wondered if Geneva was anything like it.

The past year had brought more losses, from which I was still reeling. Eight months after my father passed away, his older sister Eva was next to go. She had no children of her own, and as her goddaughter, I was closest to her among her many nieces and nephews. I had driven to Florida a few times to see her in recent years and was on my way there when I heard from the hospice people that she'd passed away. I pulled into a rest stop and had a good cry before heading back to Atlanta. In ensuing weeks, I made several more trips to Florida to pack up her condo as the executor of her will.

Next to go had been my sidekick, our sweet dog Bella. At age fourteen, she'd grown senile and was barely able to hobble outside to do her business each day. I knew it was time to let her go, although the thought of losing her broke my heart. Realizing her end was near, Stefan dug a hole in the backyard before leaving for a work trip to South Africa. I phoned our veterinarian and asked her to come to the house one day when Bella would no longer get off her bed. When the vet came, I coaxed Bella to follow me outside one last time and led her to the hole that Stefan had dug. Spreading her blanket inside it, I sat on the ground next to the hole and held her in my lap as the vet administered the shot to put her out. She lay back in my arms and sighed as I rocked her and quietly cried. The vet's assistant—a burly guy—helped me shovel dirt into the hole on top of her. After they left, I went into the house and shut the windows and doors before I knelt by her bed and started howling, letting the grief inside me pour out.

As for the kids, Aaron was only home for a week that summer after his junior year since he'd landed an internship at an aerospace company in Denver, and Elena was still trying to make a go of acting school in LA. With Bella gone, I was more alone than ever in a big empty house.

"Yes, I'd consider moving," I said after a pause. "Go ahead and apply for it."

Stefan was offered the position a few months later, and in May of 2012, we flew to Geneva to look for an apartment. He'd signed an initial two-year contract, and unlike our previous posts in Dar and Abidjan, we had to find our own housing.

Waking up in a hotel in downtown Geneva at the crack of dawn, I couldn't wait to go outside. The sun rose early in mid-May with only a month before summer solstice. Slipping on a windbreaker and walking shoes, I set off to explore the city while Stefan slept in.

As one might expect in a mountain town, Geneva's air was crisp compared to muggy Atlanta. I speed-walked a few blocks to the lake, drawn by the Jet d'Eau—a plume of water shooting up like a geyser in the middle of the port—and the oldtown tucked into the foothills under a backdrop of snowy Alps. What incredible opportunities this place would hold for us: snowshoeing and skiing in winter, hiking in the summer, and a huge lake where we could swim.

We had toured a few apartments the previous day, but I wasn't keen on living in a high-rise in the center of the city. The apartment we were scheduled to visit that morning was in a four-story complex by the lake in the nearby borough of Chambesy. After a quick walk around the oldtown, I returned to our hotel and grabbed breakfast with Stefan before we went house-hunting.

Stepping into an open foyer that led to the living area, I noticed immediately that the apartment was flooded with natural light pouring through sliding glass doors in the living-dining room. The tenant led us onto a narrow balcony that wrapped around the flat to show us the view. Below the building to the south was a pasture that bordered the lawn of a distant mansion. To the east I could see a stand of trees, and through them, Lake Geneva (or Lac Leman as the French call it). The apartment didn't face any other buildings since it was the corner flat on the top floor.

"It's amazing," I said, trying to contain my excitement. "To be in the city and see nothing but fields and trees around you."

"It's the best apartment in the complex as far as privacy and views," the tenant nodded. She led us along the terrace to where it faced the lake and pointed to the mountains beyond it. "In the winter when the trees lose their leaves, you can see Mont Blanc above the mountains and the lake over there." She indicated a dirt path that led away from the building into the nearby stand of trees. "And you can walk to the lake in six minutes along that path."

The promise of a view and proximity to the lake cinched the deal for me. As we exited the building, Stefan and I agreed to go for it.

After we returned to Atlanta, we had two months to figure out which of our belongings to ship to Geneva, which to put in storage, and what to give away. We also had to get the house in shape to rent as we'd done when we were living in Tanzania. I had mixed feelings about leaving our house and friends in Atlanta. Yet the place held too many memories—of our children when they were young, of my father and Bella—and I didn't want to keep dwelling in the past.

Stefan couldn't wait to start his new job in mid-August. He'd always wanted to live in Europe, and Geneva was situated in the heart of it with mountains on both sides. I was eager to travel too, and to explore other countries and cultures again. My only hesitation was that it would be harder to keep tabs on our kids from a distance and help them when they needed us. Elena was floundering after dropping out of two acting programs in LA. Unsure of her next move, she was working in a restaurant part time and wasn't sure if she wanted to stay in LA or move to New York, nor did she know what kind of work she wanted to do.

Aaron would soon graduate from college, and he'd accepted a job with the same aerospace company in Denver where he'd interned the previous summer. He told me privately that it was hard for him to get used to the idea of us living so far away. It tugged at my heartstrings to hear the sadness in his voice. I assured him that we'd return to the US at least twice a year, and that he could come to Europe for summer and Christmas holidays. He perked up at the prospect of skiing in the winter and traveling through Europe in the summer.

My mother, too, had come to rely on having us in Atlanta within a day's drive of her place. She depended on Stefan to give her medical advice and on me for emotional support, as did my sister Tink, who'd separated from her husband. I felt guilty and sorry about leaving them. Yet I was convinced that it was time to live my own life and stop taking on the burdens of my extended family, and to rediscover the joy of travel and making new friends. I wrote in my journal, "If you told the young woman I was at twenty—who got herself to Austria to study German for a couple of months—that she'd be living in the Alps someday after spending a decade in African countries, she'd be incredulous at the opportunities that came her way. I need to free that young woman from too many responsibilities and let her enjoy life while she still can."

We arrived in Geneva in the middle of a heat wave. Temperatures soared into the upper nineties by midday, and our fourth-floor apartment was stifling without air conditioning. My only escape was the lake.

Donning my swimsuit and preparing a thermos of cold water, I exited our building and walked the dirt path to the nearest beach. It was already crammed with people, most of them hugging the shade under a row of chestnut trees. The grassy beach had a bistro at one end of it where people sat in portable chairs, chatting with friends or reading. A few women were topless, which I'd heard was common in the francophone part of the country.

Spreading my towel in the shade, I sat back and gaped at the million-dollar view of the lake and a jagged line of Alps on the far side, with Mont Blanc towering above them. It was too hot to sit still for long, and I made my way down and stepped into the lake. As the cool water engulfed me, all thoughts fell away. With goggles in place, I could scan the shallow bottom and dodge seagrass that tickled my legs. I swam parallel to the shore because of the motorboats that plied the lake and scanned the big houses with docks and grassy lawns bordering them.

The real treat came when I flipped onto my back and gazed around me—at snowy Alps on the far side of the lake and the green flanks of the Jura Mountains behind our apartment complex. I would do a lot of backstroking while swimming in that lake to gawk at the landscape. It was pure bliss to swim in an open lake instead of a crowded pool for a change. The only downside was that immediately after swimming, I had to go straight to an outdoor shower to rinse off and rub my skin vigorously with a towel to dislodge duck fleas; harmless parasites that caused some people to get itchy red bumps that lasted a few days. I'd already discovered that I was susceptible to them, yet nothing could deter me from swimming in that lake.

Refreshed by the swim, I walked back to our apartment and was immediately felled by the heat upon entering. It was ninety-eight degrees in our apartment at 5 p.m. and stifling even with the shades closed since we faced southwest. I ran cold water on a washcloth, placed it on my forehead, and carried a portable fan to a small bedroom that faced north. Spreading my yoga mat on the floor, I lay down and tried to meditate.

A familiar hollow feeling snuck up on me as I lay there. It often surfaced in the late afternoon when I woke up from a nap or sat idly, missing my kids and wondering why I'd moved so far from them. The adjustment period was harder for me than it had been in Ivory Coast or Tanzania since it was the first time we were living overseas without our children. I worried about them constantly.

Thoughts of my father would inevitably intrude during those afternoon reveries. At home I'd been so preoccupied with concerns about my mother, Elena, and Tink that I hadn't really grieved for him. Spending so much time on my own after we moved to Geneva brought his loss to the forefront again. I ached to see him or hear his voice on the phone and felt like I would never stop mourning him. It kindled thoughts of my own mortality since I would soon spend my fifty-ninth birthday in a strange city without any friends around me.

When such loneliness gripped me, I'd remind myself to "lift up my eyes to the hills from whence comes my help" as David wrote in the Psalms. Or as Hafez said, "The place where you are right now, God circled on a map for you." While I wasn't overtly religious, such spiritual proverbs revived my flagging spirits—as did the vistas in that stunning setting.

Stefan returned from work looking happier than I'd seen him in years. Spending long days at the office—mostly in meetings with colleagues—left him tired yet exhilarated from the constant stimulation.

Working in foreign countries always energized him. Yet for me, the kids had been my anchors in Ivory Coast and Tanzania, and this post was much harder without them. It would be a challenge to make friends in Switzerland since the Swiss weren't known for being warm and welcoming to strangers, and there were few opportunities to do volunteer work in Geneva. Unlike in Abidjan and Dar es Salaam, there wasn't a strong sense of community at the US embassy or among Stefan's colleagues, nor were there receptions and private gatherings where spouses were welcome. (The actual US Embassy was in Bern, the Swiss capital, and in Geneva the embassy was smaller and the community more dispersed.)

I'd have to get used to a different scene and daily rhythm to my days, watching the mountains reveal themselves as clouds shifted in the sky outside our wall-length glass doors. Perhaps with fewer responsibilities—no children to cook for, no dog to walk or yard to tend—I'd be able to read and write more. I also wanted to refresh my French by listening to CDs for an hour each day.

As the pace of life slowed, I vowed to take a closer look at things.

I wasn't alone on my birthday as anticipated. Soon after he started working at WHO, Stefan bumped into Peter Ghys, a former colleague from Ivory Coast. Peter worked at UNAIDS, right across from WHO, and he gave Stefan the cell phone number of his wife, Angie. We had seen a lot of each other when we lived in Abidjan, even though Angie was super busy with five children, and we'd had different friends. Our family had enjoyed spending time with theirs at Assini Beach and at dinners with Stefan's colleagues. When we left Abidjan and moved to Atlanta, Peter and Angie had relocated to Geneva.

As soon as I called her, Angie invited us to dinner at their house. They lived in a borough farther up the lake, about fifteen minutes by car. When we pulled into their driveway, Angie came out to greet us with an old dog at her heels. Embracing me warmly, she pointed to the dog and asked, "Do you remember Samba?"

"I can't believe she's still alive." I shook my head, thinking of Bella.

Angie looked the same as she had a dozen years earlier when we'd lived in Ivory Coast. White-blond hair framed her tan face and deep dimples creased her cheeks, permanent fixtures since she smiled all the time. As distinctive as her hair and face were her high-pitched voice and Belgian accent. We complimented each other on how little we'd changed.

Stefan and I greeted Peter in the kitchen, his hands messy from poking fish and veggie chunks onto skewers. He hadn't changed much either and still had a full head of hair, albeit grayer, along with his signature handlebar mustache. His voice was softer than Angie's, yet he too had a strong Belgian accent and deep smile lines.

"What about Aaron and Elena?" Angie asked as soon as we sat down at the picnic table in their yard. "Are they here with you?"

We filled her in on our kids after Peter joined us with a tray of Belgian beers. When talk turned from our children to friends we knew in common, I was surprised to learn that Angie had visited Ivory Coast several times in the last year. The decade-long civil war had ended, and it cost nothing for her to fly to Abidjan since her oldest son was a flight attendant for Brussels Air.

"I always stay with Toma in Assini when I go there. You remember my friend Toma?" Without waiting for an answer, Angie went on, "We're rebuilding the primary school in the village next to Assini. The school went down during the war, and not many kids attended it. I raise money at Christmas markets and fundraisers in Geneva and Brussels with my sister's help, and we started rebuilding the school. You have to come with me and see what we're doing."

"Count me in," I said spontaneously, brightening at the thought of returning to Ivory Coast. "I'm still in touch with Gladys and Ousmane, and I'd love to see them."

Angie and Peter had deeper ties to Africa than Stefan and I did. She'd worked as a nurse in Congo and Rwanda for ten years and met Peter while he was working as a doctor in Congo. Among the many expats I'd known in Abidjan, Angie was one who fit in seamlessly. She spoke fluent French as well as a couple of local languages and managed to bridge the huge gap between her European upbringing and people she met in Ivory Coast. Though she stuck out with her white-blond hair, her body language and confidence enabled her to connect with people of all nationalities and walks of life. I had aspired to be as bold and selfless as she was when we lived in Ivory Coast, although I could never be around as many people each day as she was.

Reconnecting with Peter and Angie and seeing her kids that night was a boost to my spirits. Yet I couldn't help envying Angie her vibrant family life. After living in Geneva for a dozen years, she'd already established deep roots and friendships, and two of her kids, who joined us for dinner, lived nearby.

When we left them at the end of the evening, I hoped that this time around, Angie and I would be closer than we had been in Abidjan, and that her family might make up for the absence of mine. They would certainly be a touchstone to the rich past we'd had in Ivory Coast, and the idea of returning there with Angie intrigued me.

That fall I spent a great deal of time on my own since Stefan worked ten-hour days at his office. Most mornings I'd write, and in the afternoons, I'd explore Geneva and its lakefront on foot or by bike. On weekends, Stefan and I would go hiking—usually in the Jura, which were gentler mountains than the Alps and easier to reach.

Winter came early in that central-European city, and by mid-October it often snowed in the mountains. I wasn't a fan of winter the way Stefan was. He looked forward to snowshoeing and skiing while I dreaded spending hours alone in our apartment during the cold dark months ahead.

Christmas came and went too fast, and I was already missing our kids. Elena had visited for a week, though she had a hard time adjusting to the nine-hour time difference with LA, and she slept until noon each day, hardly leaving the apartment. Aaron stayed longer, but he went off skiing and snowshoeing with Stefan, and I found myself missing him even when he was there. We were invited to Christmas Eve dinner at Angie and Peter's, and our kids were able to reconnect with their kids, reminding us of the Christmas parties they used to host in Abidjan.

To break up the long winter, I hatched a plan to head south for the month of January and do an intensive French course in a town on the Mediterranean. I hadn't spoken French since we'd left Ivory Coast a dozen years earlier, and though I listened to instructional CDs on my own, it embarrassed me to open my mouth and speak French with people in Geneva. When someone at the Embassy told me about a language immersion program in the south of France, it sounded perfect to suit my needs.

Right after Aaron and Elena left, I flew to Nice to start the French course. On the first day of school, I hurried along the cobblestone streets of Villefranche-sur-Mer toward a white villa perched on the highest hill. A prim older woman greeted newcomers just inside the gates of the Instit de Français and directed us to a dining room on the villa's ground floor. Making my way around clusters of adults, I sat down at one of a dozen long tables next to an African American woman about my age. She was speaking English with other adult students, and all of them were welcoming.

We exchanged the usual details about ourselves as the room filled up, and everyone helped themselves to tea and coffee. When the Director called us to attention, he introduced the other teachers in the program, speaking in clear French that was easy for me to understand.

He translated his speech into English and added, "This is the only time you'll hear English spoken in this room. After this morning, you will be fined two euros every time you slip up and speak any language besides French."

I glanced around the table at my fellow students, unsure of what to make of the wiry man who delivered this warning. He went on to describe the daily schedule before passing out a test that would facilitate our placement in the proper class. I got to work, and an hour later the instructors collected our tests and went off to correct them while students stretched their legs.

Ducking outside with Rita, the woman I sat next to, we rambled around the terraced gardens of the villa. It had a spectacular view overlooking the fourteenth-century fishing port where we would be spending the next month. Rita told me she was from Macon, Georgia, and that she and her husband lived in Provence six months out of the year.

We parted ways when classes were in session; but during the break, I made plans to meet Rita and an American man from my class for dinner that evening. Because it was his second stint at the Institute, Greg knew the bistros in Villefranche that served delicious and inexpensive food. He also knew his way around Nice—a half-hour bus ride from Villefranche—and offered to take us on a walking tour on Saturday to see the big outdoor market.

At dinner that first night, the three of us tried conversing in French, although it got increasingly difficult after a glass of wine. We switched to English so I could catch the details of Rita's story. "I was in the first group of Peace Corps Volunteers (PCVs) in 1964 and served in Central America," she told us. "That's where I met my husband, who was a white PCV from Texas. After Peace Corps, I went back to Georgia and worked in the Civil Rights Movement for a while until he joined me. We had to go to Washington, DC to get married since Georgia had laws against interracial unions at the time."

"I met a lot of PCVs when we were living in Ivory Coast," I piped up, "and I have so much respect for them. It sounds like you did some hard things in your life."

She smiled graciously. "There's been a lot of water under the bridge since then. Tell me about your time in Abidjan."

It was a pattern we'd repeat in the coming days and weeks, eating dinner together while speaking French. We'd split up and go our own ways on weekends, when Rita's husband came to visit and Stefan joined me.

I never felt lonely during that month in Villefranche. On the contrary, I welcomed the occasional evenings to myself and would stroll along the beach below Cap Ferrat before returning to my one-room flat for a light supper. The school organized several group dinners and cultural outings, and they showed French movies on Tuesdays in the dining hall. We did wine-tasting at a cave in Nice and a bus trip to the medieval villages of St. Paul de Vence and Tourette-sur-Loup. It was a lot like being in college as we formed fast friendships and met up for drinks or meals after classes.

I was sorry to leave southern France at the end of the month. Temperatures were a good twenty degrees warmer than in Geneva, and there was no snow. Ahead of me were several more months of winter and too-short days, and it would be a long time before I'd see Aaron and Elena again. With a month of intensive French under my belt, I returned to Geneva with more confidence about speaking the language. But after the warmth of the people and climate of southern France, the weather and formality in Geneva seemed chillier than ever.

The constant motion in Villefranche had distracted me from worrying about my kids and other family members. But after I returned to Geneva, when Elena told us she'd dropped out of the Musician's Institute and wasn't working, my concern for her was magnified. Meanwhile Tink's divorce proceedings had turned rancorous, and she was depending on me for advice and support. After talking to Elena or Tink, I'd have to take long walks or meditate to get their problems out of my head.

Getting used to a slower pace of life, I tried to shift my focus to the outside world even though it was cold and gray in Geneva much of the winter. In our glass-walled apartment, I was more aware of the elements outside and watched the clouds race by, studying shades of gray in the sky and waiting for the mountains to reveal themselves if the sun appeared, or searching for planets in the dark sky if it was a clear night. My fondest wish in the new year was to settle into that quiet space and write. The moment had arrived, and it was now or never.

Chapter 18

Bittersweet Blessings of a Swiss Sojourn

"Hey, Skinny One," my father called in his raspy voice. "Yeah, Dad?" I responded automatically, sitting up in bed. Glancing around, I was surprised to see Stefan asleep beside me.

It was dark outside at 4 a.m. on the first day of spring in Jerusalem. As I sank back in the bed and pulled up the covers, my father's presence was still palpable and alarming. It seemed fitting that he would visit me in the ancient city where he and my mother went on a pilgrimage two years before he died. They had toured a handful of "holy sites" after he retired, Israel among them. Now I was in Jerusalem with Stefan, who was there to attend a hepatitis conference.[25]

Later that morning, as we entered the lodge's breakfast room, I made a beeline for a tall Swiss woman who was seated at one of the tables. Veronica—Vero as she told us to call her—was an accompanying spouse like me, and we'd instantly clicked at dinner the previous evening. It was one of those meetings where an onlooker might think we'd known each other for years, the way we leaned towards each other and talked nonstop, laughing a lot. At six feet tall, she had shoulder-length grayish-blond hair and steel-blue eyes that seemed vulnerable and attentive at the same time.

Over breakfast, Vero and I made plans to visit Jerusalem together that day. We asked the lodge manager how to get to the city, and he offered to drive us himself for a small fee.

Vero and I made the most of our time with him. His demeanor was warm and open, and we felt free to ask him questions about his family and about the political situation in the country. He told us what it was like to be part of a small minority—he was a Messianic Jew, a group that numbered fifteen thousand in a country of seven million—and how they interacted with other Israelis and with Palestinians.

The manager walked us through the Museum of Israel and pointed out the Dead Sea Scrolls and other artifacts from ancient history. Since attendees at the hepatitis conference would take a guided tour of old Jerusalem later in the week, he drove us instead through a couple of villages that were outside the city and off the beaten tourist track. It was a privilege to share his insider's view of Israeli society and politics and the kind of opportunity I relished as an expat living overseas, interacting with local people who could offer insights into the culture.

The following day Vero and I hopped on a bus and headed to Tel Aviv to go shopping. We had fun browsing in shops, including a crafts cooperative. Eventually we ducked into a café to grab something for lunch.

Growing lazy after lunch, we ambled down to the beach and found a spot where we could rest in the sun. Vero had thought to bring a small travel blanket that she spread on the sand for the two of us. Gazing at the sea and watching people on the beach, we talked about our families and the types of work we'd done. She was a semi-retired nurse who was doing volunteer work as a sex counselor to people with disabilities. Like me, she had complicated relationships with her mother and her adult daughter. She was thoroughly Swiss even though she'd been raised in Brazil after her grandfather emigrated from Switzerland and started a sugarcane plantation. Small wonder that she didn't conform to the stereotype of Swiss people as cold and aloof with foreigners.

After a couple of hours, we strolled along the beach towards Jaffa where we were to meet up with the rest of the conference attendees for a walking tour of the old port city. By the time we sat down to dinner in a harbor restaurant that evening, Vero and I were exhausted yet exhilarated after a day of walking and talking.

In subsequent days at meals and outings, we broached deeper subjects beyond the exchange of information about ourselves and our families. I could tell we were going to be good friends. We spoke the same language in more ways than one—mostly in English since hers was more fluent than my French.

After the trip to Israel, Vero invited us to join her and her husband at their weekend retreat in the Alps. It took two hours to drive from Geneva to their chalet-condo above the town of Aigle. Daniel built a fire in their wood-burning stove while Vero made raclette and told us about activities in Morges, the town just outside Geneva where they resided. Vero promised to invite me to the tulip festival in Morges during the month of May.

Our friendship deepened as we found ourselves in other foreign cities together when our husbands attended conferences. We were both brooders and soul-searchers who talked openly about our spiritual paths, how we found meaning in life, and how we made peace with our pasts. Vero shared her favorite books that had metaphysical dimensions to them, and I'd talk about my writing and novels that moved me.

She was the first real friend I made in Geneva, and she went out of her way to welcome me into her very full life. It was a friendship that anchored me and gave me a sense of belonging, which had been hard to achieve in Switzerland. Without my children nearby or other family ties, friends like Vero and Angie took on greater importance in my life.

Searching for other opportunities to get out of the apartment, I took yoga classes at the Embassy and sometimes stayed after to have lunch or tea with the teacher. I also joined the Geneva Writers Group, which brought writers together from all parts of Switzerland once a month to hear speakers and do writing workshops. It was helpful to be in the company of other writers, and I befriended an American woman married to a Swiss national who had children and grandchildren nearby.

It was up to me to make the most of my solitary existence in Geneva, and I did my best to make friends and connect.

Our first full summer in Switzerland was a blur as other people's needs took precedence. In May I flew to LA on two days' notice when my sister Tink had another crisis. She'd been depressed and had started drinking heavily since she and her husband separated, alone much of the time when her children were at their father's place. It broke my heart to see my fun-loving sister that way. She desperately wanted to stay in her house.

On the fourth day of my visit, I suggested we look for another place for her to live since the monthly mortgage was steep and she had no job prospects or source of income. Her husband was also unemployed at the time and wouldn't be able to pay her alimony. He was considering a move to Virginia where he had friends and better job prospects.

"I'll find a way to pay the mortgage myself," she insisted. "I'm not leaving my house."

"Mom and I have been paying your bills for a year since he moved out," I reminded her, "and $3,000 a month is too much for us when we have our own house payments. A smaller place would be easier for you to maintain, and it wouldn't have so many memories."

Our conversation was cut short when she started shaking violently and vomiting. After three hours of retching, she finally let me call her doctor, and he advised us to go to the ER.

In the waiting room, she shook uncontrollably and asked me repeatedly with fear in her eyes, "Am I going to die? I really don't want to die."

"You're not going to die," I tried to reassure her.

Before long a nurse led us inside, and an ER doctor did a quick exam. Results from her blood tests showed that her electrolytes were dangerously low, and they put her on an IV and admitted her. Tink ended up spending three days in the hospital with what her doctor termed nervous exhaustion. Relieved of her burdens for a time, she admitted that things had to change.

While Tink was in the hospital, I took Elena to lunch and broached a difficult subject with her too. "An acting career in LA doesn't seem to be working for you," I said tentatively.

"It's a lot harder than I thought, trying to get auditions and make a living at the same time," she agreed.

"You gave it a good try for three years. Maybe it's time to let yourself off the hook and try something else?"

She sat back in her chair and sighed. "I'm not even sure I like living in LA. I didn't like acting school, and I hated auditioning." Saying nothing, I waited for her to continue. "It would be a relief to get out of here and do something else besides acting."

I nodded. "You're increadibly resilient when it come to starting over in a new place. I don't know anyone who's as good at it as you are, apart from Dad."

Elena would later say that she had an epiphany that day, and that she didn't care enough about acting to stay in LA.

After Tink was released from the hospital, we started looking for a place for her to live and bought plastic bins to pack up her house. I returned to Geneva utterly exhausted and could do nothing for days except sit on our terrace and stare out at the view.

But it was a pipe dream to think I could rest after helping my sister and daughter with hard choices. My mother came to visit for two weeks in June with my sister Mary, and they were completely dependent on me for everything from meals to sightseeing excursions and trips to other Swiss cities. In the middle of their visit, Elena called us at 5 a.m. and said she was stuck on the side of a road in LA with no money. She'd had a fight with her closest friend, who had taken her car keys after Elena was drinking. We asked Stefan's brother—who lived nearby—to pick her up.

While she was with his brother's family, Elena told us she couldn't stay in LA because the temptation to party with her friends was too great. We bought her a ticket to Dallas after my brother and his wife offered to put her up until she could figure out what she wanted to do. (Nick and Amy were also the ones who'd sheltered my brother Mike when he went through his crisis.) Relieved to be around family again, Elena decided to look for a job and an apartment in Dallas.

In July I flew to LA to help Elena drive her car and belongings to Dallas. She gave away most of her furniture and fit everything she wanted to keep in her Volkswagen Jetta. We did the drive in three days, talking occasionally but mostly listening to music. She was still sullen around me and not particularly grateful since she hated having to rely on us again.

At dinner in a hotel restaurant, she voiced her unhappiness. "I'm tired of being treated like a child when I just want my independence from you and Dad, and also your respect."

Stunned, I tried to respond to her underlying wishes and not to what felt like an attack. "Our relationships will change once you have a real job and control over your own money, and you don't have to ask us for help," I said tentatively. "You interview so well, I'm sure you'll get a good job quickly." She was quiet for the rest of the meal, yet it felt like we'd connected and understood each other for a fleeting moment.

The highlight of that summer was meeting Stefan and Aaron in a mountain town near Denver, where we spent a week hiking in the Rockies. From there we flew to LA for a beach vacation with Stefan's brothers and their families. It was a noisy week and hardly relaxing as beach vacations could be. After it, I spent another week in LA, helping Tink get her house ready to sell and looking for a place for her to live.

By the time I returned to Geneva at the end of August, I was relieved to be back in our quiet apartment, even though it was hard to get used to being alone after the tumultuous summer. I woke up one morning before dawn and noticed a solitary light in the sky over Mont Blanc. The North Star glittered above the lake and lifted my sights, filling me with an awareness of the vastness and beauty around me.

At such moments, alone in a distant northern city, I couldn't help thinking about my father. It struck me that distance—like time—was whatever we made of it in our minds, and that it was an illusion to think it had a vice grip on us. Was death the same? Was it possible that the non-physical was as real and present as its opposite? Was my father always out there in some form like the North Star, even though it was often hidden by clouds? If so, I could embrace his presence when I felt alone and far from my family and friends.

When the Geneva Writers Group solicited members' work for a literary journal, I submitted a poem that I'd written about my father, and it was published the following year. It was one among dozens of poems that came unbidden after his passing.[26]

During our sojourn in Geneva, Stefan made it his goal to hike the entire Jura Crest Trail, which runs 220 miles from Geneva to Zurich. It was what he loved most about living in Switzerland: the easy access to mountains by public transport. At the first sign of snow in the Jura, he'd strap snowshoes and poles to his backpack and take a couple of trains into the mountains. I joined him on occasion, although he could walk twice the distance I could in a day and with a heavy backpack. I often encouraged him to go on his own so he could accomplish his goal of hiking the entire Jura Crest Trail.

In October, with no visitors or trips pending, I joined him for a hike along one segment of the trail. We drove to Chasseral mountain and spent the night in a lodge to get an early start for a twelve-mile hike the following day. It would involve six hours of walking and three more of taking trains, postal buses, and gondolas to complete the trek and return to our car.[27]

When we set off on Sunday morning, the fog was so thick we couldn't see much from the top of Le Chasseral, a five-thousand-foot peak overlooking Lake Biel between Bern and Geneva. An hour into the hike, the sky suddenly cleared and bright sun illuminated the breathtaking views. We could see three lakes—Neuchatel among them—and beyond them a jagged line of Alps in the distance. The hiking was as good as it gets—along a gentle ridge with sweeping views all around us—yet we couldn't stop to enjoy the vistas for long since we had to make it to a train at the end of the trail by 3 p.m.

The last hour of the hike was the most grueling as well as the most stunning. We had to maintain a brisk pace down sheer slopes made slick by fallen leaves. While my hip bursitis was a thing of the past, my knees ached as we wound our way down scores of switchbacks in the hilly forest. With the afternoon sun spotlighting yellow-gold and rust-tinted leaves, I would have loved to lie down in the autumn leaves and watch the light play on the trees for an hour. But we had to push on and plunge down a forest path with steep canyons on either side of the narrow ridge, descending almost three thousand feet in an hour.

We reached a deserted railroad platform with only minutes to spare before boarding the three o'clock train to Biel. From there, a connecting train deposited us at the spot where a gondola would carry us back up the mountain to a bus stop. Hopping on the last bus of the season, we returned to Chasseral Lodge just as the sun was setting. I had to marvel at the punctuality of Swiss transportation and at Stefan's planning.

When our kids came for Christmas that second year, Aaron joined Stefan for ski and snowshoe excursions while Elena hung around the apartment or went shopping. We took a few trips together to visit Christmas markets in neighboring towns, but there was no Christmas dinner with Angie's family since they were spending the holidays in Ivory Coast. I planned to take Angie up on her offer and join her there after New Year's.

By the time the kids left and the holidays were over, I was more than ready for a vacation that didn't involve snow. Visiting Angie in Ivory Coast for a couple of weeks was a perfect way to break up the long winter in Geneva. I looked forward to returning to a warm sunny place that had once been our home and seeing some of the people we'd regretted leaving fifteen years before.

Angie sent a driver to pick me up at the airport and take me to the small hotel where she always stayed outside of Assini. The beach town was an hour from Abidjan, the same place where her family had once owned a beach cabana or *paillote*.

Toma, the hotel manager and Angie's friend, greeted me in the lobby and showed me to my room. The hotel was only two stories, and each room had a door opening onto an outside corridor with ocean views. Angie had arrived in Ivory Coast two weeks before me, and everyone in the village knew she was there.

She reminded me of a village chief as people lined up in the morning to seek her advice on family matters or issues related to the school she was renovating. It was a startling contrast to life in Switzerland, where each day was carefully scripted and people called in advance if they wanted to see you. Here, villagers wandered into the lobby to wait for Angie to appear in the morning. She barely had time to finish her coffee before receiving the first visitors of the day.

A pregnant woman sat down at our table and told Angie she was worried about the position of her fetus as her due date approached. Angie promised to drive her to a clinic in the nearest town later that morning. Next came a shy schoolboy of ten or twelve who gripped his cheek with his hand and complained of jaw pain. He begged Angie to help him find a dentist, and she told him to send his father to see her that afternoon. After the boy left, she received a massage therapist named Nadesh. Angie had promised to help Nadesh expand her business by getting the village chief's permission to set up a wellness center. Nadesh invited us to eat dinner with her husband and six children later in the week, and we gladly accepted.

Last in line was the handyman in charge of renovating the primary school, which was just across a dirt road from the hotel. Angie conferred with him about work to be done that day and supplies she'd need to buy. The handyman went off to work on his projects, and Angie was finally able to eat her breakfast.

As soon as we finished eating, she got up to take the pregnant woman to the clinic while I set off on a long beach walk. Reveling in the warm air, I plodded along the beach where we'd spent many Sundays with our kids at Angie's paillote. The beach hadn't changed much, although most of the old structures had been demolished to make room for bigger homes.

Strolling the beach, I couldn't help pining for close family times when Aaron and Elena were small. My steps slowed and I breathed deeply into a space behind or below my heart—a hollow space that had once been filled by children. In those days I had to plan all my activities around them and was never free of worry that something bad might happen to them. It had been a time of simple needs when the children were easy to please. They were happy to stay home with me or have friends over for playdates, and happy to go to a pool or the beach when Stefan was free. Their wishes were easy to fulfill, and they'd wanted me nearby. It had been our closest time as a family, especially the Sundays we spent at the beach. I treasured the memory of those days with my children and the hours we'd pass together building sandcastles and playing in the surf.

My heart was heavy as I recalled how much I'd loved being with my children. Never again would we find ourselves together as we'd been in Ivory Coast. The loss seemed as profound as my father's passing; days that were long gone and couldn't be reclaimed.

The following day, Angie took me to the house of the local Imam whose baby she had delivered on a recent visit. We were invited to the traditional Muslim baptism for the baby that would be followed by a feast. As we walked up the road, Angie recounted how she'd driven the Imam's wife to a maternity clinic after her water broke. "No one was on duty when we got there, so I had to deliver the baby myself."

"Was it hard to deliver a baby after a long hiatus from nursing?" I asked her.

"It's like riding a bicycle," she grinned. "You never forget something like that."

The Imam greeted Angie as if she were a war hero, pressing her hand in both of his. We went to sit with the women who were preparing food and tending small children on one side of the unpaved road while the men prayed on the other side. After the customary butchering of a goat, we listened to the Imam offer prayers in which he thanked Angie for delivering his baby.

Grateful to be included in the feast, I listened to Angie converse with the women in rapid French. She was completely at home with them, dressed in an Ivorian boubou and holding the baptized baby in her lap. The sensory pleasures of being back in Ivory Coast were inundating: voices bantering in Ivorian French, the vibrant colors of the women's garments, the spicy sauces served with mutton and greens. The savory smells and tastes brought back more rich memories of our time there.

The next day Angie drove me to Abidjan so I could spend a few hours with Gladys and Ousmane. At the maquis where we met for lunch, I teared up as soon as I saw them. Ousmane chuckled when he saw the tears in my eyes, while Gladys's cheeks were as wet as mine.

Instead of filling me with nostalgia for old times, being with them was so energizing I could hardly eat. They wanted to hear all about Aaron and Elena and see photos of them while I asked about their current jobs and how their children were doing. The time passed so quickly that it surprised me when Angie came to retrieve me after her errands. There were more tearful hugs like the last time we parted, not knowing when we'd see each other again.

Angie drove me around our old neighborhood haunts, and it surprised me to see how crowded Abidjan had become. Despite a decade of civil war, the population had doubled in the fifteen years since we'd left Ivory Coast. My neighborhood had lost many of the trees that had made it a balmy oasis as new houses and shops went up. New buildings were going up all over the city, and immigrants from neighboring countries were still flocking to Abidjan to look for jobs.

It was heartwarming to learn that treatment was now available to anyone who tested positive for HIV, and that those on medication could expect to live normal lives without developing AIDS. The US Government had already spent billions of dollars to provide testing, counseling, and treatment for people infected with HIV in African countries. As a result, over half the people in Ivory Coast who were infected with HIV were getting free treatment.

The other good news was that the African Development Bank—which had pulled out of Abidjan during the civil war, taking thousands of professionals with it—had returned to Ivory Coast and brought new investments, professionals, and jobs for local staff. I was delighted to see that the international school our children had attended in the 1990s had reopened on its former campus after serving as a base for UN peacekeeping troops during the war. By 2014, the country was once again an economic powerhouse in West Africa.

On our last day in Ivory Coast, the real village chief came to see Angie and inspect the ongoing renovations at the school. After raising fifty thousand euros in Geneva and Brussels, Angie had built the first pre-school in the village as well as a clinic that doubled as a community center. The school had grown from fewer than a hundred students in 2011, when renovations began, to over four hundred three years later. Angie planned to enlarge classrooms, build a cafeteria, and add more housing for teachers. Toma would supervise the projects when Angie was in Europe.

The village chief—a short jowly woman in her eighties—shuffled into the lobby wearing a headwrap and colorful cloth around her waist. She was accompanied by a bodyguard who doubled as her counselor. Aside from settling disputes among the villagers, the chief had the power to determine what businesses could operate in the village and how much land would be allocated to them. After offering the chief something to drink, Angie led her across the dirt road to the school. She showed her the water spigots that had just been installed along with the first toilets—a novelty that spared the children from having to relieve themselves in the bush. Next, Angie led her through the clinic/community center, and the chief grunted her approval.

As we approached a shabby building at the edge of school grounds, Angie explained that the building would be partitioned into housing for two teachers and their families, earning another nod of approval. When Angie asked the chief how far school grounds could extend for added projects, the woman stuck her cane in the ground to signal her decision. Though it fell short of what Angie was hoping, she thanked the woman and didn't question her judgment. The chief then waved at us to signal she was done and shuffled off to her compound.

All too soon, it was time for us to return to Switzerland. Angie and I planned to fly to Brussels together, where she'd stay with her son while I would hop on a connecting flight to Geneva. When our suitcases were stowed in the car, I got to watch Angie in action one more time. She ducked into the hotel kitchen to thank the staff for their services and send greetings to family members she knew. Then she gave Nadesh money for her wellness clinic and handed the remaining funds for school projects to Toma. After hugging everyone goodbye, Angie climbed in the car and headed to the airport with a dozen hands waving her off.

Instead of a beach vacation, the trip had been an opportunity to revisit the past and immerse myself in a country and culture I had treasured. I was especially glad to have seen Gladys and Ousmane again, recalling how much those relationships had meant to me and my children. The stark contrast with life in Geneva—where I spent long days alone in a sterile apartment—made it hard to return to that austere existence.

Alarm bells went off in my head when I read a notice in the lobby of our building soon after my return from Ivory Coast. It laid out plans for renovating the exteriors of all four buildings in the apartment complex. A Gantt chart showed that work on our building would take four months and be completed in July.

It was an exciting time at Stefan's work since new drugs had just been introduced that could cure people of hepatitis C.[28] His team at

WHO was setting the guidelines that all countries would be advised to follow on treating hepatitis B and C. Because the first guidelines were about to be issued in 2014 and would have to be tweaked in subsequent years, Stefan wanted to renew his contract and stay at WHO for another year or two. I agreed to the extension, knowing how much he loved living in Switzerland; and I knew this would be our last chance to explore Europe before moving back to the US.

We didn't consider relocating to another apartment since renovations on our building were only supposed to take four months and we only planned to stay in Geneva for another year. Instead, I made plans to fly to the US for summer vacation earlier than usual and stay for several months with the hope that renovations would be finished by the time I returned.

When the scaffolding went up around our building in March, it felt like we were being entombed as workmen stacked floor tiles, insulation foam, and other building supplies on our terrace, blocking us in. We could no longer see out our sliding glass doors and windows, and we had to keep our curtains closed 24/7 because of the workmen trooping by all day. I couldn't stay in the airless apartment and write, nor could I stand the constant noise as they'd start drilling and pounding on our walls at 7 a.m. and wouldn't quit until 5 p.m. each day.

I fled in May and spent two months in the US with my family and friends. When I returned to Geneva in July, it was a rude surprise to find that our terrace was still full of construction debris, and they hadn't made much progress. The floors hadn't been retiled, nor had the Gantt chart been updated with a revised timeline. Worst of all was the fact that we couldn't open our sliding glass doors and windows in the summer heat. Unable to work in the airless apartment, I sought refuge in the WHO library and public parks for the remainder of the summer.

Chapter 19

So Long, Switzerland

L olling on the banks of Lake Thun outside of Interlaken, I had an inkling of what heaven on earth might be like. The temperature was a hundred degrees, and everywhere else was stifling as Stefan and I waded into the cleanest lake in Switzerland (according to our guide-book). Adjusting our goggles, we plunged into the cool water and did our usual half-mile swim.

Hunger was the only reason we were motivated to leave the lake that afternoon. Pulling on our clothes, we drove into Thun and ambled along the city's cobbled streets until we found a deli where we could buy sandwiches. We wolfed them down at a sidewalk café, but the heat was so oppressive that we couldn't linger for long. Stumbling into Thun Castle to escape the heat—it was one of the few places with air conditioning—we did a tour of the little museum. Then we walked to a fourteenth-century church and climbed the tower to get a bird's eye view of the medieval town. Again, we didn't linger on account of the heat and had to retreat to the cobbled streets to stroll along the river in late afternoon.

As we approached a stone bridge, we noticed a handful of young people jumping off it into the rapidly flowing River Aare. Stefan immediately started removing his hat and glasses, a big grin on his face. I stared at him as if he were mad. "You're not thinking of joining them?"

"Why not? It's hot."

"It's a big drop from the bridge," I said, peering over the stone balustrade. It was at least thirty feet, and I didn't like the looks of it.

"Could you hold my wallet and keys?" he asked, thrusting both into my hands. I watched wordlessly as he climbed on the balustrade and paused before jumping into the churning water. He was carried swiftly downstream to a bridge several blocks away, where he climbed out as the youths were doing and made his way back to me.

"Was it fun?" I asked.

Grinning from ear to ear, he climbed onto the bridge and plunged into the bracing river again.

It was our third summer in Geneva when temperatures hovered in the upper nineties for weeks. The *canicule*, or "heat wave," even made international news.[29] Like us, few people in Switzerland had air conditioning, which made it miserable to be in the city and hard to sleep at night. Thus, we fled the city every weekend to escape the heat as well as the noise and dust from the renovations around our building.

From Lake Thun, we drove to Grindelwald and spent three nights in a VRBO rental. The condo's balcony overlooked a scenic river valley and faced the Eiger, a legendary mountain among avid climbers. We ate all our meals on the balcony to gawk at the view, and we took long hikes in the mountains each day.

The renovation work on our building wasn't finished until late September, and they only removed debris from our terrace and the scaffolding in October. Disturbing noises and unsightly debris around the complex didn't disappear as work on other buildings continued throughout the winter. There was no reprieve from a constant rumble of dump trucks and tractors below our apartment, or from drilling and pounding on the buildings behind ours. All winter we had to walk by dumpsters overflowing with trash and construction debris in common areas, dodging trucks and tractors as we traipsed the muddy paths to and from our building.

That third year had been packed with travel and literally flew by. Aaron and Elena had come for the holidays, which we'd spent in Poland with Stefan's relatives. In January I fled for a few weeks to Africa again, this time returning to Tanzania with my former school-board mate and friend Cathy. We spent a blissful week in Zanzibar and another week revisiting our old haunts in Dar where I got to see Lucy, Wilfred, and Kambi. It was a joy to swim at the Yacht Club beach again and take walks around the peninsula with Cathy.

One year after the scaffolding had been erected, we were still plagued by construction noise and unsightly debris in the courtyards through the spring. I'd developed a chronic sinus infection on account of the dust and dirt, and the constant noise and garbage soured me on the country and made me want to leave. Yet it was an exciting time at Stefan's work as his office was updating the new hepatitis C guidelines. His boss asked him to extend his contract, and Stefan asked me if I'd be willing to spend one more year in Geneva. I reluctantly agreed, telling myself that I could stay with friends or family in the US when I needed to escape.

My other motivation was that I wanted to see as much as possible before our sojourn in Europe ended, knowing that this would be our last post overseas. I took Henry Miller's words to heart: "Develop an interest in life as you see it: the people, things, literature, music—the world is so rich, simply throbbing with rich treasures, beautiful souls and interesting people. Forget yourself."

Whenever Stefan had to travel for conferences or meetings, I leapt at the chance to accompany him. In March we flew to Turkey for a week, and in April we went to Austria for another meeting. Vero and I explored Istanbul and Vienna together, sampling pastries and ducking into museums and parks for long walks and talks. In May, Stefan and I spent a week with our Norwegian friends Bodil and Cam on the island of Crete. All four of us did an arduous ten-mile hike through the Samaria Gorge and capped it with a dip in the Libyan Sea.

In June, I flew to the US for two family weddings. While stateside, I spent a difficult week with Elena, who was unhappy in Dallas and started having panic attacks. My brother identified a therapist who might help her find her path. Tink was struggling too, with no direction for her future or what work she might want to do.

It was impossible to leave such cares behind when I returned to Switzerland, especially with my mindset on worry. Torn between embracing expat life and wanting to help loved ones at home, I found the familiar push-pull to be wrenching. When I thought about Tink and Elena, I became anxious and wanted to be closer to them in the US. Yet living far from them restored my perspective and allowed me the peace of mind to write.

Aaron joined us for a weeklong tour of the Engadin Valley that summer. I'd wanted to visit the distant Swiss province ever since I read a rapturous description of it in Stefan Zweig's novel *Post Office Girl*. Yet the book hadn't prepared me for the splendor of the narrow valley encased by precipitous mountains on both sides.

The three of us drove to the distant city of Chur—reputed to be the oldest town in Switzerland—where we spent the night before entering the Engadin. Descending via the Julier Pass, we breezed through Davos and St. Moritz with little interest in stopping. Ritzy St. Moritz had been a destination for Victorian tourists in the 1800s, and nearby Davos became famous because of the jetsetters and politicos who attended the World Economic Forum. But long before those towns became hotspots for the rich and famous, writers and artists had been charmed by the deep valleys and towering peaks of the Engadin.

Our destination was the tiny town of Silvaplana, which was situated on an emerald lake known as the kitesurfing capital of Switzerland. As a novice windsurfer, Aaron's eyes lit up when he saw scores of kites and windsurfers skimming across the lake.

Our rental was an ideal base for mountain hikes, nestled as it was in the foothills overlooking the lake. One day we took a cable car to the top of a mountain above our condo, and from a platform at eleven thousand feet, we hiked along a ridge bursting with wildflowers. Aaron ran circles around me, jogging down the steep slopes as the clang of cowbells drifted up from hillside meadows with the jade lake in view below. After two days of hiking, Aaron decided to try his hand at windsurfing. Stefan watched him skate back and forth across the lake at frightening speeds while I found a sprawling pool in St. Moritz where I could swim laps.

There were more hidden gems as we drove further into the Engadin, through ancient towns where people spoke a dialect— Romansch—that was like an amalgam of Swiss German and Italian. Along the way we explored castles perched above the winding road as well as tiny hamlets like Scuol and Susch with their cobbled streets and ancient squares.

Vero had advised us not to miss the scenic train that went up and over the Bernina Pass to Italy. Following her advice, we spent a night in Pontresina on the Swiss side of the border before boarding the train the following day. We were glued to its windows for hours while gawking at glaciers and cliffs that fell away on either side of a deep chasm as the train climbed to a meadow and lake at the summit. The train stopped at the top of the pass long enough to allow passengers to take photos before it chugged down into a verdant valley on the Italian side. We spent a couple of hours in Tirano, where we ate pizzas and ducked into shops before boarding a train for another heart-stopping ride back up and over the Bernina Pass.

The Engadin adventure was one of the highlights of our rambles through Switzerland; an awe-inspiring journey through storybook landscapes. Such trips made me forget my unhappy living situation in Geneva, as did the many friends who came to visit us in Switzerland.

After a summer full of trips and visitors, I spent most days alone in our apartment during our fourth year there. I would write in the mornings and walk or exercise in the afternoons. Then I'd meditate while waiting for Stefan to come home at the end of each day. Some days the only people I spoke to were cashiers in the grocery store or lifeguards at the pool.

I had hoped that my friendships would sustain me during that lonely time, but Vero and I only managed to see each other once a month, given the distance between Geneva and Morges and the neediness of Vero's mother. Angie, too, was often unavailable because of family demands in Brussels and her frequent trips to Ivory Coast.

I'd come to associate Geneva with a profound loneliness that only deepened with time. Loneliness grips you when you feel isolated and disconnected from the setting and people around you. My loneliness in Geneva had a lot to do with circumstances—our newly empty nest, the loss of my father, the problems of family members far away—and it was exacerbated by the weather and our sterile surroundings. The renovation fiasco at our apartment complex—which dragged on for a year and a half—was the crowning blow.

Loneliness also implies a longing for something or a desire to be somewhere else. That somewhere had a lot to do with the people I worried about, yet it also had to do with a sense of belonging. I longed to feel at home and part of some community, which was impossible in our complex since most of the neighbors were foreigners like us and only stayed for a year or two. Occasional walks with a writer friend, Jane, and with Vero and Angie hadn't been enough. If my children had been with me in Geneva as they were at our other posts, I would have been much busier; or if I had an office job, I might have mingled with colleagues and got out of the apartment more. But in overseas posts, there were strict laws about work permits, and spouses of people with jobs at international agencies weren't allowed to work outside the home.

I didn't tell Vero how often I felt lonely in her country. It was something I had to reckon with in myself, and I knew that the situation would end when we moved back to the US. Vero had her hands full with her ninety-year-old mother who called several times a day begging her to come over with food or medications. She also had two adult children living nearby.

Compounding my loneliness were long-standing concerns about Tink and Elena, with my mother also weighing on my mind. Despite a few good friends and the stunning landscapes in Switzerland, my mindset was worry and there was no shaking me out of it.

Perpetual gray skies in winter didn't help. Because Geneva is situated in a bowl between two mountain chains, clouds would hover over the city for weeks. The winter was relentlessly gloomy, and the cloud cover and cold often lingered into May. I was prone to brooding and self-searching anyway, and the weather had a big effect on me.

The despair that accompanied my sense of alienation usually lifted when I lost myself in meditation. It was the surest way to loosen the grip of ego and its attendant anxieties. My perspective would also broaden when I left the apartment to take a walk or a bike ride. As Essayist Pico Iyer observed in a 2013 TED Talk, "When you live in a foreign place, you can't help being jolted awake every time you step outside your door and take in your surroundings. The beauty of being surrounded by the foreign is that it slaps you awake, and you can't take anything for granted."

I'd known beforehand that living overseas wouldn't always be fun and easy, and I was profoundly grateful for the many experiences I had in Switzerland. But with an eye on my own mortality and my mother's and sister's, I preferred to live closer to the people who needed me.

I had agreed to Stefan's request that we spend another year in Geneva because he loved living in Switzerland and was immersed in his work, and because I still wanted to travel in Europe. He would have liked to stay a fifth year, but he didn't balk when I said I had enough. My chronic sinus infection wasn't getting better, and I was too worried about people at home.

It was Stefan's idea to sign up for weekly salsa dance classes in the center of Geneva. On the first night of class, he walked to town from his office while I biked along the lake to meet him for dinner at an Italian bistro we liked. After eating, we strolled up a side street and found the salsa class in the basement of a dingy jazz club.

The teacher was warming people up by doing exercises to salsa music. We were the oldest attendees among several couples in their fifties and a handful of younger singles. The Puerto Rican teacher, who had a quick wit and was smooth on his feet, dared to call Stefan "Papa." Bristling at first, Stefan eventually warmed to him, and the nickname became a private joke between them. We changed partners often during the ninety-minute session, and I relished the chance to dance with the teacher, who whirled me deftly. It was a good workout and also fun.

On our walk home along the lake, Stefan and I stopped several times to admire the city lights reflecting off the water. The beauty of the foreign did indeed slap us awake at such moments. We reminded each other how lucky we were to be living in a pristine city at the foot of the Alps where we could walk or bike into town in a matter of minutes. It had been a privilege to live that way and to find something new to marvel at each day.

During our time in Geneva, Stefan and I had grown closer as we agonized together over crises with Elena, and he supported me when I worried about Tink or my mother. If one of us was down, the other would pick him/her up by suggesting a walk or a weekend outing. We had fully indulged our passions for nature and travel together in Europe. With our children and families far away, we'd come to rely on each other more than ever.

In late October, Elena called us in tears and said she couldn't stand living in Dallas any longer. She said she didn't fit in and didn't feel at home anywhere in the US. We certainly understood why. She'd spent her first year of life hearing Polish, and after her adoption, we spoke only English to her. When we took her to Ivory Coast, she was surrounded by French-speakers until we moved to Atlanta. When she moved to the US at age six, it was more foreign to her than it was to the rest of us. Yet her resilience and adaptive nature had been remarkable, especially since the move from Tanzania to Atlanta when she was sixteen had been harder on her than anyone else.

Now, at twenty-four, she thought she might be happier living in Europe. She had a friend from high school who was living in Paris, and we agreed that it might be good for her to move while we were still in Geneva and near enough to help her. Elena moved to France in November of 2015, and we helped her find a furnished apartment in the hip district of Le Marais through a contact of my brother. We were confident she'd be able to find a job since she already spoke French and was impressive in interviews.

She was able to renew her Polish citizenship and passport, which would allow her to work in any EU country. A month after she landed in Paris, she found a job at a law firm as an executive assistant, and she was doing French-English translations of letters and documents.

It was a relief to see how happy she was when Stefan and I took a high-speed train to Paris and visited her in December. She and her friend accompanied us to Christmas markets, where we shopped together and warmed ourselves with mulled wine.

Elena and Aaron came to Geneva for the holidays, and all four of us drove to Belgium to spend Christmas with close friends in Arlon. Having our children under one roof again made it a happier holiday for me and Stefan.

In March I flew to Atlanta to take care of business with our house. We'd decided to sell it since Stefan was ready to retire from CDC and had no desire to live in Atlanta. I walked around with a lump in my throat, feeling as empty as the vacant house and sad to see it in poor condition after four years of renting it to tenants.

Even sadder were memories that flooded over me in that house: of my father's last visit when we celebrated his eighty-fifth birthday, and of my children when they were young and had friends running in and out. Neither Aaron nor Elena considered it "home," nor did Stefan for that matter. None of them had been as attached to the house as I was. For me, it had been a touchstone when I felt rootless living in foreign countries.

Spring was the time of year I'd enjoyed it most. Without leaves on the trees or curtains in the windows, unfiltered light permeated the house, and I could see pink and white buds on the azaleas in the front and backyard. A recent delivery of pine straw made the grounds look fresh, and Lenten roses decorated Bella's grave. There was a light dusting of green sprigs on trees in the dense woods behind the house, portending an early spring. I'd be sorry to let it go.

The fact was that none of us—including the children—cared to

hold on to the house. It was time to find a home that would be easier
to maintain and the right size for Stefan and me. We were considering
a move to Seattle since—like Geneva—it had reliable public transportation and lakes and mountains nearby. I knew the city well after my
closest friend from college had settled there with her husband, and I'd
visited them a dozen times over the years. Seattle seemed like it might
be a good fit for both of us.

I found a competent realtor in Atlanta who would oversee the
painting that needed to be done before listing the house. Then I flew
to Florida to spend a week with my mother. We drove to Sarasota
and basked in the sunshine from a beachside motel. She told me how
grateful she was to have me there, which confirmed my resolve to
move back to the US. Even if we didn't live in the same city, just having
me in the country would be a comfort to her.

The day our house in Atlanta was listed, we got an offer for the
asking price. After we accepted the offer, I made another trip across
the Atlantic to finalize the sale in June. During my weeklong visit, I
had lunches and dinners with different friends each day. Those visits
convinced me that I didn't want to live overseas again. Being at home
in my mother tongue reinforced my sense of belonging, as did being
part of a community again.

Stefan and I said goodbye to Vero and Daniel over dinner on our
terrace a week before we were to leave. The night before our departure, we drove to Angie and Peter's place for a last supper with their
family. Our goodbyes weren't terribly sad since they had offered to let
us use their house as a base where we could store our valuables while
traveling.

Stefan had accepted an offer to join the faculty at the University
of Washington in the Global Health Department, and he intended
to take a sabbatical between jobs. Our plan was to travel in Europe

for three months before moving back to the US. We'd fly to Norway in early September and stay with Bodil and Cam before going on to Sweden, Finland, and Estonia. In October we planned to visit friends in Germany before traveling through Italy, ending our trip in Marseilles in November. After that we'd visit Elena in Paris before saying our final goodbyes.

Now that the time was coming to an end, I had mixed feelings about leaving Switzerland. Stefan's job at WHO had been the perfect capstone to his career in public health, and the setting had been idyllic too—minus the renovation fiasco. We had seized opportunities to visit places like Corsica and Sicily and had seen many countries and cultures from our base in Geneva. But the pull towards home was too strong to resist, and my heart would be lighter if I were living closer to Tink and my mother.

It was beginning to dawn on me that worry was a long-ingrained habit that needed to be examined. Perhaps I was even addicted to worry, as well as to a desire to be a linchpin in my family. The paradox was that moving overseas kept me from drowning in family responsibilities, yet a sense of duty invariably drew me back. I hadn't stuck to the resolution I'd made years earlier—not to hold on to people and places in my past too long. Here was another opportunity for growth: to detach from roles I'd played reflexively in the past and try to live my own life while letting my children and siblings do the same. Kierkegaard said that, "Our life always expresses the results of our dominant thoughts." It would take a complete reboot for me to allow joy in the moment to become my mindset instead of worry.

Chapter 20
Settling in Seattle

It was pouring rain when Stefan and I stopped in front of a house in the University District that a realtor had flagged for us. Oozing with charm, the house was unlike any we'd seen in our search thus far, with a landscaped yard and an arbor-like arch over the front gate. Though it was early March, daphne bushes and daffodils were in bloom after a mild winter with tons of rain—so much rain that it would be termed the wettest winter on record. That's saying something for Seattle.

It was more like a bungalow than the ranch-style house we'd recently sold in Atlanta. The For Sale sign in the front yard drew lots of interested buyers who traipsed in and out the front door. Strolling up the walk, it felt oddly familiar—as if I were home and the other house hunters were there to sightsee. The feeling intensified as I stepped into the cozy bungalow with dark oak floors. While Stefan examined features like the crown molding and double-glazed windows, I wandered through the rooms on the main floor.

We met in the kitchen, which had a breakfast nook overlooking the backyard. A kitchen update had included granite counters and Mexican tiles on the floor. But what drew my eye was the yard outside. Making my way through French doors in the dining room, I was surprised to see a small pond with an even smaller river rock waterfall. The backyard had terraced flagstone walls and a garden that was appealing even at the end of a soggy winter.

When Stefan and I finished touring the house, we looked at each other and sighed. It appeared to be in pristine shape even though it was built in 1905. The real estate market in Seattle was so tight that houses like this would have multiple offers on it by day's end.

We decided to go for it anyway and inserted an escalation clause that automatically increased our offer against competing bids. Per our realtor's advice, we also wrote a letter telling the owners why we wished to buy their home. It was like writing a student essay to gain entrance to an exclusive college.

Three days later we were informed that our bid—one among five—had been accepted. We suspected that we got it because of the escalation clause and not the college essay.

We'd been rootless for so long that the move-in date couldn't come fast enough. After leaving our apartment in Geneva and traveling around Europe for three months, we had moved to Seattle after the Christmas holidays. While looking for a house, we'd been renting a place in the University District that allowed Stefan to walk to his new job at the University of Washington.

We moved into our house in mid-May, and the first thing I did was dig out my gardening tools. The front and back yards were brimming with rhododendron and iris blooms along with weeds in the garden. After excising the weeds, I planted columbine, cosmos, dahlias, and salvia that I'd picked up in a nursery. Like a dog in a city park, I was marking the terrain and grounding myself by pruning and planting again. It felt like home right away even though Seattle was new to Stefan and me. I thought of the Wendell Berry Poem, "The Peace of Wild Things."

When despair for the world grows in me

and I wake in the night at the least sound

in fear of what my life and my children's lives may be,

I go and lie down where the wood drake

rests in his beauty on the water, and the great heron feeds.

I come into the peace of wild things

who do not tax their lives with forethought

of grief. I come into the presence of still water.

And I feel above me the day-blind stars

waiting with their light. For a time

I rest in the grace of the world and am free.

My primary focus—once boxes were unpacked and excess items given away—was to set up my study with everything in place so I could get back to writing. I wanted to start a new project, and the idea came to me to write a book about our experiences of living overseas. The prospect galvanized me more than the idea of rewriting my unpublished novels. Staying in one place and feeling grounded would allow me to reflect on where I'd been. As Leonard Cohen said, "Going nowhere is the grand adventure that makes sense of everywhere else." Or as Pico Iyer wrote, "After traveling, the beauty of sitting still is to turn the sights I saw into insights."

My next priority was to look for connections in our new environs, and my first impulse was to do volunteer work in the neighborhood. I didn't have to look far for it in the University District. There was a day shelter for unhoused women two blocks from our house, and I ventured in one day to ask if they needed help. The volunteer coordinator escorted me to their kitchen and introduced me to the cook. She was an older African American woman, a retired minister who'd recently moved to Seattle herself. Under her direction, I helped prepare breakfast and lunch one day a week for sixty-some clients and afterwards load the dishwasher.

Aside from the urge to plug into the community, I was motivated to do this volunteer work because I wanted to understand why so many people in the city were experiencing housing insecurity. Seattle's homeless problem seemed near epidemic, especially compared to Geneva where we didn't see people living on the streets. Underlying this urge was my concern for Tink, who hadn't had a job in months and had been without stable housing for short spells.

On a drizzly Monday in January, a year after we moved to Seattle, I stepped into the office of the Language Institute in a U District church and introduced myself to the director. Valerie's eyes lit up when I told her I was a writer who had done some ELL tutoring (English for Language Learners) and that I'd lived overseas. We chatted for an hour, at the end of which I didn't want to leave. We had so much to talk about, and she was so engaging that I wanted to work there just to be her friend. Later, she would tell me she knew as soon as I walked into her office that we would become friends.

I started volunteering one morning a week as a classroom assistant in an ELL class. At the end of my second week, Valerie asked if I would take over as lead teacher in a mid-level class. I gulped and said yes even though I'd never taught a formal ELL class. Fortunately, Valerie was full of ideas and resources for teachers. Most of the students were from China, Korea, or Japan, and they were visiting scholars or spouses of researchers at the university. It was easy to teach adults who were highly motivated to learn English while living in the US, especially with only eight students per class. I enjoyed the work and seemed to have a knack for it, empathizing with outsiders after having been a language learner and a foreigner myself.

A month after I began teaching, Valerie invited me and Stefan to meet her and her husband on a trail near Snoqualmie Pass. They went cross-country skiing most weekends when there was snow at the Pass. Stefan and I snowshoed alongside them, and we ate lunch together at the top before they skied down, and we trekked after them. It was an outing we'd repeat several times that winter since Stefan—like Valerie and Wes—was eager to be in the mountains when there was snow.

As winter wound down, I attended a benefit dinner for the University District Food Bank and happened to sit next to a woman my age. She was open and friendly and asked right off the bat where I was from and what brought me to the dinner. As luck would have it, she was a neighbor and a writer like me. Trained as a journalist, Misha had been theatre critic for the *Seattle Times* until her recent retirement. We made plans to meet for lunch later that week, and it went so well that she started inviting me to plays that she was reviewing for online publications.

Both Valerie and Misha became close friends in no time. It was as if the universe—or God, the law of attraction, or whatever one might call it—brought me the companions I needed during the settling-in phase. Apart from my new friends, I reconnected with two other women in the area from the past: my oldest friend from college who lived a mile away, and Carol who had been my anchor during a difficult first year in Ivory Coast.

In 2017, a year after we left Switzerland, Stefan had to return to Geneva for work, and I went with him to spend time with Vero. She took the train from Morges and met me at the hotel where I was staying. We strolled along the lakefront as we had in the past and stopped at a café overlooking the Jet d'Eau. After we caught each other up on our doings, she invited me to go to her chalet while our husbands were at the conference. I jumped at the chance to spend three days in the Alps hiking and talking with her.

The most challenging part of our discussions was hearing her criticisms of the US after Donald Trump assumed the presidency. She was appalled by his policies—particularly in foreign affairs—and by his behavior. "I'm sorry for you," Vero shook her head. "It isn't easy to be an American in Europe these days. Many people will attack you on account of Mr. Trump."

"It's definitely more challenging for American diplomats oversees these days," I agreed. "The world looks at us differently now, and Americans increasingly have to watch out for terrorist activities." After reflecting for a moment, I continued. "It was easier to represent our country when we lived in Ivory Coast and Tanzania. People knew that Stefan was there to work with local doctors to stop the spread of AIDS and help infected people get medication. It wasn't a political job, and they didn't resent our presence."

"Yes, but Europeans think that Donald Trump's ideas are dangerous and that it's time to pull away from American influence."

"If you look at what our country is doing in other sectors, America still has a big influence—in public health, for example." She canted her head and considered this.

"Do you know the filmmaker Ken Burns?" When she nodded, I went on, "He made a series for public television called *America's Best Idea* that was about National Parks in the US. But I think America's Best Idea from a global perspective has been pumping money and manpower into improving public health around the world. US taxpayers have spent almost $90 billion since 2003 on AIDS treatment and prevention through PEPFAR, and every five years Congress keeps funding the program whether Democrats or Republicans are in charge. Billions more are spent on tuberculosis, malaria, and other diseases. To me, that's America's Best Idea."

Vero nodded graciously. "You have a right to be proud. No country spends as much on public health around the world, and before Mr. Trump, no country accepted as many refugees."

"That's true," I sighed. "These days we aren't so willing to accept the huddled masses from other countries."

The rest of the weekend, Vero and I discussed our daughters, our mothers, and other concerns we had in common as we hiked in the surrounding mountains. At the end of our time together, we talked about meeting the following summer when Stefan and I returned to Europe, and I urged her to visit Seattle so I could show her around the Pacific Northwest.

In December of 2019, I got an email from Daniel instead of Vero. He broke the startling news that Vero had a cerebral aneurism that had ruptured just before the Christmas holidays. She'd lingered in the hospital for two days before passing away, devastating Daniel and their son and daughter.

The news was so shocking and the suddenness of Vero's passing so distressing that it shook me in a way my father's death hadn't. Watching his slow decline, I had braced myself for the eventuality that he'd be felled by a stroke someday. While I missed him terribly, I was grateful that we'd moved back from Tanzania in time to spend the last two years of his life living nearby. Vero's death came without warning to a woman who was physically fit and exactly my age. She was my vigorous friend whose presence had been critical to so many people, including me. Her son was about to have a baby, and her daughter and mother still needed her, as did a dozen friends. It was hard to accept the news and simply let her go. How could someone so full of empathy and life have hers snuffed out without notice? Her death didn't make sense to me.

For months I felt a profound sense of loss every time I thought about Vero. In time, I had to acknowledge that we didn't have a choice about whether to accept death or not. It doesn't matter if we accept it since it's inevitable for all of us. What we *can* choose is to live each day to the fullest and not hole up in our houses or apartments to avoid risk and worry, which is what I did during the early anxious months after we moved to Ivory Coast. After meeting Carol and Angie, I'd mustered the courage to drive around town on my own and was happier once I got to know Gladys and Ousmane as well as my neighbors and colleagues. When we moved to Tanzania, I knew that our time was limited and decided to take advantage of any opportunity to explore the country, meet new people, and get to know the culture around us. It was a richer life when I looked outward and didn't let fear and anxiety hamper the chance to connect with others.

My urge to leave Switzerland had been motivated by a longing for deeper connections—to a physical place and to people I could talk to. While I found those things upon moving to Seattle, I also realized that a meaningful life wasn't about being rooted to the point of being stuck in one place. It was about embracing change and not trying to hold onto certain people or places too long. In appreciating and making the most of the time we have with those around us, we won't be dogged by regret or nostalgia.

Friends would come and go in our lives just as our children did, and I had to be resilient while adapting to change—which wasn't going to stop once we got our belongings out of storage and arranged in a house. Every five years on average, our setting had shifted when we moved to a different city or country, and it probably would continue to do so. We would move, and close friends and family members wouldn't always be around. In not grasping onto them or to a fixed place, we make room in our lives for other people and ways to connect.

Watching Carol climb into a yellow kayak from her dock on Whidbey Island, it was hard for me to square the lone figure who began paddling across Penn Cove with the businesswoman who ran a bustling household in steamy Abidjan. That's who she was when I met her in the early 1990s. She was married to an Ivorian and had become a true insider in political and business circles in Ivory Coast.

Soon after we moved to Seattle, I'd seen a photo on Carol's Facebook page of her kayaking off Whidbey Island. I messaged her that Stefan and I were living in Seattle, and she immediately invited us to her house in Coupeville. It took less than two hours to reach by car, including a ferry ride across Puget Sound.

As soon as Carol and I saw each other, we hugged and started talking as if we were resuming a conversation we'd begun twenty-five years prior. We had seen each other only twice since she moved away from Abidjan, yet she looked much the same, her eyes the color of tanzanite and her face scored with smile lines.

Her house was set in a madrona grove overlooking Penn Cove. The home's interior echoed the woods outside—with arched ceilings, hardwood floors, and huge picture windows facing east and south. Stefan and I were bowled over by the view from her airy living-dining room—of the bay glistening below and Mount Baker on the horizon.

While cooking together that evening, Carol told us about her job on the south side of Whidbey Island. As director of the Good Cheer Food Bank and Thrift Stores, she worked with other NGOs and organic farms that supplied the Food Bank with fresh produce. She also advised civic groups on the Island and ran strategic planning retreats.

Over dinner we talked about our children, and I mentioned that Aaron had finished his PhD and landed a job with an aerospace startup in Seattle. "It's such a joy to finally have one of our children living nearby."

"You're lucky," Carol smiled. "My daughters attended universities in the US, and as soon as they graduated, they moved overseas. One of them is in South Africa and the other in Abidjan."

"Did she move there to be near her father?"

Carol shook her head. "Mamadou died of cancer a few years ago. We never officially divorced even after his mistress moved in and took care of him through his illness. Bi moved to Abidjan for work, and she's married to a guy from Mali."

"I'm sorry to hear about Mamadou," I said before switching subjects. "Elena was eager to move back overseas too. She never really felt at home in the US and moved to Paris to find work there. After a year, she got a job offer in Luxembourg and our friends put her up for a while."

"Is that where she is now?" Carol asked.

I shook my head, a smile spreading on my face. "She's a dynamo. She ended up in London and got a high-paying job as head of Human Resources and Recruiting for an online university. She also met a British man she's crazy about, and they had a baby."

"How exciting! I have a grandchild too, with Bi in Abidjan."

"Do you miss anything about your life in Ivory Coast?" I asked after a pause.

"I don't have a nostalgic bone in my body," she said dismissively. "If I'm happy in the moment, why would I want to be anywhere else?"

Carol launched into the saga of how she'd found her true passion some years ago. After working for Population Services International in Pakistan, she had moved to India and run PSI's office in Delhi for a decade. It was there that she took classes with a woman who taught George Gurdjieff's philosophy and movements. On a whim, Carol quit her job and moved to Goa to devote herself to learning the practice. After five years she became a teacher of Gurdjieff movements herself, following a spiritual path unlike anyone I knew.

Carol bought the house on Whidbey Island with the intention of giving classes in Gurdjieff movements as well as retreats and workshops. She asked us if we wanted to join her class in the morning, and I said yes, curious to see what had become the center of her life. Stefan opted to sleep in and go for a hike instead.

Rising early as usual, I made my way to the studio behind Carol's house where four other adults had turned up. Standing an arm's length from each other, we faced Carol as she demonstrated the first set of movements with her feet—a heel-toe, step right and left, back and forth exercise that we had to master quickly so as not to throw each other off. Then she put on syncopated piano music—Gurdjieff had been a pianist and a composer as well—and we tried to stay in step with each other and with her. Once we mastered the steps, she added arm and head movements to be done at the same time. The exercises required utmost concentration as we moved in sync with each other doing intricate motions with our arms, feet, and heads. It was like walking meditation in a way since you had to give up your "monkey mind" and concentrate on what you were doing at every moment, only it was more frustrating than relaxing to me.

After an hour of practice, Carol led us upstairs to a carpeted room where the six of us sat in a circle on the floor and shared feelings that came up while we were doing the movements. "I got frustrated whenever I forgot steps and felt a little foolish," I admitted.

Carol grinned. "That's the point of the work. It's to get you to examine feelings that arise without judging them. You try to learn what triggers negative feelings and look at them in a new light." For my benefit, she reviewed some of the central tenets of Gurdjieff's teaching.[30] Later, she would tell me that the movements were a way of praying with the body.

Carol had found her passion in ways she'd never envisioned when she was living in Ivory Coast. Her spacious house on Penn Cove had become a kind of Gurdjieff retreat center, and she often had students staying with her for weekend workshops or for months at a time. She treated me and Stefan like family and made us feel welcome just as she had twenty-five years earlier when we'd arrived in Abidjan.

As in the past, Carol challenged some of my statements and caused me to examine my thinking from other perspectives. She was a longtime adherent of Transactional Analysis (TA) and had recently started studying the Enneagram, which also figured in Gurdjieff's writings. Her purpose in studying it was to examine the automatic responses of her personality type so she could temper them, with the aim of growing into an integrated and awake individual.

Differences in our personalities were reflected in our surroundings. Carol's house was sparsely furnished, and she had few knickknacks or keepsakes, whereas mine had African masks, paintings, tablecloths, and other memorabilia from our past. It meant a lot to me to recall where an item came from or the person who gave it to me, like a painting I'd bought from Kambi that was titled *The Way Home*. It depicted Masai figures moving along a road and evoked images in my mind of people trying to get home.

Carol's statement made me wonder if my life might have been easier if I—like her—didn't have a nostalgic bone in my body. The word "nostalgia" comes from the Greek "nostros" meaning "return" and "algos" meaning "pain or grief." The dictionary likens it to homesickness and a longing to return to some grief or pain in the past. A related meaning is "a longing for something far away or long ago" and implies a sentimental or wistful yearning for the past. I didn't think of myself as longing for the past so much as being intrigued by it. Examining the past was my way of learning from jarring life events. My father had often repeated the saying "know thyself" when I was young, and I tried to do just that and also to make sense of the world around me.

Whenever I thought about the past, Tink and my other siblings came to mind because of our tight bonds and the concerns I felt for them. It was a big difference between Carol and me—that she was accountable to no one other than a high-achieving sister, whereas I was the second of seven children born within a decade. All of us had gone through difficult childhoods, and as one of the oldest, I had assumed responsibility for them. While I didn't pine for the grief or pain of the past, I couldn't shrug it off or ignore my responsibilities no matter how far I moved from my siblings. That sense of obligation to others had set up an internal tug of war that motivated me to move overseas and pulled me back time and again. Those bonds also gave me a sense of purpose and meaning, and my siblings had often helped when I or my children needed them.

The handful of people I'd bonded with in Tanzania and Ivory Coast also had places under my umbrella of concern. I still felt connected to Ousmane, Gladys, and Kambi, and they maintained regular contact with me. If the opportunity arose to go to Tanzania or Ivory Coast, I'd jump at the chance to visit the people with whom my children and I shared key life events, just as I regularly visited the European friends I made in those countries. It wasn't so much a pining for the past as it was treasuring the time and people who shared life experiences with me.

When I was young, I had wanted to leave home and reinvent myself by living elsewhere. Maybe it was less about reinvention and more about exploring different aspects of myself while discovering who I was in relation to others. Some of us could only come to know ourselves by moving far from home. After I did so, I didn't yearn to be in a certain city or house as much as I longed for the sense of being at home, and of being grounded and connected to those around me. The challenge was to find stability and a sense of "home" inside myself instead of in a physical place. And the trick was to transform nostalgia about "home" from wistful yearning for the past into understanding it. Thomas Wolfe wrote in *You Can't Go Home Again*: "To lose the earth you know for greater knowing; to lose the life you have for greater life; to leave the friends you loved for greater loving; to find a land more kind than home, and more large than earth."

After Geneva, Seattle immediately felt like home even though we had never lived in the Pacific Northwest. Having a place of our own where I could write and tend the garden was fundamentally grounding, but so was knowing how to find my center whenever I felt adrift. Sometimes that meant reaching out to a friend or my partner, and sometimes it meant gardening, meditating, or walking on my own.

When I moved to West Africa with small children in the 1990s, I needed people more than I liked to admit. I wasn't as brave as my mother-in-law had been, or as intrepid as younger generations of women who've had the courage to move abroad on their own—as Peace Corps Volunteers, health professionals, and foreign correspondents. I applaud their courage and wish I could have been more like that myself.

Starting over in a new city was never easy, but what made things smoother was that I didn't have to do it alone. Stefan has been the companion of my head and heart for forty years, and he pushed me beyond my comfort zone and took me places I hadn't dreamed of going. While living in other countries, we grew closer over the years and became more sensitive to each other's needs. I was lucky to find a partner who shared a spirit of openness and adventure, and who respected and believed in me. We had fun together too and knew how to put petty grievances in perspective.

Perspective was one of our biggest gains from living elsewhere. To my mind, it helps enormously in processing the changes that life will inevitably bring. Neither Stefan nor I ever joined a church or religious group, which is something that set me apart from my siblings and made it harder to find a community. Yet both of us wanted to connect and work with people who were unlike us. Believing in Stefan's work as well as my own enabled me to put up with the hardships that expat life often entailed. I couldn't have done it with a partner who pursued his own goals above all else. Stefan always took my opinions and needs into consideration and valued consensus when it came to decision-making in our family.

It's what I wish for my children, who moved every few years until they were eighteen and kept moving of their own accord into their thirties. I hoped that they would find trusted companions through the many changes life would bring, including unforeseen circumstances like illness and accidents, pandemics and climate disasters.

Our children gained what Stefan and I did in living overseas: perspective. They came to view themselves as part of a larger world after living in other countries; after seeing the splendid landscapes in Tanzania, for example, alongside poverty and disease. They witnessed the daily struggle to survive in Ivory Coast and Tanzania by coming to know and love Gladys, Ousmane, and Wilfred. We may have deprived our kids of a fixed sense of home, yet they gained perspective and learned how to navigate the world with confidence; and how to connect with people of other cultures after embracing individuals who weren't like them.

For all of us, the concept of "home" would keep evolving.

Perspective enables us to feel at home almost anywhere when there's an inner grounded-ness. Both of my kids are adept at making friends and finding ways to engage. They've found jobs that interest them, yet at the end of the day, connecting with people matters most. I devoted a lot of energy to cultivating friendships, and my children do too. We had the courage to relocate time and again because we had each other and we knew how to make friends.

For my children, discovering who they were meant having to accept the discomfort of feeling foreign. There was only so much we could do to protect them from the sense of alienation and rootlessness that accompanied relocation and change. The best thing we could do—and did—was to give them a safe place to land and open arms when they needed them.

Epilogue

Sitting on a rocky outcropping above Summerland Meadows, I couldn't imagine a more fitting way to celebrate my sixty-fifth birthday than hiking around Mount Rainier with Stefan. We'd walked up the northern flank of the volcano and reached the end of the Summerland Trail by lunchtime. It was a path that I'd hiked with friends thirty years earlier, and I had wanted to do it again with Stefan on a peerless September day.

Exhausted from the hike, we ate our sandwiches and watched a pair of hikers disappear around some boulders. "I wonder if they're going on to Panhandle Gap?" I remarked idly.

I had wanted to hike up to the Gap when my friends showed me the Summerland trail years before, but eight miles up and back had been enough that day. The trek to the Gap would have added three miles and another thousand feet in elevation gain, after which we'd have to hustle the remaining five miles down the mountain to reach the car before dark. "The view is worth it," Piroska had told me. "You should do it someday."

The hike with Stefan on my birthday had already held enough adventure on the way up. We'd run into two backpackers who told us to watch out for a bear that was munching on salmonberries near the path. Not wanting to startle a hungry bear, I asked Stefan to sing with me along the way, and we'd run through several renditions of our favorite oldies. It must have scared the bear because we never saw him. Now, eating lunch on a rocky outcropping with Mount Rainier in view, I told myself it was reward enough for one day. It was already 2 p.m. and the rigorous climb to the Gap would add another two hours to our hike.

Still, a stellar view from the top of the Gap sounded intriguing, and if we didn't do it then, there was no guarantee we'd be in shape to hike it in another year or two. "Let's just walk around those boulders and check out the path to the Gap," I suggested after we finished eating.

Stefan heaved the backpack onto his shoulders and nodded. "It's your call today."

Following the trail around the boulders, we discovered a moonscape on the far side as the path wound up a rocky scree. We babystepped across a log that traversed a milky creek still running fast with glacier melt in early autumn. Picking our way across the scree, I spotted a couple of figures at the apex of a saddle between two peaks. "That must be the Gap," I pointed. "It doesn't look that far. Do you want to go for it?"

Stefan grinned and let me lead the way.

My breathing became labored as we climbed above the tree line, but I talked myself into going as far as the next switchback and then the one after that. It was three o'clock, and I tried not to think about the trek down the mountain at dusk when bears and cougars might be foraging in the woods. I'd have to goad Stefan into singing again to feel safe on the way down.

Nearing the Gap, we had to scramble along a narrow path that hugged a cliff face, and I didn't look down. It was the type of path that scared me since one misstep could send us tumbling off a precipitous slope. My stomach was in my throat as I sidestepped along the path, hoping we wouldn't meet other hikers on their way down.

Before I knew it, we'd edged past the cliff face and reached the crest of the saddle. I felt a ridiculous rush of pride—much like I had at the summit of Kilimanjaro—to have made it to the top of Panhandle Gap. This time it wasn't Stefan who'd pushed me out of my comfort zone and urged me to keep going. The achievement was my own, and it hadn't been too painful.

Nor was it a letdown after all the hype. The view from the Gap was exquisite with the verdant slopes of the valley on the far side dotted with mountain goats and paths that wound through stands of evergreens. We sat on a rock in reverent silence and gazed at the collapsed dome of Mount Saint Helens in the near distance, the pointed peaks of Mount Adams and Mount Hood on the horizon. Though the sun was waning and we still faced a long trek down the mountain, nothing could tear us away from the panoramic view on that autumn afternoon.

It was indeed a long slog back. Still wary as I tromped through the twilit forest, my knees were complaining that I'd pushed them beyond the norm. Yet my heart was light as I sang for the bear, grateful to be able to hike twelve miles and climb three thousand feet in a day. An added gift was knowing that I was farthest from my anxious ego-self when walking in nature as we did that day.

When Stefan asked me to move with our children to a West African country with high rates of malaria and HIV, it required a leap of faith to override my fears and trust that things would turn out okay. He pushed me beyond my comfort zone at a pivotal point—when I was a new mother just finishing my PhD and without a clear path ahead of me. I agreed on the premise that I could stand anything for a couple of years. Going on faith and trusting my instincts allowed me to settle in a foreign place and make myself at home there.

Along the way I had to wrestle with many challenges. One was being called a "trailing spouse" and another was knowing that certain jobs—in the medical field, for example—were more highly valued (and paid) than the work of freelance writers. I fell prey to that bias and considered Stefan's job more critical than mine, partly because he earned a lot more than I did and because his work could save people's lives. It took a great deal of resilience to come to terms with the fact that it would be hard to publish anything while living overseas—there was no internet when we were in Ivory Coast, and it was in a nascent stage when we were in Tanzania–and that Stefan's work took precedence over mine.

Resilience was key to being content and adjusting to change. Equally important was my willingness to question preconceptions and judgments about events (e.g., crime in Abidjan) and people (e.g., the Ambassador in Tanzania) and remain open to whatever came my way. I'd already decided to live as Michael A. Singer would later advise in *Living Untethered*: "The moment in front of you is special, and you might want to practice appreciating it and noticing the effect on your life . . . not whether you like or dislike it. You're being given this wonderful opportunity to experience a moment in creation that took billions of years to get here. Be sure you don't miss it."[31]

The long and winding road that took me to foreign countries and brought dozens of rewarding relationships into my life wasn't designed or foreseen by me. After years of living overseas, I concluded that connecting with people instead of focusing on differences was the most fulfilling way of being in the world. Bonds with people around me have mattered most in life, and I've been richly rewarded by connecting with people from many countries, starting with the international friends I made at American University. It was a gift and facility that I developed early on—relating to people of other cultures and walks of life—and such people had a huge impact on me.

Gregory Boyle, a Catholic priest who worked with gang members in LA, wrote about the healing force of compassion and love in his book *Barking to the Choir*. "The gulf in our present age could not be wider between 'us' and 'them.' How do we tame this status quo that lulls us into blindly accepting the things that divide us and keep us from our longing for the mutuality of kinship—a sure and certain sense that we belong to each other?"[32]

My children learned how to be resilient in the face of change and to connect with people of different cultures. So did my sister Tink, who moved to Florida to take care of our ninety-year-old mother. It was a happy solution that I didn't orchestrate, and it taught me that worrying about them didn't serve any of us. It was resilience that got us through the many changes and moves that came our way, and all of us know how to summon it when needed.

Big and varied as our country is, I feel at home anywhere in the US and can find common ground with people everywhere. Growing up in Maryland and having siblings in California, Ohio, Indiana, Minnesota, Idaho, Texas, and Florida, I'm attached to those places even though I live in a distant corner of the country. The parameters of our world have narrowed, yet Stefan and I enjoy exploring landscapes and towns in the Pacific Northwest that have a history and character all their own.

I've written about the joys and challenges of living overseas as well as the tradeoffs, and of experiencing exotic places versus being far from friends and family. My biggest regret is letting fear and worry rule my mindset instead of appreciation. Less worry would have freed me to enjoy the present more, wherever I happened to be.

Instead of worry, what absorbs me now is walking in a state of wonder and staying open to the people who cross my path.

Notes

1. Tadeusz Wiktor worked at the Wistar Institute as a research virologist until his death in 1986. He developed a human rabies vaccine that was safer and more effective than previous vaccines, and it's still in use today.

2. In the 1990s, cooks, nannies, and housekeepers were the highest paid domestic workers. Guards at private residences earned the least since they were employed by local companies.

3. Terry A. Repak, *Waiting on Washington: Central American Workers in the Nation's Capital*, Temple University Press, 1995.

4. Robert Kaplan, "The Coming Anarchy," the *Atlantic* (February 1994).

5. Chimamanda Ngozi Adichie, "The Danger of a Single Story," TED talk (2010).

6. I was told that few American men married to Ivorians stayed in Ivory Coast since Ivorian law made it harder for foreign men married to Ivorians to get citizenship than for foreign women, and because job prospects for American men were more limited.

7. None of the other women or men I interviewed were involved in polygamous relationships.

8. We learned later that Adama's brother had gone to the guard

company to collect his pension, and he kept it without giving anything to Adama's widow. Adama's younger wife died of AIDS soon after he did.

9. Roughly one third of Ivorians were Christians—predominantly Catholics—and 43 percent were Muslims, while 20 percent followed traditional African religions. Most men who practiced polygamy were Muslims from neighboring countries where polygamy was still legal.

10. Even in the 1990s, an impressive proportion of doctors, lawyers, and pharmacists in Ivory Coast were women, and the civil code legislated equal pay. Yet women in all professions, from housekeepers to MPs, were still subjected to sexual harassment as in the US. It started as early as primary school when young girls might be asked by older men to be their "fiancées."

11. Unexplained illness and deaths in African countries were often attributed to poisoning. Gladys's brother graduated from high school and died suddenly as he was preparing to go to university. She believed he was poisoned by another student who coveted his place at university.

12. Alan and Stefan hired and trained dozens of West African doctors, many of whom went on to hold leadership positions in such organizations as WHO, UNICEF, and CDC. Most notable was John Nkengasong from Cameroon, who ran the HIV lab in Abidjan and went on to head CDC's Global AIDS Lab. He then became the first director of Africa CDC and was later appointed by President Biden to direct the PEPFAR program, an ambassadorial position.

13. Stefan Wiktor et al., "Short course of oral zidovudine to prevent mother-to-child transmission of HIV-1 in Abidjan, Côte d'Ivoire: a randomized trial." *Lancet* 1999, 353: 781–85.

Stefan Wiktor et al., "Efficacy of trimethoprim-sulphamethoxazole prophylaxis to decrease morbidity and mortality in HIV-infected patients with tuberculosis in Abidjan, Côte d'Ivoire: a randomized controlled trial." *Lancet* 1999, 353:1469–75.

14. Site visits were a critical aspect of Stefan's work because he had to monitor the testing and research at clinics in Abidjan and upcountry. He also had to review work sites of partner organizations that received CDC funds for counseling and treating people with HIV.

15. I was acutely aware of this historic moment for personal reasons. When I studied in London in the 1970s, I'd befriended a few South Africans who'd left the country on account of apartheid. I visited South Africa after apartheid was dismantled and my friends had moved back.

16. The mayor presented Stefan with a carved wooden stool and a *Chasse Mousse* (bamboo fly swatter) to "chase away his troubles." Then they asked him to sit on the stool while the chief wrapped a bolt of Kente cloth about his shoulders. They had me sit on a stool beside Stefan, and the chief wrapped a woven *pagne* with blue and gold threads around my shoulders. Though I didn't like being in the spotlight, I was happy to see Stefan honored for his hard work.

17. Fewer indigent people were homeless in part because of the social policies of Julius Nyerere, Tanzania's first President. His homegrown brand of African socialism ensured universal health care and education after the country's independence. He forbade favoritism in jobs based on nepotism and tribal affiliation, and he united the country under one identity and language (Swahili). As a result, Tanzania has never had a civil war or a coup as in Ivory Coast.

18. Approximately 75 percent of the country's twenty million residents lived below the poverty level of $2 a day in 2019, and the annual GDP per person in Madagascar was a little over $500.

19. After antiretroviral therapy proved effective in treating people in the US, the PEPFAR program focused on treating people with HIV/AIDS on a global scale. The medication allowed HIV-infected people to live longer and prevented transmission.

20. A selection of my columns from Dar Guide Magazine are available on my author website: www.terryrepak.com

21. At 16,893 feet, Mawenzi Peak is the second-highest summit on Kilimanjaro after Kibo Dome, which is 19,341. Unlike Mawenzi Peak with its formidable spires, Kibo Dome is rounded with several "peaks" on top of it: Uhuru is the highest at 19,341 feet and Gillman's Point is the second at 18,885. Gillman's Point is considered an official summit point on Kilimanjaro.

22. It was easy to organize the Kilimanjaro climb since we used the same local company that guided us up Mount Meru. Our trek followed the Rongai Route, and we stayed in primitive campsites instead of the huts along more popular routes. Along with five Tanzanian guides, we had a cook, two camp attendants and cleaners, and twenty-five porters carrying tents, bottled water, food, and a portable shower as well as a toilet tent.

23. Rachel Aviv, "How Elizabeth Loftus Changed the Meaning of Memory," the *New Yorker* (March 29, 2021).

24. The aim of the PEPFAR program in Tanzania had been to get as many HIV-infected people on treatment as possible. In two years after Stefan started working there, the number of people on treatment jumped from ten thousand to one hundred thousand and was growing fast.

25. I found it ironic that I heard my father's voice while staying at an inn on the road to Emmaus. In the New Testament, Jesus had appeared to two of his disciples incognito on the road to Emmaus before telling them that he'd risen from the dead.

26. My poem, "Lists," appeared in the 2015 edition of *Offshoots: World Writing from Geneva.*

27. I wrote about this hike for the US Embassy newsletter and called it "A Ridge too Far." I authored other articles for the Embassy's weekly newsletter, Geneva Talks, as well as for a Swiss journal called "Hello Switzerland."

28. As Team Lead for the Global Hepatitis Program, Stefan's work focused on hepatitis B and C, which killed more people each year than AIDS or malaria. In 2012, 257 million people worldwide were living with chronic hepatitis B, and 70 million had hepatitis C compared with 37 million with HIV/AIDS. 1.3 million people died of hepatitis-related illnesses every year, while 1 million died of AIDS. Like HIV, hepatitis B, C, and D are transmitted through blood and body fluids. Yet funding for AIDS treatment and prevention dwarfed that of hepatitis B and C. Few people in Europe and the US could afford treatment and far fewer in Africa and Asia. WHO negotiated with drug companies for lower prices to make treatment affordable worldwide.

29. Such heat waves—a new phenomenon in Europe—were attributed to climate change.

30. George Gurdjieff was a controversial spiritual teacher born in 1866 in the Russian Trans Caucasus. His "Fourth Way" posited that people functioned as unconscious automatons and had to "wake up" to become more alive in the world. This awakening involved considerable effort—through study and discussion and the practice of dance-like movements.

31. Michael A. Singer, *Living Untethered: Beyond the Human Predicament*, (New Harbinger 2022) Chapter 10.

32. Gregory Boyle, *Barking to the Choir: The Power of Radical Kinship*, (Simon and Schuster 2018).

Acknowledgments

I relish the task of acknowledging some of the people who helped me along the way—first and foremost the many friends who became like family at key points in my journey. In London I was blessed to meet Gitte, Tess, Noreen and Harry, and later Halinka and Kamal who always welcomed us with open arms whenever we transited between the US and Africa.

I thrived in Cote d'Ivoire thanks to Lorna, Jeane, Carol, Gladys, Ousmane, Martine, Marybeth, Christine, Kristin, Francoise, Nina, Leo, Regine and Joachim, Angie and Peter, Michele and Alan, John and Susan. In Tanzania I was incredibly fortunate to befriend Cathy, Kambi, Lucy, Wilfred, Dominique, Candy and Randy, Nancy and Michael, Bodil and Cam. In Switzerland I grew closest to Vero, Angie, Jane, Alice, Samira, and Aliya. Friends who repeatedly opened their homes and hearts to me whenever I landed in Atlanta are Kathryn, Anne, Patty, Jane, Jennifer, Judith, Paul and Dianne, Clyde and Kim. New friends who helped ground me in Seattle are Misha and Paul, Valerie and Wes, Marta and Tom, and my oldest friends Don and Piroska. My first and closest African friend, Kadafo, came from Afar and had a profound influence on my life, as did Piroska. When I look back on my life and lament my few literary achievements and honors, I think of the many people I can count as friends and am satisfied. In that sense, I won the lottery.

My mother, father and siblings supported me and my children over the years. My deepest attachments started with Pete and Beverly, Becky, Nick, Mike, Mary, Patsy, and Tink, and extend to my in-laws Amy, Celia, Bill, Scott, and James; not to mention their children—my dozens of amazing nieces and nephews—and grandchildren. If I started to list the ancestors who seeded my journey, I'd have to begin with Aunt Ann and Aunt Didi, Julia and Helen.

Invaluable help on this manuscript came from my former writing group—Kathryn Legan, Anne Echols, Elizabeth Nelson Brown, and Greg Chagnon—as well as from the dedicated team of women at She Writes Press. Brooke Warner was the dream editor who has coached many a memoir writer and helped me refashion this book. Lauren Wise competently steered it through the publication process, and Krissa Lagos provided a critical editorial eye and advice. Jane Ward, Donna Miscolta, Jennifer Haupt, Melissa Fay Green, Misha Berson, Michele Greenberg, Peggy Barlett, and Pam White gave generous support and advice. A handful of friends read and commented on drafts of this book, including Lorna McFarland, Jeane Harris, Carol Squire, Kathryn Legan, Helene Gayle, Stefan Wiktor, and my brother Mike (his penname).

My immediate family—Stefan and my children—traveled many of the paths with me that led to this book. My hope is that they find enough truth and happy memories in it to forgive me for writing about them. They are the ones who've made my life complete in every sense that matters.

About the Author

photo credit: Meryl Schenker

Terry A. Repak is the author of *Waiting on Washington: Central American Workers in the Nation's Capital* (Temple University Press 1995) and *Edward Kennedy* (Houghton Mifflin 1980). She studied journalism in college and worked as a reporter for syndicated columnist Jack Anderson for a few years before earning a masters degree in International Relations at the London School of Economics and Political Science and a PhD at Emory University. She and her husband lived in East and West Africa and in Europe where he directed AIDS projects and she wrote, raised their children, and worked in the community. She is the author of numerous travel articles and her research has been published in academic journals. She lives in Seattle where she continues to write, teach English to foreign language learners, and to garden, hike and swim.